MANIFEST VICTORY

1974

Our very best regards

Love Shirley, Hal & Neil

From the very nature of God and the things of God and from the very nature of evil and the things of evil, God and the things of God must win. Manifest victory has not only been achieved in the experience of Jesus but is being achieved in the experience of everyone in union with Him. Ultimate manifest victory is predestined; God is working everything together for its achievement in us and in creation.

MANIFEST VICTORY

A Quest and a Testimony

by

J. R. MOSELEY

"The Sign of the Dove"
119 Nanimo Ct.
Antioch, CA 94509
754-4476

LOGOS INTERNATIONAL
Plainfield, New Jersey

CONTENTS

IT HAS BEEN SAID:

There are four empires. The first is the empire of Nature and the second the empire of Spirit. The third, which reconciles these two, is the empire of the Divine-Human. But the fourth, which is the empire of the Human-Divine, is where all three are raised up, fulfilled and made perfect members of a perfect whole. Now the Divine-Human is the Christ, who is God made Man. The Human-Divine is the ascended Jesus, who is Man made God. In union with Him, the fourth empire is experienced and revealed.

FOREWORD

<<<<<<<<<<<<<<<<<<<<<<<<<<<<<<<>>>>>>>>>>>>>>>>>>>>>>>>>>>>>

For over forty years the author of this book has been my close and intimate friend. Yet I must confess to a surprised admiration for what he has here written. Our approach to life and its problems has, as regards terms used and formulations reached, been so very different that for friendship's sake we have avoided probing our differences. I was, therefore, unjustly to my friend, not prepared for a book that would make so universal an appeal. His aim for the book has been to give a straightforward account of personal religious experiences. The result is such an objective account as promises, in my judgment, to enrich the world's literature of the inner life.

First of all, what appears is absolutely genuine, a frank and exact account of the author's own experiences. No one who knows Mr. Moseley will for a moment doubt either the authenticity of the experiences described or the precise accuracy of the statement; and it is hard to see how anyone, knowing only what appears in the book, can fail to reach a like conclusion. To be sure, not all will accept Mr. Moseley's explanation of certain happenings—it could not be expected—but this will carry no implication of doubt that the author believes precisely all that he says. The experiences are, as such, authentic beyond any question.

As suggested, the book includes a portrayal of mystic experiences. These are remarkable, as is the whole tone of the book—and indeed the author's whole life—for the joyousness that pervades them. Many, when they think of the deeply religious life, think of it as denying essentially life in this world. Not so for Mr. Moseley. There is nothing of the sort here. On the contrary, for him life is properly rich and fine for living here and now. So far from being other-worldly, the almost sole emphasis here is on this present world of ordinary human living, only this is to be lived, as life itself should be lived, in such a way as to be on its own account best worth living.

What has just been said needs elaboration in a certain direction. The reader may begin with the idea that the author's use of certain customary religious terms implies a prerequisite underlying theological system. If he does so think, he will be happily disappointed. Hardly in literature can one find a treatment of authentic religious experience that is, on the one hand, so real and concrete to him who described it and yet is, on the other hand, so free of specific theology. And still, strange as it may seem, hardly anyone who is genuinely religious will miss this absence of theology, however much he may be used to thinking his religion in such terms. In rare degree Mr. Moseley has been able to transcend all theological formulations, without in any way antagonizing those who think they need such formulations.

Most admirable, perhaps, of all is Mr. Moseley's consummate ability to deal in kindly fashion with any and all groups from whom he has felt compelled to separate him-self either as regards ties of defined organization or as re-gards systems of thought. One will look long before he finds anywhere words more nicely chosen to say, on the one hand, nothing that is not strictly true and, on the other hand, nothing that is not in fullest degree kindly. These things show the author as the man that he is, determined not to judge his neighbor, determined always to enhance life, never to mar or reduce it.

Many readers, it may be added, will enjoy with this writer the author's clear style. It is easy to read and as attractive as it is easy. Would that others who deal with life's funda-mental problems might be induced to follow also this part of the author's example.

Finally, this book, while the work of a saint—a modern saint to be sure, but as true a saint as ever lived—can be

FOREWORD

read by all, whether saint or sinner. No one will partake so much of the saintly as not to find his deepest yearnings here clearly recognized and stated. No one that is a sinner will fail, if only he will read discerningly, to find here the good that he himself at his best most deeply cherishes. He may, as does this writer, use other language when he communes with himself, but he will recognize, cannot fail to recognize, in this saint a true friend to his deepest insight. There is that in this book which will appeal to any honest seeker for the true way of life, whatever may be his faith or outlook; and this it is that constitutes the unique contribution and appeal of the book. And the essence of that appeal is the man himself, speaking through his life to all who may come thus to know him.

WILLIAM HEARD KILPATRICK

MANIFEST VICTORY

*"When life's all love 'tis life;
Aught else is naught."* Lanier

INTRODUCTION

Timid conformity is death; there is only life in the quest.

◄◄◄◄◄◄◄◄◄◄◄◄◄◄◄◄◄◄◄◄◄◄◄◄◄◄◄◄◄►►►►►►►►►►►►►►►►►►►►►►►►►►►►►►

Jesus wrote no books. He was too busy at better things, but if all that He did and said had been reported in detail, as the author of the Fourth Gospel says, "Even the world itself could not contain the books that should have been written."

Jesus, through the Holy Spirit, and in and through disciples who are in identification and fruit-bearing union with Him, continues to act and speak in a way that man apart from Him never did nor could. It seems expedient for me, who by His grace have been so favored by His manifestation of Himself to me, and by His presence continuing with me, to put in accessible form a report of how He has revealed Himself and His way of life in His quest for me and for my best in terms of others, as well as of self. My quest for Him at first appears to have been a feeling out for Him as that SOMETHING rather than SOMEONE, that I was in great need of, which later was revealed to be Jesus, His Spirit and His way of life as love. This finally came to be my seeking for union with and likeness to Him, who is perfect everything, not for myself only, but for each and all.

My young friend, O. T. Binkley, encouraged me to give expression to the quest in written form. What he said I would need to go through to get my material into shape I have found exactly true; namely, suffering, crucifixion, and resurrection. I have found that the experience of putting in cosmic order the nebula of ideas and impressions, the chaos of book stuff, and the clothing of my earth of spiritual experience with green and flowering things, have

1

been somewhat after the order that the Great Author made the earth to bring forth universally.

To be of most value this report must needs be intensely personal; but, to use the words of Emerson, I hope what is most personal can be "purged of the last taint of egotism," and that I may do the work of the reporter in the awareness that "From within or from behind [and from above] a light shines upon things that makes us aware that we are nothing [apart from the light], but the light is all." Yet in identification and union with Him all things are ours. The branch apart from the vine is of no value, but it becomes of infinite value when it is in fruitful union with the vine, and is of the same nature and life and urge to bear fruit as the vine.

In the chapters that follow I hope to give in a much fuller and more human-interest way the story and the fruition of the quest. Even so, the mind of the Spirit seems to desire and even to urge that I attempt to report certain precious experiences that are so much needed to be known and experienced.

Today there are many who may ask, "What can Jesus mean to me—a man who lived on this earth some two thousand years ago, whose actual existence some have doubted? How can a life so distant in time and in a setting so different from ours, have a direct bearing on my life today?"

Jesus as revealed and manifested to me is both the most real, alive and life-giving of all beings and persons, and the historical and eternal personification of love as life, and life as love. Jesus and life are revealed as limitless love going to the fullest limits and possibilities of love. The love, the life, which Jesus is and calls for is limitless good-will, the longing and the urge to work and to see achieved pure good to everybody and to everything; its self-giving is unbounded. Like water and sunshine love is wholly non-resistant, self-giving, and self-adjusting. No resistance or opposition can keep it from being true to its nature and doing its best (even when most opposed, hated, and crucified) without expecting any return. It is always beneficent and re-creative. Like light, warmth, and rain it remains faithful to its purpose whether we coöperate or oppose it—"for He maketh His sun to rise on the evil and on the good, and sendeth His rain on the just and on the unjust." The rain makes no discrimination between the fields of industrious and lazy farmers; the only discrimination is man-made.

Love is personal and impersonal, personal at its source but flowing out impersonally to all the world. In Jesus we have love and the personal incarnation of love as one, so that Jesus is love and love is Jesus. If Jesus is not yet a real personality to you, think of Him as the embodiment of this love that I am seeking to describe, so that when you read His name in the following pages you will be unhindered by theological doubt in grasping the spirit that pervades this book. You will then discover the possibility of real fellowship with Jesus through love, even before you know Him as a person.

The essential thing is that Jesus, according to His last night's promise to His first disciples, and after a manner similar to His appearance to them on the night following His Resurrection, is manifesting Himself still—from without, and breathing and infusing Himself within, giving the keys and the secrets of an abiding, fruitful and transforming identification and union with Himself.

Through the medium of conscious need, of desire, by invitation, and by yielding to the free and freeing control of the Spirit, the risen and ascended Jesus manifests Himself, enters into and makes His abode with all who are made ready to receive Him. Those who receive Him, by conscious, yearning desire and need, by asking and knocking, by leaving on the outside everything that has kept them on the outside, by humbling themselves as little children at His feet, and by using the master key of holy love, may enter consciously into Him and into the Kingdom of Heaven here and now. While all live, move and have their being in God, the fullest appreciation and awareness of its reality is found only in submitting to the qualities and disciplines of Jesus; only in yielding to the Spirit of Jesus, can we be consciously entered into Jesus and His Kingdom. One must go through Gethsemane and come to "Thy will be done," and not mine, until mine becomes Thine; also through Calvary, crucifixion and death to everything that prevents entering fully and freely.

If anything that belongs outside of Jesus and of Heaven could enter, it would not be Heaven. The door into the union with Jesus and the Kingdom of Heaven is the perfect condition by which we enter. The door is just the right size. If it were larger, something could enter that belongs on the outside; and if it were smaller, something would be left on the outside that belongs on the inside. All that is unloving, unmerciful, and unforgiving, all that is impure, insincere, false, fearful, and unbelieving, all that desires, wills or works harm or injury has to be left on the outside. Everyone who enters must humble himself as a little child at His feet. The master key of Love unlocks the door into the Holy Realm. All must enter at the lowest and humblest place. No matter where you later go in Jesus, you must enter at His feet. To be least in Him and in His kingdom is far better than to be greatest on the outside.

As we choose to please Him, to think and feast upon Him, and to manifest Him and Him only, as we concentrate upon Him and His way of love, as we always go in love and manifest nothing but the loving spirit, His presence goes with us and gives us rest. He keeps us and we keep ourselves within the most holy place, within Himself. Within this holy place there is but one responsibility, namely the responsibility of remaining there. There is but one law, the law of love, which fulfills all other laws. Here is the place of perfect safety and freedom, and of the beginnings in experience of the perfect universe. We do not need many things; we need this all-important thing. This is the "pearl of great price" which has such high value that they who are wise will let go everything that keeps them from possessing it and being possessed of it. Since Jesus has overcome fully and passed through death to resurrection, ascension, and to the throne, it is even better to be in union with Him now than it was to be in union with the Father prior to this. In this union with Him in the Spirit we are already dead to what He died for and already raised with Him from the dead and seated in the Kingdom of Heaven with Him. Even our human bodies are feeling something of the quickening that raised Him from the dead. God came in the flesh as Jesus, and was gloriously manifested in the body as well as in the Spirit. As he brought the Kingdom of God in the visible and external, so Jesus through the Holy Spirit comes into our bodies and spirits and is beginning the work of their full redemption and transformation.

Dying to the things that keep us out of identification and union with Jesus is not sacrifice but great release. We give up nothing worth keeping; we get everything. The life of overcoming is far easier than the life of yielding to false desires and being overcome. The Cross of Jesus is far easier than the crosses of the world. Jesus gives us an easy yoke for pulling the loads of life. Moreover, it is far easier for us to enter into union with Jesus than it was for Him to enter into union with us. He came out of life into death to get to us; and He came to the bottom of our needs to minister to us. We go out of death into life to get to Jesus, and to the heights of privilege in Him. He took upon Himself what we have to give up. We take upon ourselves His Spirit and His perfect everything.

This yielding and responding to Him, this consent to manifest Him and His love, is made divinely easy, natural, and happy as, led by the Holy Spirit even in our desiring and praying, we learn to ask Him to write His nature and love in the whole of our being. Thus, as we follow, as we delight to abide in Him, and to do His will, our will also becomes one with His. This is the place where we find that we did *not* want what we thought we wanted, that is, to have our own way; that we *did* want what He wanted for us, His best possible. Only His best will completely satisfy us, and satisfy Him, and work pure good to the whole of life. To adapt the words of Augustine, He has made us for Himself and for the very highest and best for us and all, and nothing short of fully yielding and fully expressing His will and purpose can satisfy us. He delivers us from the things that we thought we wanted that He may bring us to what He knew we really wanted and needed.

This place of loving to do what we should, what we can do better than anyone else, is the place of complete freedom and complete fulfillment. Here we are free from our old wills and desires, and from all lower wills and leaderships, free to do through redeemed desire what we best like to do. Here we go to our best place and work as naturally as birds go to the air, and children to their play, more from what is within than from any teaching from without. As Emerson would say, only our Maker can lead us and teach us what we can do better than anyone else and just where we belong in relation to Him and to all the rest.

This doing what each of us can do best, what nobody could buy us off from doing, what nobody has to pay us to do, and what we would gladly pay for the privilege of doing, is the very order of life, the only order of life that will satisfy us. This way of life will make each of us a divine artist in thinking and in doing. In the words of Kipling, each of us is going to be free and inspired "to paint the thing as he sees it for the God of things as they are." There is no more fear of false opinion, no more low conformity to customs and traditions that limit and enslave, no more effort to save the old bottles that will not hold the new wine, "that never grew in the belly of the grape." This is the new wine of the Spirit, the wine of God, the wine of life. As Ibsen says, "The wine of the world has grown old and insipid." The old bottles will not hold the wine of God.

The holding on to the old bottles, as well as the old wine, has been the special perversity of the custodians and profiteers of the *status quo* in religion, in the social order, and in the whole of conventionalized life. Life, to be spiritual and aglow with the life of God, must be forever responsive to the fresh movements of the Spirit. Institutional life has never been thus responsive. This reminds me that Wycliffe Rose once asked me if I could tell him what was the matter with an unusually good college that had let men go who would have made a college fashioned after the order of the Academy of Plato. My reply was that in the institutional life of the college some new wine was causing the bottles to crack, and it was decided to keep the bottles.

The free flow of the Spirit must have even its own ritual that will be as free and spontaneous as the Spirit Himself. And yet, a flowing thing like a river knows how to keep within its banks and is far more permanent than icebergs floating toward the equator. Of high necessity all of us, if we be true disciples, must become immediate disciples of the Perfect One. All disciples of disciples are pale and anæmic in comparison with an immediate disciple of Jesus.

As we are led by the Spirit, and only those who are led by the Spirit are free and growing up into divine sonship, as we obey the new law of love urged within and written without, as we go on loving and praying for all, and for the whole of life, and serving as best we can, our understanding is opened and we see with Jesus that it is even better to give than to receive. Then we can say with Emerson, "Do you ask my aid? I also wish to be a benefactor. I wish more to be a benefactor and servant, than you wish to be served by me, and surely the greatest good fortune that could befall me is precisely to be so moved by you that I should say, 'take me and all mine and use me and mine freely'—for I could not say it, otherwise than because a great enlargement had come to my heart and mind which made me superior to my fortunes."

With the opening of an understanding that makes us good soil for the seed of the Kingdom, we also see that it is infinitely worse to do evil, even the least of evil, than to receive the worst that men and devils can do to us and against us—infinitely worse to crucify than to be crucified. To quote Emerson again, we come to know that "only the law of love and justice can effect a clean revolution," that

evil can only be overcome with good. Only the cross can conquer the sword. Only Christ can conquer anti-Christ.

In the will to work pure good and nothing but good at
all, to give out as much heaven as possible to all, and no hell
to any, the deepest secret of the Kingdom of Heaven is
given us, namely, that we are in, and that we are, what we
give out. If we give the love of God to all, we open ourselves
even wider to Him, and to His love, and find ourselves increasingly in Him and His Kingdom. If we give out heaven
all the time, we are in heaven all the time; if we give out any
hell any of the time, we are not in heaven all the time. For
a man's own good, he has to be in whatever spirit and realm
he yields to by giving voice or expression to it. If a man
could give out hell and yet be in heaven here or anywhere,
he might remain hellish; but because he has to be in whatever he is giving to others, he is taught by all experience the
folly of giving anything that he would not like to receive and
be in himself. Thus we discover the wisdom of giving out
and desiring pure good and the greatest possible good to all.
When a man's understanding is opened to the beautiful
Laws of the Kingdom as taught by Jesus, he becomes the
good soil that will bring forth abundantly the seed sown
by the Sower. It is not that we are good, but that when our
understanding is opened we see the way of perfect love, the
way of Jesus, as the only way. All other ways are unreasonable and dangerous.

In the spirit of revelation of Jesus, and in His way of love,
we are delivered from the spirit that judges and condemns.
We are brought rather into the heart and secret of the gospel, the victorious judgment of love and mercy. If a man
were the worst of all, His judgment of love and mercy for
such an one would be that by His grace the man might
become the best possible. He longs to make a divine interchange with us, taking away everything in us that should not
have been and should not be, and giving us in its stead
everything that we should be. A man may have been His
chief enemy and may have made it harder for himself than

anyone else, but Jesus longs to deliver him from his tragic position and miserable state, and make him a chief among friends, witnesses, prophets, and apostles. This is the way that He dealt with Saul of Tarsus. The way He dealt with him became Paul's Gospel, the Gospel of the immeasurable love and grace of God. There is no limit to the possibilities of this Gospel when one sees it, and becomes its incarnation.

To the degree that one becomes an incarnation of the Spirit of Jesus, he enters into identification and union with Him. He also is given the measure of love and light that causes him to identify himself with all that he can bring to this light and into this love. As blessed as it is to be identified with Jesus and to be receiving freely from Him and for Him, it is even better to be giving out freely from Him and for Him, and identifying ourselves with every need in the world until it is met, or as St. Paul put it, "finishing out that which is lacking in the sufferings of Christ" to bring the creation to God.

It is not true that Jesus Himself, in His own body which is lifted above death and every shaft of evil, has to come and be crucified over and over again, but it is true that His Spirit in His disciples will continue His work of redemption, through the cross, until the creation is reconciled to God and the earth is filled with His love and justice and glory. With the understanding that the Spirit of Jesus in those in whom He is being successfully incarnated and reproduced and not Jesus in His own body has to keep on being crucified, how magnificent are the words which Ibsen put in the mouth of the Emperor Julian, who tried to revive the old Roman religion and make the world Galileanless: "The Galilean, the Carpenter's Son, sits enthroned as the King of Love in the warm believing hearts of men.

"Where is He now? Has He been at work elsewhere, since that happened at Golgotha?

"I dreamed about Him lately. I dreamed that I had subdued the whole world. I ordained that the memory of the Galilean should be rooted out the earth, and it was rooted out. Then the spirits came and ministered to me, and bound wings on my shoulders, and I soared aloft in infinite space till my feet rested on another world.

"It was another world than mine. Its curve was vaster, its light more golden, and many moons circled around it.

"Then I looked down on my earth—the emperor's world, which I had made Galileanless, and I thought that all that I had done was very good.

"But behold, Maximus—there came a procession by me, on the strange earth where I stood. There were soldiers and judges and executioners at the head of it, and weeping women followed. And lo, in the midst of the slow moving array, was the Galilean alive, bearing a cross on His back. Then I called to Him and said, 'Whither away, Galilean.' But He turned His face toward me, smiled, and nodded slowly saying, 'To the place of the skull.'

"Where is He now? What if that at Golgotha, near Jerusalem, was a wayside matter, a thing done so to speak in passing a leisure hour? What if He goes on and on and suffers and dies and conquers again and again from world to world?"

In His people, yes. But thanks be to God that He can die no more and that in His Spirit and in His people he conquers and conquers until even death is dead.

An English officer in the first World War had the feeling that every shot fired on either side was fired at Jesus, and that every shell which passed through another also went through Him. As "the lamb slain from the foundation of the world," He will continue to be slain until all slaying gives place to healing and resurrection. What the English officer felt, all sensitive souls should be feeling, and feeling increasingly, until all that defiles, hurts, wounds, and kills gives place to the reign and splendor of His good spirit. This victory, as I understand it, is to be gradual like the dawn of the early morn, and yet sudden like the rising of the sun.

In Jesus, through union with Him, all conflicts are resolved in sublime and inconceivable harmonies. All the good and every possibility of good are fulfilled. The things that seemed impossible to reconcile are not only reconciled, but are brought to perfection through the union of seeming opposites. The spirit of wisdom and revelation in the knowledge of Jesus, which Paul had in such rare measure and which he prayed for us to have in fullness, not only reconciles us to God and His best for us but also puts us in the beginning and makes sure of the consummation of the reconciliation, the fulfillment, and the perfection of all things in Jesus Christ.

Take, for example, the conflict between the so-called ideal and the so-called actual realms: in the harmonization that is already beginning to be felt in us and that has already been achieved in Jesus Christ, the ideal is realized in the so-called actual realm, and the actual is transformed into the ideal so that the two together become the ideal-actual and the actual-ideal. The earthly and the supernatural in Jesus are wholly in unity. The highest reality is higher than the purely ideal and spiritual can be, apart from their incarnation and victory in the visible, tangible, bodily, or earthly. In turn, the visible, the tangible, and the bodily through yielding to the use and transformation of the supernatural become the highest expression of the supernatural. The last becomes first and the first last. Though the body is only a corpse when separated, with the spirit it becomes the highest reality of all, bringing God into visibility, and into concrete reality so that His reign extends to the fullest limits of His love and power. And not only are the natural and the supernatural, God and the world, spirit and the body, brought together in a great synthesis, but all other conflicts are likewise resolved into dynamic coöperative harmonies.

The surpassing wonder and preciousness of Jesus above all other divine and human names is that in Him God appeared in a human, external body on the plane of our suffering and need, went the way of perfect love and self-offering (the way of the cross) to resurrection, ascension, and the highest throne. But it takes the Holy Spirit to reveal this. Do not condemn those who do not see it. As they yield fully to the Spirit, He will reveal it to them.

Those who repeat the sacred names and teachings and fail to yield to the Holy Spirit that brings the revelation have only the letter and miss the reality that cleanses and makes alive.

Jesus brings together in one body those who are easiest to convince and those most difficult—the so-called Fundamentalists, and the so-called Modernists. He did not drive away Thomas because he required extra proof. He gave the proof.

In the love of Jesus the conflicts between the liberal and charitable spirit, on the one hand, and the orthodox spirit that magnifies the letter (and too often at the expense of the spirit), on the other hand, are harmonized to the enrichment of each. Each has a value needed by the other, and the orthodoxy of the Holy Spirit gives to each the very thing needed. The temptation of the orthodox has been to substitute Lord, Lord, and the other shibboleths of the correctness of the letter, for keeping His commandments, and for entering and abiding in fruit-bearing union and identification with Jesus. They have tried to be the branches without vital union with the vine, and without bearing the fruit of the vine. The temptation of the liberals has been the effort to bear the fruit of the vine without being in union with the vine. The liberal is easy to get along with in comparison with the unconverted and unchristianized orthodox man, who is the hardest nut of all to crack and the poorest meat of all when cracked. Such men and women are in desperate need of the Spirit of Jesus, the only possible bond of union with Jesus Himself. But notwithstanding the spiritual deadness of formal orthodoxy, its factual content is essentially true, truer than the spirit in liberalism that denies. When both of the types yield to the Holy Spirit and receive the revelation of Jesus, they will be at His feet and in each other's arms.

In my own experience, I was born naturally and spiritually in an orthodox environment. In my quest for God's best, I sought Him, if happily I might find more of Him among the liberals than I had found among the orthodox. He was with me all the way in the quest, and was with me to the degree of hunger and receptivity, irrespective of names and labels. When by the leading of the Spirit, I left all groups of opinions, and was dedicated to be led by the Spirit, I asked for the truth and the baptism of the Holy Spirit, if this was the best for me. Finally I asked Jesus, if He could, to come within me and be in me the very principle and life of His own good life and teaching. He quickly (as soon as He could get me ready to yield to the Spirit and receive Him) manifested Himself without and came within. Jesus longs to get us to receive Him, to enter and abide in Him, and to bear the fruit of the union. Then He can give us of His orthodoxy, the orthodoxy of unity and spirit and understanding. I magnify my office at this point because, having been both orthodox and liberal, and having found Him no respecter of dividing labels, I desire to make emphatic His great desire and longing to receive all who will come to Him, to take the responsibility of correcting theories, philosophies and theologies, and of guiding men into all the truth, and into the fullness of perfect life.

I have been much helped by fundamentalists like Moody, and the Gordons, and by liberals like Swing, Gunsaulus, Hillis, Drummond, Foster, Newton, Buttrick, Stanley Jones, Rufus Jones, the Poteats, and Fosdick. Jesus was with me when I sought Him among the Hindus, the philosophers, the poets, and in the Christian science movement. I have found in the free romantic spirit of the poets more of what I am feeling after than I have in the philosophers and the theologians. More than any other mortals the poets have succeeded in giving glimpses of the shape of things to come. Plato, a poet as well as a philosopher, gave me idealism in such a perfect form that his appeal has been tremendous. It was while reading Plato that I had my first experience of being lost in the beauty of the ideal realm. Emerson, more than any other modern, has helped to induce me to cut loose from all other leaderships and to be led by the Spirit. He has also said for me in the language of rare beauty and appeal much that I have been longing to say for myself.

While I had not read Ibsen's *Emperor and Galilean* prior to the revelation of Jesus, and my entering into the new world through identification and union with Him, of all modern writers Ibsen has helped me most to find words to express the reconciliation that is seen and felt, in part, between the realms of the natural and the supernatural. His expressions are poetic and are not to be taken as more than suggestive, but they point to that third realm, or kingdom, or empire, to use the words of Royce, "Where the rigid order of nature shall be one with the most miraculously significant divine truth, where Caesar shall become a spiritual, and God an earthly ruler, is precisely the realm where not so much our philosophy, but our age, whose echo this philosophy is, is even now seeking to comprehend, and with prophetic voice to proclaim."

Ibsen felt that we were in the last scene of the last act of the drama of history; "that the consummation stands at the threshold."

What Ibsen calls the third empire, the prophets saw as the reign of the Messiah on earth, and the early Christians looked forward to as the manifestation and reign of Jesus in visible victory. The visible reign of Jesus will be the empire of the human-divine that fulfills the three former empires, the natural, the spiritual, and the divine-human, where each of these three has been consummated. What has been made so precious to me is that in this fourth realm both the natural and the supernatural, the human and the divine, and everything that has been separated and incomplete are brought together in miraculous harmonies and fulfillment. To me, this fourth realm is the realm of perfection, of complete happiness, of everything prophesied and more. At the times when I have been caught up in the Spirit in

this realm, I have found myself in the state where I saw
that everything in reality was good or permanently real,
where there is "thanks for everything." All that could be
desired in the natural is there; all of the holiness and immortality and glory of heaven is there; and the four realms
have become one. The natural has been purified and become
immortal, and the supernatural has become concrete and
appears supernaturally natural. In this realm each of us has
just what he would have chosen. A part of my happiness is
that you will be just as well pleased with God's place for
you as I am with His place for me. Each of us in a body like
the ascended Jesus Christ will, in the spirit, possess the whole
creation and be present in every part of it. All will be mine
and all yours. I am all the richer because of you. You are all
the richer because of me.

Not only was Ibsen feeling out for the bringing together
of the empires of the natural and of the spiritual, but all of
the finer and freer and more sensitive spirits who have had
the genius to voice this feeling in literature have left in their
writings the most appealing intimations and fragments of it.

Goethe sensed the wonder of the ideal actualized in the
so-called actual and of the so-called actual transformed into
the ideal. Alfred North Whitehead has seen the whole movement of the Spirit as seeking "Concretion," incarnation, and
triumph in externals. As he observes, there is something
about Christianity that will not be satisfied until the perfect
is realized in the realm of the actual. The best feeling and
longing of our time is for this very synthesis.

Tennyson, either by fortunate guessing or by inspired seer-
ship, saw over a hundred years ago: "The heavens filled with
commerce," and, "The nations' airy navies, grappling in the
central blue; and from which there reigned a ghastly dew."
He also saw the "parliament of man, the federation of the
world," where "The common sense of most shall hold a fret-
ful realm in awe, and the kindly earth shall slumber lapped
in universal law."

Our own poet-musician Sidney Lanier saw the perfect

harmony between truth, beauty, and goodness. He saw that these three shining as one light, and burning as one fire, are essential for high being and achieving. He realized that life had to be all love to be life, that enough love would even heal the body, and that when love rides in, hell moves out.

Oliver Wendell Holmes saw even Emerson a "Soaring nature ballasted with sense, wisdom without wrinkles or pretense, in every Bible faith to read and every altar helping to shape his creed, an iconoclast without a hammer, removing our idols so gently that it seems an act of worship."

In the life we are feeling after, all things that have had values we have held on to will be carried over. Things that seemed opposites will be found necessary to each other. Only hate and the things that destroy, mar, or defile will be left out. Nothing good enough to get in and make a contribution will be left out. Where Jesus sowed in tears, we shall reap in joy. Jesus will be seen again in an environment achieved by Him, and by His spirit and His people, a fitting place for One so loving and self-giving. We will yet see Him as the man of joy. Even while on earth, until the persecutions set in, what He brought was more like a wedding feast than a religious service. Let us not forget that Jesus conducted no funerals; in His presence no one remained dead. He was and is the superlative biologist, the giver of perfect life, the abundant life, the victorious life, the life of joy, peace, and gladness. He did not bring a new religion. He brought perfect life, and all that goes with perfect life. In the new Jerusalem, where He has a city to His liking, even the temple, a place of worship, apart from the normal life of a perfect city is no longer seen. Even now the hunger is to transcend what has passed historically for religion and enter into perfect life through union and fellowship with Jesus, the triumph of His way of life in the individual, in the social and economic orders, and in the creation itself.

In these words spoken through me but seemingly from

Him: "I am perfect everything; I give perfect everything; I give you perfect everything," we find a summary and fulfillment of all that Jesus and the Spirit have said concerning Him, and what He gave and is forever giving. He will not fail nor be discouraged until He has brought forth His judgment of enlightenment, love, and mercy unto victory.

He brings forth, and must succeed in bringing forth, in us and in the creation, not only perfect spirit and mind and body, but also perfect harmony and blessedness with relation to each and all. "BLESSED BE HIS NAME," saith the Spirit. His ministry of love and light is individual, social, and cosmic all in one.

In the new covenant which brings us into the new nature, and prepares us for the new realm that we are glimpsing, we will not only delight in His will and work and predestination, but we will find that in Him and in His life for us there is no more darkness, or evil, or harm, or discord, or sickness, or death. None of these things is in Him; and in the perfect union and life and victory, they will not be in us. He is the life, and the love, and the redemption, and the health, and the healing that dispels the darkness, that masters hate and brings forth the kingdom of love and harmony. He is the life that heals wounds and diseases and supplies the full needs of the whole man, and of the whole of life; that banishes death; that brings forth life, immortality and cosmic as well as human perfection. This is the great way, the true way, and in the end will be found the only way.

J. R. MOSELEY

BOOK ONE

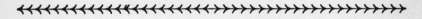

LIFE AS LOVE

CHAPTER I

SEED, SOIL AND CLIMATE

‹‹‹‹‹‹‹‹‹‹‹‹‹‹‹‹‹‹‹‹‹‹‹‹‹‹‹‹‹‹›››››››››››››››››››››››››››

Happily, the divine when planted in the human and allowed to bear fruit has the power to change the human, while the human has power to become the channel of expression for the divine. The kind of plant accords with the seed; the way in which it grows will accord with its soil and climate. One event stands out in the dim memories of childhood which I can clearly recognize as the seed of all that I have desired to be. When I was not more than six years old, my oldest brother read me these words of Jesus: "Whosoever drinketh of this water shall thirst again; but whosoever drinketh of the water that I shall give him shall never thirst; but the water that I shall give him shall be in him a well of water springing up unto everlasting life." As I listened, something within me leaped. However undeveloped our powers of ordinary understanding, there is that in us which learning can make no wiser and immaturity of years cannot impede. There is a power to grasp deep truth in the heart, even though it be beyond the comprehension of the head, a "light that lighteth every man coming into the world." Such moments of insight come to many in early years, to people of every type and race, and in every variety of circumstance. The background of tradition and environment will greatly determine the way in which these insights are ultimately developed and expressed; and this is well, for the wholeness of human life demands the greatest variety of gifts so that each personality may become a unique expression of God's will.

Therefore my own manner of endeavoring to express His will has its beginnings among a primitive, unspoiled folk in the backwoods of the Blue Ridge Mountain foothills of North Carolina. In his *Blue Bird* Maeterlinck pictures children before they are born planning some great benefit to bring to earth. I once heard a learned Hindu say that each of us chooses his parents. Whether God alone chooses them or we also have a part in the choice, most of us who have had good fathers and mothers feel that a happy choice was made. But we are not in the happy place, in God, to which He wants to bring us, until we say in the words of Ibsen, "Thanks for everything."

I was early impressed with the sincerity and honesty of my father. When he offered for sale, or in a trade, a horse or a mule, he first told its faults to the full. When he took a load of watermelons to sell, he sought to have the larger ones at the bottom instead of the top. When he listed his property to be taxed, he told the assessors what he thought it was worth, or what he would want for it if he offered it for sale. He was an absolutely honest man and free from sham and pretense—humble, gentle, and considerate. When we children would start to the field to work, his last words were, "Don't get too hot," or "Don't work too hard." He used a red mule in ploughing and rode the same mule to public speakings, elections, and other places of community interest. I rode behind him. It seemed to me that he sought to tell me everything about his plans and interests.

His health was unfortunately undermined in the foolish war about slavery and states' rights, when there should have been a love feast over setting the colored people free and generosity and magnanimity over states' privileges. But in spite of his health, he was a tremendous worker.

My mother's determination that the children should have the best education and life advantages, and her hard work, wise planning, rigid economies to that end, were almost beyond belief. Even when she was weaving at the old-fashioned loom, she taught the children and heard them recite their lessons. She dried blackberries, apples, and peaches, spreading them out on planks in the sun, and kept beehives. In her world she was the wisest economist. She told me late in her life (she lived to be eighty-seven), that she had been guided even as to when to plant her crops, so that the planting would suit the weather conditions to follow.

The way my mother prayed, when there was a new door of opportunity or a new step which seemed to be upward for any of us, awed me. She would go out at night in the dark and pray and pray until she had the answer, the assurance that the new venture would be well. She had, she felt, the promise that one of her children would be used in a special way to help usher in the Kingdom of God and that Millard would be that one. Millard is my brother, six or seven years younger than I, who has a wonderfully good heart.

My oldest brother, Charles, now a physician in Greensboro, North Carolina, was the best educated and most mentally alert person in our neighborhood. I was quite young at the time of the Charleston earthquake. Charles is five years my senior. I was sleeping upstairs and when I felt the shaking of my bed and of everything about me, I jumped out of bed and ran downstairs. I found Charles fearlessly calm. He remarked, "I don't see why we make all this disturbance. It is only an earthquake."

Charles watched over me with kind domination. After the first baptizing he attended, he took me to the creek to see if he could baptize me. That night I complained that my ear hurt and he appeared fearful that I would tell about my bath in the creek. I had no idea of doing that. I prized too highly the privilege of being with him and imbibing his knowledge. He kept nothing back from me, nothing that I should have known and, I fear, one or two things that I should not have known.

My father's family, consisting of a baby brother, a widowed mother and four or five unmarried aunts treated each other with such astonishing kindness that the only times I ever heard any dissension among them were times when they were trying to make one of the group stop work, or get new clothing which could not be afforded for all. "You are more tired than I am, let me finish the work." "You need a new dress more than I do. I won't get another until you have had yours." So great was their unselfishness.

Mother's oldest brother, Uncle John, was almost a saint. He was tender-hearted, somewhat after the manner of Saint Francis, and lectured the neighborhood boys if he saw any of them throwing a stone at a bird or inflicting unnecessary pain. He taught me something of what I later learned from Emerson, to "name the birds without a gun," to "love the wood-rose and leave it on its stalk," to "sit at rich men's tables to eat bread and pulse," and "unarmed face danger with a heart of trust."

The doctor in the neighborhood, Ed Hampton, was a rare soul. In spirit he was much like the Quakers, although he did not want to belong to any denomination. He wanted to be baptized in water in order to acknowledge Christ openly before men and fulfill the forms of righteousness, yet he had a minister baptize him as a member of the church rather than as a member of any particular sectarian group. When he had a patient who was very ill, he changed his home to live with the patient until he was out of danger. He prayed for his patients and for guidance in doctoring them. He said that if he could get a patient who had not been hurt too much by home doctoring and was not an eater of meat to excess, especially of pork, the patient usually got well. He married a girl of sixteen when he was fifty-six and brought up a large family of children who loved him and admired him greatly. He lived to be more than ninety-two.

John Park, the neighborhood school teacher and a county commissioner, was another leading citizen of the community. He and my mother seemed to be more interested in our school than any other folks. He bought the first Jersey wagon, a kind of cross between a one-horse wagon and an uncovered buggy, for himself and the neighborhood. We all used it freely on special occasions. If he ever felt we made too free a use of it, he never intimated it.

When he was about thirty-five years old, he was ill and the doctors of our region decided he had tuberculosis. His belief in their opinion hurt him terribly. Through a wise providential guidance, he decided to make a twenty-five mile trip over rough roads driving a mule to the Jersey wagon to see Dr. Hollingsworth of Mount Airy, North Carolina, who had the reputation of being the most successful doctor in our part of the state.

We saw him as he left and he looked like a man going to his own funeral. When he came back, he was aglow with joy. He yelled out to us that Dr. Hollingsworth said to tell his wife that if he would live temperately and sensibly and eat plenty of turnip greens and such, she would have to put up with him for a long time, that he had a good chance of living until he was seventy. That was the last of his "consumption." He remained on the earth until he was eighty-two. His wife is now more than ninety years old, the only one of the grown-ups of my boyhood memories who is still alive.

The schoolhouse in the neighborhood was also the Primitive Baptist Meeting House. It was the center of neighborhood interest and talk. The neighbors came to hear us spell and speak, and if any of us did measurably well, he became the neighborhood talk. One year the school term lasted only seven weeks. The longest public school term I remember was three months. My brother Millard says it was the best school he ever knew, and the number of boys who went to college from that school was extraordinarily high.

I did not like to study and be confined in school. On my way to school the first morning, I had the wicked wish that I might find that the schoolhouse had burned the night before. Having little interest in Webster's blue back speller and a great deal of interest in life on the outside and in mischievous funny things on the inside of school, I was naturally a very dull pupil.

I believe I re-learned my ABC's three times, but I found such keen delight in arithmetic that I learned to read in order to understand the problems that were stated in words rather than in figures alone. Then I woke up, and within a few years stood examination and received a first grade certificate. As I remember, I was then between sixteen and seventeen and small for my age. I went up near the Blue Ridge Mountains to Gum Orchard to see if I could get a school. I went because the neighborhood Baptist preacher, whom I had met, suggested it. One of the three committee-men had been in the war with my father and loved him greatly. He was for anything that he felt would please father. He took me to one of the other committeemen, who was a country wit, humorist, and philosopher.

The second committeeman said it was wonderful for a boy my size and age to have a first grade certificate. He wasn't sure, he said, but that the grown boys and girls, some of them twice as large as I, might dispose of me through the cracks of the schoolhouse. After all this fun he said that if the third committeeman agreed, they would have a summer term and employ me to teach it. The implication was that if I could make good I would get the winter term also.

When the big boys and girls were told that I was to teach the school, they said I would be there but a short time before they made it so uncomfortable for me that I would give up. The committee came out the first morning of school and read the law to the pupils, but before the opening of the school I had found out who was the leader of the opposition and had a walk with him. I told him I wanted to make a success of the school and that I understood he had a great deal of influence. I told him if he would help me I would be very grateful. He surrendered on the spot and said, "I'll do it." He did. They first tested me out to see if I knew my arithmetic. After that the pupils helped me main-tain good enough order to make the school satisfactory.

In the country section there were more Missionary Baptists and Methodists than there were Primitive, or "Hard-shell," Baptists, though there was quite a scattering of the latter. As I was resisting an inner urge to yield to the good Spirit and become a follower of Jesus, the Primitive Baptists disturbed me less than the Methodists and the Missionary Baptists, especially at the time of their protracted meetings, which were sometimes revivals. I loved life and I was bent on a career. I was afraid of what I thought religion was. Had I known then that God is love and that Jesus came to give abundant life, joy, peace, health and healing, I am confident that much of my resistance to the drawings of the Spirit would have disappeared.

Such urges had come upon me before. I remember once feeling a sense of tragedy when I heard two grown people quarreling, and something moved me to make peace between them. Though I knew nothing of Jesus' way of making peace at the time, I nevertheless managed to heal the quarrel by appealing to each of them alone. I remember too how I was instantly cured of rheumatism in the arm when one of my uncles rubbed it with kerosene oil. Since that time I have never been too ill to get up and walk. I was not anointed or rubbed as a religious rite, but because somebody believed and acted upon the belief that kerosene oil when rubbed on the body is a cure for rheumatism, the trouble vanished. Would the healing have occurred anyhow just at that time, without the oil? To what extent did the oil and rubbing have healing virtue? How far did faith in the oil and the rubbing act upon the body? How much of it was an act of divine love and purpose? I do not know. The God of love, health and healing, as I understand, is always doing His best, with or without coöperating faith on our part, to keep us well, or to restore us from sickness to health.

Most of us remember our boyhood by these small but significant incidents. Once I made a pet of a calf. I sometimes rode the calf, but more often drove him before a small cart which brother Charlie had made for me. I would go to the woods to get pine knots and lightwood that we used for fire-light to study by on winter nights. I decided that in the steepest and muddiest places I would pull with him, and would go and take my position by him, pulling on one of the shafts. I had done this only a few times when the calf began choosing places for me to pull. Later he refused to pull at all unless I pulled with him. This taught me never to do anything even for a calf unless it was good enough to keep on doing.

I remember how I used to look up with wonder at the mountains around our part of the country. I was willing to climb to their tops that I might have the freshness of their altitude and the great views. I still like this. In principle this has been both a strong and a weak point in my life. I have been so concerned to get large views and great sweeps that I have not given enough attention to technical details.

I was ambitious for public life, and wanted to be a lawyer as a stepping stone to that end. I also wanted a college education. We did not have the money and I could not think of putting any new burden on father and mother. Soon after Charles came home from attending a business school at Bowling Green, Kentucky, he told me about Peabody College at Nashville, which gave scholarships of two hundred dollars a year, in addition to free tuition. (I remember the very place on the farm where he told me that.)

I ascertained that a competitive examination would be held by Major Finger, the State Superintendent of Education for North Carolina, as a basis of award of some of these scholarships. I stood the next Peabody examination, but wrote no better hand than I do now. Major Finger notified me that I had not been appointed to one of the scholarships, but that my examination papers showed that I was entitled to enter the sophomore class at Peabody. He wrote that if I made good for one year and Chancellor Payne would recommend me, he would grant me a scholarship for the following year.

Mother said, "We'll sell the creek field." That was about the best land we owned. I could not accept such a sacrifice.

I found three friends who would lend me fifty dollars each. My father stood as my security and with the extra thirty-five dollars I had saved from my pay as school teacher, I set off for college.

Saying good-bye was a severe ordeal for all of us. I remember well the scene, but recall nothing any of us said, except the words of my father, "Rufus, I know nothing about the world you are to be in. I have no advice to give. I trust you."

CHAPTER II

THE WITNESS OF THE SPIRIT

◄◄◄◄◄◄◄◄◄◄◄◄◄◄◄◄◄◄◄◄◄◄◄◄◄◄►►►►►►►►►►►►►►►►►►►►►►►►

Four years at Peabody College; four quarters at the University of Chicago; five autumns and winters, and one whole scholastic year at Mercer University; two spring and summer quarters at the University of Chicago, where I taught one course as a Fellow; one semester at Heidelberg; several summers at Harvard University, and one spring there when I was the guest of the philosophical faculty in the days of Royce, James, Palmer, Everett, Munsterberg, and Santayana: these gave me unusual cultural advantages.

It was in these years that I began having increasing intimations of the possibility of a wholly different principle of living than is generally known or lived. This principle was associated for me with Jesus as I had read of Him in the Gospels. The possibilities of this way of life so stirred my imagination that I began yielding to its urge. This yielding brought days of great peace and joy. I was given moments of bliss that more than compensated for all that I had ever suffered in spirit, mind, and body. These seasons of being actually in the Kingdom of Heaven spoiled me for everything outside this realm. I had been slow to yield and respond to the Spirit's predestination of perfect love. Not until I had given myself to the quest of God's best and had given up the expectation of a secular career did the secrets of identification and abiding union with Jesus become known to me. There have been many hindrances, but the joy on the way has been exceedingly great. He who gives himself and all that he has to be led by the Spirit is headed rightly, no matter how imperceptible his progress may be.

In college life I was enriched by various cultural influences and by contact with dynamic men and women. I especially value knowing and studying under President W. H. Payne and Professor Wycliffe Rose. President Payne started his career as a country school teacher and advanced to the top of his profession. Wisdom fell from his lips. He knew that the only way to success was the way of love. When I remarked to him one day that no man is ever won and no situation is ever solved except in love and mutual respect, he was so pleased that he sought to advance me beyond my attainments.

Professor Rose was a graduate student during my first year at Peabody and one of my instructors the following three years. He was one of the best balanced and most inspiring of men, putting more of the ideal into the practical and lifting the practical more into the realm of the ideal, than is generally the way of college professors. I learned from him that the ideal divorced from the practical goes "thin," while the practical divorced from the ideal becomes "muddy."

Professor A. P. Bourland introduced me to Emerson, Arnold, Ruskin, and other Victorians who have meant much to me. We took long walks and he seemed to believe that impossible things were possible for me. He had faith that if I went immediately to the university a way would be found for me to continue, offering to furnish money if it did not come to me from other sources. During my first year at the University of Chicago he sent me a cheque which carried me through a difficult period. Soon afterward I received a fellowship which made it possible for me to stay on as long as I cared.

During that first year at Peabody a small copy of the Dialogues of Plato, dealing with the trial and imprisonment of Socrates, fell into my hands. Plato so gripped me that I completely forgot my body. For the first time in my life

I was lost in pure intellectual delight. When I started to read, I felt uncomfortable from nervous indigestion; when I put down the volume my body felt entirely comfortable. But when I relapsed to a lower level of thought and feeling, the old discomfort returned. Some years later when I was listening to Hamilton Wright Mabie at the University of Chicago, I had another experience of intellectual absorption and delight that brought relief and healing. Later I became aware that to live in the Spirit heals the body as well as the spirit.

While I was a student at Peabody, I heard Sam Jones many times. Through him I became aware that moral and spiritual life, lived well and presented intelligently, is what every awakened soul is most interested in. But even truth in the mouth of one who has not been made alive by living it, seems dead and of little appeal. As Royce says, "It is even humbling to belong to a race that has so many 'wooden minds' [even in high places] who can make such an interesting thing as truth dull and uninteresting."

During my second year at Peabody an evangelist from Texas named Penn conducted a meeting at the Central Baptist Church near the college. The first time I heard him was on Sunday morning. His subject was Naaman the Leper. He preached by making pictures—every detail so vivid that it was but a short time before it seemed that he was preaching to Moseley the Leper, instead of about Naaman. Every objection attributed by the evangelist to Naaman was my own objection to obeying the urge of the Spirit. When the evangelist made the altar call it seemed that I stood in jeopardy if I did not respond. Some of my college teachers and many of my student friends were present. Their presence made it all the more difficult to take up the cross by acknowledging my need to yield to the Spirit and follow Jesus. Going to the altar that Sunday morning was the most difficult step I had ever taken, or have ever yet been called upon to take.

Monday night was rainy and only a few people were

present in the lamp-lit barn of a church at the service to witness my open dedication. Going to the altar was far easier this time. But the great difference was, really, because the second step in the path of God, as always, was easier than the first. The evangelist, as he stood near and over me, remarked that this small congregation with only one at the altar might seem of minor consequence, but that he had the witness, which he felt was from God, that the young man at the altar would mean far more in the Kingdom of God than he himself had yet meant.

The next morning, alone in my room, there came the certainty that I believed, when I read in the Gospel according to Saint John, "He that believeth hath everlasting life." More than ever before I felt sure of being at that moment in the joy, peace, and fearless love of the Kingdom of Heaven. But I did not yet treasure it enough to keep it as a conscious perpetual possession. For years I would go out and return, not always understanding why. There was much I thought I wanted that experience had to teach me I did not want, before I was ready for the secrets of the Kingdom. More and more, being in conscious identification and union with Jesus, being in the Kingdom of Heaven, became so precious (and everything on the outside so unsatisfactory) that I was made ready to let go the things that led me out and kept me out.

I soon joined with the Baptists and expected the baptism of the Holy Spirit to accompany the baptism with water. While I had never heard baptism with the Spirit taught or preached as an actual spiritual experience, I sought to follow Jesus. At that time this baptism carried with it no definite meaning other than the New Testament report concerning the baptism of Jesus. Jesus received this baptism in connection with the baptism of John, why should we not receive it? I went away from the baptismal service disappointed, having received the baptism in water only, and missing the opening of the Heavens and the descent of the Holy Spirit. Later I realized that Jesus, while being baptized by John with water, was praying so hard that His whole heart and mind was on the Father and the doing of His will. I had failed thus to pray and dedicate my life to God. I had my mind too much on the water, the minister, and the people present to be receptive to the gift and presence of the Spirit.

During the early years of my life, the reading of the New Testament accounts of the sufferings and the crucifixion of Jesus melted me into great tenderness. What a loss it is not to abide in such tenderness and compassion, not to be deeply touched by every memory of His cross! Even so, it is ours to be stirred by the presence of the crosses under which men and women about us are stumbling and falling from day to day.

My first communion service brought the unexpected experience of seeing a gentle glowing light over the table, the bread, and the wine, which gave me a deep sense of the quiet presence of God. Years afterward, when I was a student at Harvard, I went to the Christian Science Church in Boston one night, where a communion service was being held without the symbols. Judge Hanna, the first reader, asked all present "to unite in communion with the one God Who is life, truth, and love." I said to myself, we Baptists do not invite others to join in our communion services, but I am going to divest myself of all prejudice and commune with God with these unknown friends. I humbled myself and fell at His feet. I was overshadowed and became lost in the Spirit. It was as if I stood in a great ocean of love and became at one with it. I have no conscious memory as to how I got from the gallery to the main floor of the church.

Neither the earlier experience of the glory of the Lord upon the table and the bread and the wine, nor the overshadowing that came when I first sought to commune in the Spirit without the material symbols, have ever been repeated, much as I have longed for them.

Sensing the reality and wonder of everything depends upon the spirit of approach. A recent convert from the English high church to the Roman Catholic faith, Harry

Orchard, has said in his book on the cross, "One may enter into communion with God through love, apart from the sacraments of the church." Nothing without love and the good Spirit of Jesus has any real value. Everything in His love and Spirit has eternal value. Ritualism does not avail anything of itself, neither does the lack of it. This same principle applies in the practical affairs of everyday life. Nothing has value outside of the Spirit and love of Jesus. True worship must be in Spirit and in truth, in Spirit and in love, in Spirit and in life. Perfect worship and perfect living are one. We can have the presence and the glory of the Lord everywhere and miss them anywhere.

At the University of Chicago I entered the world of the question mark. Yet, to use the great lines of Tennyson, "There lives more faith in honest doubt, believe me, than in half the creeds." As Plato observes, it is preferable for children to deny the existence of parents than for them to attribute unworthy characters or deeds to them. One reason for the lack of whole-hearted loyalty to God is that He has not been seen and worshipped as perfect love made real in human relations.

The first thing I heard in the University which sounded a positive note and gave me keen joy and a new zest for life was this from Professor George Bernard Foster: "Faith is the feeling or conviction that there is a meaning in things and that that meaning is good." Men of faith see the hidden good in all experiences. They are aware that everything is working together for their good, with the hope that in the fullness of time all things may also work together for the good of all. Faith that works by love and increases with love, sees that there is no experience which does not turn to good as one turns to God to do His will of love.

The preacher who helped me most in Chicago was David Swing. He had been tried for heresy, but not convicted. He grew tired of being tried by his Presbyterian brethren and went to the Central Music Hall, where he preached until his death. He preached almost as well as Emerson wrote, with the same happy way of seeing and explaining the truth of life apart from its specifically religious form. Swing was a liberal with the spirit that affirms. I have been repelled from what seemed the over-religiosity and unreality of the conventional religionist, and Swing gave me the spirit apart from its conventional forms. But, having discovered the spirit, I found that the conventional forms could live again. I had to become liberal in order to become orthodox. After listening to him I was given a new zest for life. My feet hit the sidewalk in a new way. I realized that I could make it for at least another week, although it looked as if I might have to leave the university for lack of funds. That would almost have broken my heart.

My first year in Chicago brought me in contact with one whose influence upon me has been unforgettable—an influence exercised by a man's *being* rather than his *saying*. This was Henry Drummond. Though he spoke and wrote with high command and clarity on the spiritual order in the natural world and the natural order in the spiritual world, his greatest value is expressed for me by a boy who, seeing him speaking to English miners, exclaimed, "Here is the first *man* I have ever seen!" He seemed to me a man whom it would be impossible to bore, so great was his interest and appreciation for the smallest things of life and for those around him. Of him Emerson might have said, when speaking of a visit to Rome, "I would have given everything I saw there to see a man worthy to be there." I watched him one day in the electrical building at the World's Fair. There was nothing on display which interested me so much as his countenance and manner.

In the class and lecture rooms of the university there were others whose influence has always remained with me, notably Herman von Holst, Harry Pratt Judson, and John Dewey, who stands out in my memory for surpassing humility, kindliness and brilliance of spirit. Seldom have I seen a man so moved by the account of another's suffering, and in my hearing he once spoke of the guilty sense of shame that follows failure to visit friends who are ill. I have the feeling that it was his good heart that enlisted his clear head in the interests of unpopular reforms. What he was and what he did appealed to me much more than what he said and wrote.

The Mercer days were especially happy. I liked Macon from the first and the college boys were an inspiration to me. I was thrown constantly with them and joined them in forming a health club where we found that we could live well at a cost of twenty cents a day. It was about the best human society I have ever known. Our club was referred to by the outsiders as the "Transcendental Club" from the variety and profundity of our meal-time conversation. Walter George (now U. S. Senator), John Roach Stratton, A. E. Ramsaur, S. E. Stephens, P. S. Carmichael, B. H. Grover, P. J. Christopher, J. E. Sammons, and I, as both Sammons and I remember, were the charter members.

J. B. Gambrell, the sage of the Southern Baptists, was president of Mercer when I first came to Macon and remained in office for two years. He was succeeded by P. D. Pollock, who made Mercer University his "life and likeness." Both presidents and their families were good to me almost beyond belief and made rich contributions to my Mercer days. W. H. Kilpatrick came to the college as professor of mathematics at the beginning of my fourth year. I discovered in him one of the wisest, kindliest, and most helpful friends who has ever come into my life. From then until now he has always been glad even to stop his own work to help me with mine.

While engaged in this work at Macon, I became connected with a boy of great promise who, through loss of sleep and the excessive use of cigarettes, became mentally unbalanced. Under very clear guidance I went to his room to care for him. I was at that time reading Lombroso's *Genius and Insanity,* and felt that enough friendliness and common sense would enable this boy to return to sanity. It was only a few hours before he had lucid moments. Through the best

influences that could be put around him and cheerful
drives and walks, he was saved the humiliation and shock of
being taken to an asylum or sanitarium. He recovered rapidly. Within a few weeks he was back at work, making his
accustomed high record in his studies. The last time I saw
him he was State Commissioner of Education in a pro-
gressive eastern state. It was in doing work of this kind that
it became clear to me that visiting the sick in love is especially pleasing to the Lord of love.

During the Mercer-Chicago and the Mercer-Harvard days,
I came to know something of the contemporary effort to
achieve physical and mental health through the resources of
the spirit. When I was giving a course of lectures at the summer assembly in Monteagle, Tennessee, in 1895 or 1896, the
friend who was reporting my talks for the *Nashville American* and the *Chattanooga Times* told me one evening, at the
conclusion of my lecture, that she felt as if I were a swimmer
striving to reach the shore and about to sink before reaching
it. She explained something of the influence of the mind and
spirit upon the body. She suggested that even when a man is
suffering, he should remember and say to himself, "In God
I live, move and have my being." I glimpsed something now
as to how I could coöperate with God and with the forces
resident in myself, in the interests of better health and better
living. I saw, and said, "I am going to be well some day."
As I said this, I leaped for joy, or the Spirit within me
leaped, a witness to its truth.

At Harvard I listened to William James prior to his
going to Europe to give his lectures on *Varieties of Religious Experience*. I came to know something of the whole
movement designated as New Thought, which James said
constituted, together with Christian Science, a spiritual
movement as significant for our day as the Reformation was
for its time. I found out that the Christian Science effort
was the most daring and radical of all current efforts to lay
hold of the resources of the Divine Spirit for doing again
at least some of the works of Jesus.

Some of the Christian Scientists appealed to me as being deeply in earnest, unusually loving and very radiant. Others repelled me. The more I lived with the poets and the prose writers who stressed the transforming power of the Divine Spirit, the more I felt that I should follow out the ray of light that was increasingly lighting my life, and which I saw at that time in Christian Science, as it appeared to me. I knew that to apply the Golden Rule to the college and to be true to every ray of light that was given, meant that I must put this whole matter before the college president, faculty and trustees, and resign my place on the faculty, because I felt that they might be embarrassed by my interest.

While I was seeking to lay down everything, to be led by what seemed to be the Spirit and the pressure of circumstances, I had an experience of such bliss and satisfaction that I realized that a moment of it more than compensated for all the sufferings and privations of my life up to that time.

It came about this way. One of the professors, my friend B. D. Ragsdale, had come to feel that I did not speak the language of orthodoxy. He came to see me to tell me so. He also let me know of the struggle he was having as to his duty in the matter. He was the teacher of the Bible in the college. Some of us had the feeling that he had been appointed as a kind of guardian of the college's orthodoxy. He said he recognized that my whole life influence was good; he stated that what was worrying him was concerning my orthodoxy. I reminded him that if the fruit is good, the tree is also good and that, furthermore, it is well to guard against the temptations of the custodian of popular orthodoxy, namely, the temptations to judge others according to conventional viewpoints, rather than according to the fruit of the Spirit. I urged him to pray through to God's will and to do it regardless of its possible effect on me personally. He left me to get God's answer. The next night when I stepped out of the main college building, where I lived, to post a letter, I met Ragsdale and saw that he was transfigured. He said something like this, "I have heard from God. You will never find me doing anything against you or against the fruit of your spirit and life." I tried to tell him that I had always loved him. We found ourselves in each other's arms and the Lord put me in the purest happiness and the greatest bliss that I had experienced up to that time.

Shortly after that, when I was taking a walk with Professor Edward Holmes, to whom I owe so much, I told him I felt I should call the board of trustees together and put the whole matter before the members and offer my resignation. He agreed with me in the conviction that this was God's way. I asked for the privilege of meeting with the trustees, who were soon to convene at Griffin, Georgia, in connection with the annual session of the Baptist State Convention.

Happily for me, I yielded enough to the Spirit to pray the prayer that is always answered: that I might have the Spirit of Jesus and manifest His Spirit entirely in all the steps I was under pressure and free necessity to take.

President Pollock did his best to keep me. Professor Kilpatrick came to me and told me that if I would remain at Mercer for ten years more my spirit and the spirit the boys were receiving through my influence would change Georgia. I told him that if I were to trim, or seek to save my position, even in order to have a good influence, I would lose the very thing that made me vital and worthwhile. He smiled and said, "You are right."

Every time an effort was made to influence me to keep silent and conservative enough to continue in the college, the spirit of courage and humility that comes from looking to Jesus would be manifested quite convincingly. Sometimes I would find myself unconsciously kneeling at the feet of those who sought to out-argue me. This was the beginning of a whole series of experiences wherein I came to find that the Spirit has a perfect ritual that all enter as they yield and respond to the Spirit.

Every time I thought of writing out a statement to read

to the board of trustees, I would be stopped with the overwhelming certainty that I would be given what I should say only at the time for saying it, that I should not plan or prepare, except to be in the Spirit and will of God.

Just before going before the trustees, I went to a side room and was overshadowed by His presence. When I commenced speaking I was so helped that I was enabled to say the right words in the right spirit. The board of trustees, made up largely of the leading Baptist ministers of the state, responded heartily. I had not talked long before one of them said, "This boy has got religion and doesn't know what is the matter with him." It became the order for reticent men to melt in tenderness and throw their arms about me.

The trustees tried way after way to leave me free, and at the same time to keep me from giving up my college work. One of the most orthodox of the group, Mr. E. Y. Mallory, Sr., first suggested that I continue both my teaching at Mercer and my study of Christian Science, but that I do this without associating formally with the Christian Scientists. I told him that would be like studying chemistry away from chemists and chemical laboratories, because of their unpopularity. He next proposed that my position be left open until I found out what would be my attitude toward Christian Science, so that if it were such that I felt free to return to Mercer, the position would be waiting for me.

I told him and all the others who sought to find a way for me to be true to the light as I saw it and at the same time remain at Mercer that, taking into consideration the contemporary order of Baptists and orthodox opinion in general, there was nothing left for me to do but to follow the course I had indicated to them and that there was nothing they could do but accept my resignation.

About midnight they came to see that the only course was for us to part in love. They left it to my judgment as to when I should leave the college. No restrictions were made upon what I might teach. They trusted me.

In leaving the Baptists I entered into genuine fellowship with them. Ever since they have seemed a little more loving to me than the rule is for them to be to each other. When I left the Christian Scientists years afterward, I had a very similar experience.

That night at Griffin when I went to the hotel, I was so enveloped by the Presence that I had another experience of being immediately in the Kingdom of Heaven. People are usually happier in getting positions than they are in giving them up. I have been made most happy in giving mine up, when the unfolding light and Guide have led me forward.

When I left the college about two months later, the kindness and consideration of President Pollock, the faculty, and the students were so great that I seemed to float out from Mercer upon a sea of love into a new world of spiritual adventure.

CHAPTER III

THE APPEAL OF CHRISTIAN SCIENCE

‹‹‹‹‹‹ ‹‹‹‹‹‹‹‹‹‹‹‹‹‹‹‹‹‹› ›››››››››››››››››››››

When the urge came to write this book I realized that this chapter would be my most difficult, both to please Heaven and be the most help both to the Christian Scientists, who believe that Christian Science is both the truth and the unfolding spirit of truth, and to those of the orthodox who believe that it is from beneath rather than from above.

It was not until I began to write this chapter that I fully appreciated what God did for me in my association with Christian Science. I tried several writings and two dictations. They were displeasing to me and seemed equally displeasing to the Spirit within me. I considered inserting a page with the explanation that since I have sought to leave all to be led by the Spirit, the revelation has been concerning Jesus rather than Christian Science. By prayer and by a new death of all points of view and prejudices, and in the desire to write to please the Inspirer and True Judge, this much was made clear: "Start by recounting the appeals that Christian Science had for you." I had not gone far in writing out these appeals before I found myself in this new appreciation of Jesus and in a happier realm than I had known for a long time. This new realm of such exceeding sweetness, satisfaction, and increased guidance continues. I have lived in a new sense of immediate dependence upon Him, feeling myself as dependent upon Him for life, joy, revelation, and victory as the limb is dependent upon the tree.

I love Jesus all the more because of the certainty that

43

He loves the Christian Scientists more than I can do. It may be that I was not permitted to write freely about the Christian Scientists until I was ready to write entirely in terms of my clarified intuitions and leadings.

I was in quest for health, for complete wholeness; but it is seldom recognized that in seeking wholeness our approach must be whole. In Christian Science I had glimpsed new aspects of the spiritual approach to health. But at that time the equally necessary physical approach was little understood, even among doctors, especially in the field of scientific nutrition, which was my own chief problem. How simple it would have been for me to regain health had I known the foods that produce acidity and the foods that are alkaline in their reactions in the body. Man is what he eats— physically and spiritually.

One of my doctors, a lecturer on physiology in the college where I was teaching, was not in his office one day when I went to seek his help. I was told that he was at home and when I found him he was in bed, suffering with the same trouble as my own.

Even Billings of Chicago, an ex-president of the American Medical Association, and a noted authority on disorders of the digestive tract, told me that the only way I would ever be well was to return to the country and live and work in the fresh air and sunshine. But I wanted that something that I knew later to be God Himself, even more than I wanted health.

This was brought home to me one afternoon when I went to the English Kitchen in Macon, owned and run by Mr. and Mrs. Chapman, who sought to prepare food for me that I could digest. I asked myself, or was asked, if I could have only one thing and have that by asking, what it would be. I replied I would not ask for physical health, if it meant that I could have it without knowing the laws of life that make one healthy, that I would not ask to live forever unless I could learn to live better than I was then living. And coming as a flash of light that expressed my deeper need and longing, I concluded I would ask to know the truth. Most of the pain and physical discomfort disappeared. I was for hours in the border land of the Kingdom of Heaven. When the desire to know the truth becomes great enough to be chosen above health and human immortality, it brings health and healing. Later I learned that to seek perfect love as the way of life, and identification and union with Jesus, opens the way for us to receive God, love, truth, and health.

It was not Christian Science as a book, as an organization, a visible church and a human leadership, with their necessarily human limitations and imperfections, that had appeal for me. It was the Spirit behind the letter, the reality behind the visible forms and effort, the healing touch of Heaven that I sought. I liked especially Mrs. Eddy's statement that she was only a pioneer, a child as it were, glimpsing and seeking to report the truth that saves, heals, and transforms. The Christian Science she had glimpsed (as distinct from the historic movement) includes all the truth that ever has and ever will be revealed and discovered and excludes all the error that ever has or ever will be manifested.

As I understood Mrs. Eddy, she had been permitted to see and was seeking to report and to put into saving and healing action nothing less than the Spirit of truth, the Spirit that guides all into the truth and makes free from every limitation and bondage. Of course all real divine healing under any and all names is the action of the Divine Spirit upon the human spirit, mind, and body.

It was only in this sense that I could think of being a Christian Scientist, for I was keenly aware of much that did not appeal to me in the first efforts of Mrs. Eddy and her associates to move out of the realm of human imperfection into the realm of perfection. I was never meant to be a disciple of any disciple; I can only be a disciple at first hand of the Teacher of Teachers. When the Oxford Group had a house party in Macon years ago, Sam Shoemaker, the most vital and interesting person I have met in the Oxford Group movement, said, after I had had hours with him, "I greet you as an ally." Such I seek to be to all engaged in any good work. But I cannot be anything other than an immediate disciple of Jesus and the Spirit of truth, getting my orders direct from the Source, not through imperfect and too often blind guides. It is the purpose of Jesus to bring all to this immediacy of leadership as there is sufficient yielding and responsiveness to him.

I was an idealist and was familiar in a general way with the teachings of the most daring idealists in the history of religion, poetry, and philosophy. The idealists from Plato to Emerson had opened my mind to see that Spirit, mind, and ideas are more real than the appearances and forms that are called matter. "The things that are seen are temporal and unsubstantial in comparison with the things that are unseen, perfect, and eternal" and are, as Emerson puts it, "the creed of all idealists." Plato saw that the things made and seen are but shadows; the form, the idea, the ideal, is substance.

Professor Horace Williams, of the department of philosophy at the University of North Carolina, once asked his students if they were going to make a wheelbarrow what would be the first thing needed. The pupils answered in terms of materials and a workman. Professor Williams replied, "You would start with the idea of a wheelbarrow!"

Plato saw that before the real remedy for even a headache could be administered, one must attain to temperance. Bronson Alcott, who helped to create the atmosphere of New England transcendentalism in which Mrs. Eddy was born and lived, saw clearly that when we humans become sane, wise, gentle, and loving, nature itself will respond and be what it should be. Shakespeare sends the raging Lear out into the raging storm, the fitting environment for his rage. When spirits, minds, and souls are fully healed and whole, so will be the bodies of men and the creation. When the inner climate changes, the outer climate will also change. The two are really one, the inner and outer of the same thing.

I hoped that Christian Science had the key to unlock new resources from the unseen perfect for the health and healing of the soul, the body, and the whole of life. At any rate, its claims were so enormous and the hopes it raised were so precious that an experimenter like myself must investigate such possibilities.

Most important of all there was the pressure of what seemed to be the Spirit urging me to seek and find out the reality. At times I felt the healing touch in some of their meetings, but not in all of them.

I liked and still like many of their songs. Just recently when I dropped in to one of their testimonial meetings here in Macon, they were singing, "God is Wisdom, God is Love," and I felt God in the singing, more of God than in their testimonies. Two hymns of Mrs. Eddy, "Shepherd Show Me How to Go," and "O'er Waiting Harp Strings of the Mind," are to me alive with the healing touch. I wrote Mrs. Eddy soon after the Holy Spirit had revealed Jesus to be God as man and man as God, that I felt these two songs of hers would be sung by all lovers of the Healing Presence, possibly long after much of what she had written in prose was forgotten.

I knew before I had even heard of Christian Science that the only way to overcome evil is with good. As Judge Black put it in an address to the Mercer students, "You can't fight the devil with his own fire without getting burnt." The devil has so much more fire of his kind than you have and is so much more skillful in the handling of it, you will always be burnt when you fight with his kind of fire; he is always defeated when you fight him with God's fire. I once heard Edward Kimball, the keenest mind I knew in the Christian Science movement, say, "When beasts fight, the biggest beast wins." Even if you could whip the devil by being worse than he is, by out-fighting him with his own weapons, you would be a worse devil than the one you had conquered and succeeded.

It was while I was seeking God's best in association with

the Christian Scientists that I saw in the love and wisdom of Jesus a scientific certainty, an understandable law, and a workable principle that I had not seen so clearly before. I saw that the teachings of Jesus are really provable or demonstrable to all who dare honestly and bravely to try them. When we yield to Jesus, the Holy Spirit, and His way of life, we are not in the realm of opinion but of fact, not in the realm of belief, but of highest self-evident truth.

There has been no natural scientist so scientific in spirit and in method in the realm of appearances as was and is Jesus in dealing with both the spiritual and natural.

No Christian Scientist that I knew in those days had yielded sufficiently to the Holy Spirit to have Jesus revealed to him as He was revealed to the early Christians and as He was revealed to me two days after I left the Christian Science church to be led by the Spirit. Nevertheless, God seems to have honored the Christian Scientists in their partial blindness to the wonder of Jesus as God more than he has the orthodox literalists who stopped by saying, "Lord, Lord," and did not even attempt to do what Jesus said those who believed in Him would do. "Not everyone that saith unto me, 'Lord, Lord,' shall enter into the Kingdom of Heaven, but he that doeth the will of My Father which is in Heaven." Only he who comes to Jesus, listens to Him and does what He says to do, builds on the rock.

During the period covered by this chapter some remarkable healings occurred, but the efforts at peace making, according to the Spirit and technique of Jesus were the more successful. This has also been true since I left all organized systems to be led by the Spirit. God evidently longs to heal all of our diseases, as well as to forgive all of our iniquities and to give us a new start, but as S. D. Gordon said when he was in Macon a few years ago, "God seems like a good mother trying to give her child the beautiful apple, but waiting until there is capacity developed to receive it."

The fault is not His but ours, but no effort on our part to reach up for God and His gifts is in vain. There is no real defeat for those who are striving in the right direction. Where they seem to fail, others going their way and profiting by their advances will succeed, and it will be found that those who seemed to fail and those who succeeded because of their contribution have both succeeded, and will rejoice together.

I have already referred to some of the healing touches that came through the word of light that was given me from the time I was a college boy on through the period preceding my knowledge of Christian Science. The first case of healing I remember during my study of Christian Science was that of Mr. Eugene Smith of Geneva, Georgia. He was very pale and weak. He told me that his doctor said X-ray plates showed an abscess on the brain. I felt so utterly helpless that I sought the help of the Lord more in the orthodox Christian way than through my conscious ability to give a Christian Science treatment. To my great joy, it was not long before another X-ray plate made by the same physician revealed that the abscess had simply disappeared. When I saw Mr. Smith a little later, he looked like a new man. After that I visited him several times in his home and I never heard of any return of his former trouble.

In the spring of 1901, a child who was badly afflicted with eczema, and whom I was seeking to help, felt an almost instantaneous release and was soon well of the trouble. The child's mother was again pregnant, although her husband was nearly dead with consumption. The doctor warned her that owing to the condition of the husband at the time of conception, the child would die before it was brought to birth. A few days later she telephoned me that the child had been "essentially lifeless" for about six hours. I was so overwhelmed by the plight of the mother that I knelt and almost fell on my face. Then these words of Jesus were flashed before me and spoken through me, "Verily, verily, I say unto you, the time is coming and now is when the dead shall hear the voice of the Son of God and they that hear shall live." At that very moment, or soon afterward, the mother felt "the sense of abounding life in the child," and on June 12, the child was born, "a normal and healthy child and lived as such for fourteen months, until an attack of membraneous croup caused its death." (The mother helped me dictate the above.)

Some time later when I went to the men's ward at the city hospital, a lady whom I did not know came to me and said, "Please come over and see my husband. He was badly scalded in a railroad wreck and suffers terribly when the scalded parts of his body are dressed." There was so much pain registered in his face that I closed my eyes and looked up physically as well as spiritually for refuge in the contemplation of the Perfect One. When I opened my eyes, the man who had been in such great pain just previously was smiling. All the pain had suddenly left his body. His release came to him as I looked and appealed to the Perfect Savior and Healer. It was remarkable that this had involved no conscious effort on my part, indeed I had sought refuge in God from the sight of such suffering. Beholding as in a mirror His perfection and glory changes us and may change those for whom we intercede.

In the summer of 1901, because I did not know how to feed and care for my body and did not live enough in the high joy and healing peace of the Spirit, I had days of terrible suffering from what appeared to be appendicitis. Dr. Billings of Chicago had previously diagnosed a similar but lighter attack as appendicitis. While Miss Alice Jennings was giving me a treatment which consisted of an affirmation of God's goodness, allness, and healing presence and control, I felt something unloose or untie in my intestines. This brought considerable relief, but not the healing I was seeking. A few days later when I was alone in an upstairs room, I awoke with a cold spongy feeling of death working in my body, especially in my lower limbs. My first thought was the grief that it would cause my mother and the unjust criticism it might bring to my Christian Science friends. This somehow opened the windows of Heaven. I was flooded with heavenly love that brought life, warmth, and healing. I arose and went to the bathroom. There was so much poison on my body that the water I used for the bath became tinged with green.

In my Mercer days, when I had these attacks of intestinal pain due to bodily poisoning, I usually sent for a doctor who administered an opiate, the after-effects of which seemed worse than had been the acute suffering. The last time I sent for him I was somewhat improved when he reached me. I told him that I preferred suffering the acute pain to taking the opiate. He commended me generously. The next attack I had, although it lasted about thirty hours, left me feeling so well that I rode my bicycle to Bellevue, a distance of about five miles, taught a Sunday School class and rode back to the college.

In the autumn of 1903 there came a call to render a service to Peabody College that required much of my time for several months. This work made me keenly aware that God is genuinely interested in and seeking to help in all the legitimate affairs of this life, that he hears and answers prayer, gives guidance, shapes decisions, and directs events, and that the best way to insure the success of things of secondary importance is to put and keep uppermost the Thing and things of first importance.

The call came first in the form of a letter from Professor A. P. Bourland, Professor Charles E. Little, and Doctor J. M. King, the college committee. It said, among other things, that the very existence of Peabody College as a teachers' college for the Peabody territory was at stake, that Senator Hoke Smith, former Secretary of State Olney, Senator Hoar, Pierpont Morgan, Sr., and other members of the Peabody board were favoring a move to withdraw financial support from the college and to use the income from the million dollars that had been going to the college for educational campaigns to be conducted throughout the South.

The college committee was asking for one man from each state in the Peabody territory to come to Nashville for a conference. I was invited as the representative from Georgia. I advised them to get one of their graduates holding a high position in the state, as the prejudice against me because of my Christian Science affiliation might make me of less help than would be either of two men whose names I suggested. They replied, "We want you."

On the way to Nashville to attend the conference, I joined President A. A. Murphree of the State Women's College of Florida, at Tallahassee. After a little visit with him on the train, I went alone and prayed and sought guidance as to the best help we could be to the college. It was made very clear that our effort in behalf of the college would succeed and that it would be my work to prepare and present our case to the Peabody board.

When the alumni representatives met the next morning with the college committee, I was asked to make a statement as to the strength of our case. When we reassembled in the afternoon, J. B. Aswell, the representative from Louisiana, later famous as a Congressman from that state, rose and said that just one thing was clear for us to do, namely to bring the Peabody board and Moseley together, and that if the board had been at our meeting that morning and heard the statement, nothing more would be necessary. As much exaggerated generosity as there was in Friend Aswell's statement, the essential arguments in behalf of our case had been stated, although it took much work with the help of others to get the statement ready to put before the board in written and oral form.

I had told the friends that the work I was seeking to do to help people in desperate need must be kept first and that in order to do this I would have to be kept free to give up the work for the college at any hour that a higher call seemed to require it, but if they would give me an assistant who would be ready to take up the work if I should need to put it down, I would accept their call. S. H. Bowman, a lawyer, the representative from West Virginia, was selected.

The first man that I consulted after leaving the conference was W. H. Kilpatrick, who was then acting-president of Mercer University. He offered me his time and all the assistance within his power. He worked with me night after night, preparing letters to go to the Peabody board, and helped formulate something of what the new Peabody should be.

A little later I went to see Senator Hoke Smith. He told me that I was wasting my time, and gave me to understand that the majority of the board had already decided to abandon the support of Peabody College. But he sought to give me the consolation that after the board had conducted popular educational campaigns throughout the South, he hoped to induce the board to establish in Atlanta a new Peabody College for teachers. That was what we had suspected, and it stirred us to all the greater effort. The alumni all over the Peabody territory went to work to win new friends for the college. The Southern and the Nashville, Chattanooga and St. Louis Railway systems gave me passes so that I could present our case to key men. When the time came to go to Washington and stay there two weeks in advance of the meeting of the Peabody board, the alumni had won the support of leading educators throughout the country, and had the majority support of the United States Senators from the Peabody territory.

Through Judge Griggs, a member of the Ways and Means Committee of the House of Representatives, an interview was arranged with President Theodore Roosevelt, who was a member of the Peabody board. The President did most of the talking and told me he was going to invite Harry Stillwell Edwards of Macon to second his nomination at the forthcoming Republican Convention in the summer of 1904. He said this wise thing to me, that so far as I know has never reached the general public: he had a contempt for a man who, because he had won a reputation in one field, presumed to pass upon matters in other fields until he took time to inform himself well. He added, "I have the Panama

Canal, Congress, and other small affairs on my hands for the
present. I will not attend the forthcoming meeting of the
Peabody board, but shall inform myself on the subject and
be ready to attend a later meeting."

Judge Dickenson, a former Secretary of War and a friend
of the President, some time afterward arranged with him
for a bear hunt in Mississippi and helped to inform Roosevelt of the college situation. At the next meeting of the
board the President appeared and said, "I understand that
you are to vote on these propositions . . ." and, naming
them, voted on each question. All of his votes were cast for
the things we were seeking and had the effect of bringing
the other members to voting instead of appointing new com-
mittees, a habit with them.

One morning while I was in Washington so many tele-
grams and special delivery letters poured in that I failed to
take time first of all for meditation and prayer and to write
letters to humble people who were seeking help. I accomplished essentially nothing that day for the college, but
learned the necessary lesson to put first things first.

With the assistance of former President John Franklin
Crowell of Trinity College, North Carolina, who held a high
position in Washington, we had made ready a typewritten
brief to put in the hands of each member of the board
before starting the verbal argument. When Bowman and
myself went to the Arlington Hotel, where the board was
to have its meeting, we were informed that a majority of
the members offered objections to breaking a long established custom of allowing only their agents to appear before
them. We remained in the lobby and prayed. It was not
long before President Gilman of the board, former president
of Johns Hopkins, came to me and said, "The college committee will hear you and the other members of the board
will listen in." We got the substance of what we asked for
and the board saved its precedent. They gave me twenty
minutes to present our case and gave Bowman sufficient time
to present the petitions. I sought to bring home to them

the immense assets, particularly the spiritual assets, that had accumulated during the thirty-five years of the board's work in connection with Peabody College. For the spiritual work of the college consisted in forming a nucleus of trained pioneers who were going out and leavening the whole South with a new educational spirit. With the foundation already laid they could achieve many times more than could be achieved by any fresh start, which, if made, would be a failure to use the splendid material already at hand. I had talked but a few minutes before many members of the board were smiling assent. President Gilman soon told me he would extend my time if necessary. The board immediately began to take steps to give us all that we had asked.

The next move was to get Wycliffe Rose back to the college in charge of the work of getting all the local factors to coöperate with the Peabody board in making the college what they had in mind. When I spoke to Governor Porter, the president of the college, of our desire to get Rose back, he commissioned me to go to the University of Tennessee, where Rose was teaching, and induce him to return. He authorized me to offer Rose the dean-ship of the college, with the understanding that he would have a free hand. Rose returned upon those conditions and accomplished the work we had in mind with great skill and success. Later the Peabody board made him its agent and still later the new board offered him the presidency of the college. He could not be induced to accept the presidency, because he felt that the heroic work the situation had called for on his part made it unwise for him to attempt to work with factions that might refuse to let their wounds heal quickly. He thought that a new man would find better coöperation.

With a genius like Rose in charge, I felt that I was no longer needed and returned to my simple and more humble services. Rose wanted me to live on the campus of the new Peabody even if I did not care to be a teacher. I told him that all I knew vital enough for me to be concerned in sharing could be told in three hours. He replied, "That is true of all of us. The rest is padding." I did not want to give my life to so much padding, but to the seeking, finding, and sharing of the greatly vital.

An all-important truth of life that I was taught in connection with the work for the college (for which work I refused to accept anything but actual expenses) is, that the highest human success comes not from self-seeking, but by the whole-hearted giving of oneself to the quest for God's best.

CHAPTER IV

LED BY THE SPIRIT

‹‹‹‹‹‹‹‹‹‹‹‹‹‹‹‹‹‹‹‹‹‹‹‹‹‹‹‹‹‹››››››››››››››››››››››››

The things reported in this chapter, as in Chapter Three, occurred during my association with the Christian Science movement, but I recognized them increasingly as acts of the Holy Spirit. It became increasingly apparent that the Holy Spirit as looked to, yielded to, and responded to, is the light and light-giver, the way and the guide, the life and life-giver, the One who "doeth and enableth the works of God," and without whom all our efforts are fruitless.

This was brought home to me with emphasis in the spring of 1906, by a letter from a friend in Monteagle. Years before she had opened my eyes to the healing touch that comes to the whole being whenever we turn our thoughts away from the body and all else to God and rejoice in the fact that in Him and His love and care we live, move and have our being. She now wrote me that she had done something that had caused her to condemn herself, and that the condemnation was making her sick in mind, spirit, and body, and bringing her under the obsession of a destructive idea. Having already become a Christian Scientist, she asked me to give her "absent treatments." By this she meant for me to affirm and realize as best I could God's healing and loving Presence as being with her, rebuking, denying, and removing the claims or appearances unlike Him and His perfect man and creation. In other words she wanted me to pray the prayer of realization and thanksgiving; as Jesus says: "Whatsoever ye pray for and ask, believe you have got it and you shall have it." Orthodox Christians, who offer this prayer of faith believing they have already received what they have asked for according to His will, and the Christian Scientists, who offer the prayer in affirmation and realization, may be closer together in their praying than either realizes.

I tried to help her by absent treatment, by the prayer of petition, which I never gave up, and by the writing of letters. These each and all failed to bring the help desired and needed. Finally, I made a trip to Monteagle to see what might be accomplished. The friend was so obsessed with her problem that not a word or a prayer reached her. I left her with a sense of defeat, and with the feeling that any of us, by getting the wrong reaction in any situation, may become the victim of self-destructive condemnation.

As I was leaving Monteagle for Macon I inquired of the Lord for His remedy for the condition in which the friend had put herself. The answer came: "Justification by faith." As Paul Wernle has said, Saint Paul meant by Faith nothing less than receptivity and response to God. On the way to Macon I read Paul's epistles on faith to the Romans and to the Galatians. This was Saturday. The following Tuesday a letter came from the friend out of the same gloom and condemnation in which I had found her the previous Friday afternoon and left her the following morning. When I went to my desk to answer her letter, I said to the Helper, "All I have done, all the letters I have written, all of the prayers I have made, all of the treatments I have given, and the trip to Monteagle have availed nothing. There is no need to write another letter unless You give me the right word or words to give her."

I found myself writing, seemingly under the guidance of the Spirit: "You are making the mistake of identifying yourself with your past sins, blunders, and mistakes, and with your brain and nervous system. Cease this and identify yourself with God, with Jesus Christ, with your ideal selfhood, and with the good that you can do in the world." I felt myself in the Holy Presence and the holy burning and cleansing of the Spirit, in the Kingdom of Heaven. I went on to say that the whole secret is in our identification, and the highest of all identifications is to be in union with Jesus Christ. This explains why Saul of Tarsus was such a monster while identified with the enemy and enemies of Jesus, and became so much like Jesus as soon as he yielded and identified himself with Him. This also makes clear why salvation can be instantaneous and why those who come in last are paid off first. It is not a question of how long we have professed Jesus, but how whole-heartedly and thoroughly we are identified with Him *now*.

As one may be out in the mist all day and yet dry at night, so one may be identified for the most part with other things and only partially with Jesus for a long period of years and consequently be far from the Kingdom of God. As one may have been dry all day and made suddenly wet by falling into the creek that night, so one may have been out of Christ up to the eleventh hour and yet by yielding whole-heartedly to Him enter into the Kingdom of Heaven before those who entered His service early in the day.

The revelation concerning the inestimable wonder of being in identification with Jesus continued and kept me for days in the light, joy, and peace of the Holy Spirit. I sent this message at once to my friend in Monteagle sharing with her what had been given me for her concerning the tragedy of wrong identification and the redemption and transformation that come through identification with God, Jesus, the ideal selfhood, and the good that one can do in the world. She wrote me the same day and about the same time. Her letter, to my great joy, stated that the gloom and depression had lifted and that she had become free, happy, and well. The change had come to her at or near the time the revelation was given to me, so that our letters actually crossed.

I wrote a long article for the *Christian Science Journal* on "Salvation through Identification with God: through Union with Jesus Christ." One of the editors wrote me that the

article was excellent but rather too theological. It was published in the July, 1906, issue, under the caption, "Salvation
through Identification with Divine Principle and Its Idea."
Slight changes appeared, evidently to make the article appear more scientific and less theological. God, of course, is
divine principle, divine love, divine life, and divine perfect
everything. He is also a divine person and He hears and
answers all righteous prayer as a loving Father, as well as
responds when we act according to perfect law and principle.

Soon after the article was published, I received a letter
from a lady in California saying that twenty years before
she had been healed by reading the writings of Mrs. Eddy,
but had relapsed and that neither her own treatment nor
the treatments of others had reached her need, but that
while reading my article she had received her healing.

In the summer of 1908, I was called to see a friend who
was over eighty. He had made the request that when the
time of the end came a certain doctor be sent for to minister
to his body and that I be sent for as a spiritual friend. When
the telegram came asking me, I took the first train, but upon
arriving was told that there was no need to see him as he
was unconscious.

I spent the night with his daughter, a Christian Scientist.
Early the next morning we were called to come quickly as
the doctor said the man was dying. Without any conscious
faith that I would get any response from him, I said aloud,
"E——, in God you live, move, and have your being. He is
your life. Though you walk through the valley of the shadows there is nothing to fear. In Him there is no death, only
life and resurrection." To my surprise and to the astonish-
ment of the others, he awoke from the dream of seeming
death, smiled, began talking, and later took some nourish-
ment. I remained with him and had a greatly blessed time
until late in the afternoon, when I went uptown for a short
time.

On my return his daughter told me that when I left her
father, he had lapsed into the dying condition from which

he had awakened that morning and that her sister and brother-in-law, in whose home her father lived, did not want me to see him, believing that if he could not get well it was better for him to go, rather than to linger in the condition that he had been in for some time. My friend added, "He is my father, too, and I want you to stay with him." But I could not do that against the wishes of those in whose house he was living.

I went to her home to spend the night, expecting to take the first train for Macon the following day. Early next morning a telephone call came, saying, "Papa is dying, come at once and bring Mr. Moseley." I took this to mean that the son-in-law and daughter who had objected to my being with their father had repented, so I went immediately.

When I entered the sickroom, I began to speak aloud after the manner of the previous morning and the miracle of awakening re-occurred. The son-in-law took me aside and said that as the sick man wished me to be with him, I might stay, but only upon condition that I did not speak a word in his presence. I thought, if I should ever be in the hands of such relatives I would be glad for someone to stay with me, even if not permitted to speak to me. So I stayed about a week, until the end came. When I would leave the dying man to get some sleep, the daughter who wanted her father to live would get the feeling that he was dying and would awaken me. On each return, there was clear evidence of reviving life.

By the following Monday afternoon the doctor was so sure that the end had come, he informed the family and they appeared to get themselves in readiness for going through with their part. As worn out as I was, I said to the Lord, "Every minute this man lives will be well and a rebuke to the apparent desire for him to die." About ten o'clock in the evening the doctor came into the room and an expression of awe came over his face. During the night the coldness of death came and went according to our faith and our holding on to the truth that God was this man's life and breath and everything. When daylight came the son-in-law and wife came through the room. They looked frightened. I said, "For God's sake, let me speak to E———." They passed quickly out of the room without answering.

I was being put in a realm of glory where it seemed that anything might happen. When the breath left the body I spoke to the friend, calling him by his first name, and said "Arise." There was distinct recognition and movement registered in his face. I spoke to him a second time and the movement on his face was repeated. It seemed both to the faithful daughter, who had been with us during the night, and to me that he was seeking to make known to us that he did not want to come back. So I did not speak to him again.

During the week I spent with him, seeking to apply the Golden Rule in an unusually difficult situation, there came another experience of being in the Kingdom of Heaven. A friend in Mrs. Eddy's household informed me that an article coming out of this experience, published in the *Christian Science Journal* of September, 1908, interested and pleased Mrs. Eddy so much that she lived with it for days. A condensed supplement of the article was published and circulated by the Christian Scientists.

On Saturday, while I was going through this battle with the forces of death and the forces that make for death, I was walking among beautiful trees. The trees and all the world became so beautiful that I said, in effect, what is the use of all this battling with death and disease? Would it not be better just to be kind, to delight in the beautiful world, and let things take their course under Your direction? The answer was, "If nature is so beautiful to you, how much more beautiful it must be to Me. You see it only in part and have an imperfect human concept. I see the whole and see it as it is, and have the perfect idea of everything."

Then it was made clear that the human concept has a part of the reality that is the divine mind, but only a small part of it. Yet as we move Godward the human concept will become more and more like the divine idea or ultimate reality, and when we see through God's eyes, we shall take on this immortal form. It was also made known to me that the transition from the human-imperfect to the divine-perfect should be made without a break of consciousness and by rapture or translation rather than by the loss of the body. I was permitted to glimpse the spiritual law by which the ultimate victory over even the appearance of death will be achieved.

In the article that appeared in the *Christian Science Journal*, September, 1908, under the title, "Divine Idea and Human Concept," I stated, among other things, that while to God there is but one universe and creation, and that that one is good, holy, and perfect, so long as there appears to us to be two, the finite and the infinite, the material and the spiritual, Christ, the perfect being, is the mediator between the two. The article closed with this statement: "The resurrection and ascension as well as the other events in the life of Christ Jesus are unfolding stages of consciousness as well as facts that are possible of recurrence in the experience of all who go His way. Everything in God is always a present and eternal possibility for each and every son of God. Through identifying ourselves with Jesus, everything of Jesus is ours, now and forever."

I did not at this time see the superlative wonder of Jesus because of the fact that He was and is God on the plane of human need and man lifted up to the throne of God. It takes the Holy Spirit to make this revelation.

Rather early in my association with the Christian Scientists, I read in the twenty-third chapter of Matthew (Twentieth Century translation), "You are not to be called leaders, for one is your leader, even the Christ." This light was so clear and authoritative that never again could I call Mrs. Eddy or any one else "leader" in a religious sense, or even "reverend." The best we can be is servants and friends, servants and friends of God and of one another and of all. One day while reading the Gospel according to John, it was also made known to me with authority that Jesus never meant to have any successor except the Spirit of truth, the other Comforter, the Holy Spirit. Mrs. Eddy and her associates were very generous to me in every way that could be desired. She told friends that I was to be called to her home, which was considered the greatest of privileges. I was made a special paid contributor to the *Christian Science Journal and Sentinel*. A short time before the announcement of the publication of the *Christian Science Monitor*, a letter came from a friend who had been in Mrs. Eddy's home, asking me the most searching questions. Happily I had come to see that the whole worth of the Christian Science movement depended upon the ability of its students to do the things that Jesus did. I repented of even the desires I had had for any place in the movement other than doing those things of which all life is in such great need.

One of the questions in the letter was, "Have you reached the place where you are willing to leave all for Christian Science?" I replied, "This question cuts deep. I hope I am ready to leave all to follow the Unfolding Good, but if the time comes when my sense of the Unfolding Good differs from my understanding of Christian Science, I shall follow the Unfolding Good. And if I understand Mrs. Eddy correctly, she would want me to do this very thing."

I already felt the time was coming and near at hand. The throwing of myself upon the Unfolding Good with the announcement of my dedication to its authority, rather than my understanding of Christian Science, gave me great release and joy, and brought me another experience of being in the Kingdom of Heaven.

Not long after, as I remember the sequence of events, the Christian Scientists in Macon wanted me to be their first reader, which would have required reading a statement saying, among other things, that the Christian Science sermon consisting of selections from the Bible explained by the Christian Science textbook was free from human error and authorized by Christ. I could not read this statement with utter sincerity as I interpreted it, so I wrote Mrs. Eddy asking whether she meant that Christ as a person had appeared to her and given her His authority for saying this, or whether she meant that it was so true to her that she felt it was authorized by Him. She replied that she meant it was true and divinely authorized. A very short time after this a telegram came from the Christian Science directors in Boston to the Macon church instructing a change in the prefatory wording of the lesson sermon from "authorized by Christ" to "divinely authorized." I infer that this telegram went to all Christian Science churches.

Still later, when I was in Boston, Archibald McClellan, editor-in-chief of the Christian Science publications and chairman of the board of directors of the Boston church, called me to his office for an interview. He was very generous in praise of the quality of my writing, but said that Mrs. Eddy had expressed the belief that I sought to write simply what seemed to me true and helpful, and had no particular interest in correlating this with Christian Science. I replied that Mrs. Eddy understood me perfectly. I had reached the place where I could write only the things that were most true and vital to me and that I felt would be most helpful to others. I find in re-reading the last articles I wrote for the Christian Science publications, especially an article entitled "Redemption of the Past," which appeared in the *Christian Science Journal*, September, 1909, that they struck essentially universal notes. Previous to that time I had yielded to the temptation of conformity beyond utter sincerity. I regret that I did.

After I received the baptism of the Holy Spirit described in a later chapter, I made the statement to a Christian Science friend that all my published writing, while seeking to report the light as truthfully and helpfully as I could, pointed to the true revelation, but contained false notes so far as the motive had been to please and to succeed.

One Sunday night while reading the fourteenth chapter of John, I came to verse twenty, which says, "At that day (when I send unto you the other Comforter or the Spirit of Truth or the Holy Spirit) ye shall know that I am in My Father and ye in Me and I in you." A wonderful glory enveloped and overshadowed me. This was something that I did not understand then, but I came to understand later when this very promise became a reality of experience.

While I was associated with the Christian Science work in Macon, a minister and author of distinction, Samuel Chadwick, preached for several days at the Mulberry Street Methodist Church until his audience became so large that the meetings were held in the city auditorium.

One afternoon at a meeting in the auditorium he preached on the baptism with the Holy Spirit. He said that it was so tremendous an experience that one who receives this baptism knows it for a certainty. At the conclusion of his sermon he asked that all who desired the baptism with the Spirit come forward and give him their hands. I was the only one who went forward. I told him that I wanted God's best, and if the baptism with the Holy Spirit was His best, that was what I wanted. He was very loving to me and said, "Here is a young man who wants God's best, and God loves an honest soul." I wonder if you have ever felt that exhilarating sense of release and freedom that follows the absolute abandonment of oneself to a high purpose. It is an experience no man should miss. Those of us who have felt this freedom feel an almost irresistible compulsion to share it with others, for it is the very condition of mind which makes that baptism of the Holy Spirit possible. This desire and prayer for God's best which is union with Jesus and going on through this union in the quest and to the attainment of perfect everything, I found later would open every door to God.

At several different times I sought release from all formal obligations to the Christian Science movement, but there were so many calls for help from Christian Scientists that I would be drawn back into its organized activities. No one is ready for the freedom of the Spirit until he is ready to be led by the Spirit.

Nearly a year before I asked the Christian Scientists to release me that I might be free from all external obligations to be led by the Spirit, I began to pray definitely for the baptism of the Spirit. I had become aware that the healings and the successful efforts at peacemaking, and all the revelations that had been given me, were really gifts and acts of the Holy Spirit.

On Monday, March 14, 1910, a Pentecostal Holiness minister, J. H. King, started a meeting in Macon. I was the first one to indicate publicly the desire to receive the baptism with the Spirit. I had sought only a few days until I felt the Spirit moving in my body as well as giving new light to my understanding. By Friday the Spirit came into control of almost my whole being. Sunday morning, before I had arisen, it was said to my understanding with authority, "You are ready for your release from the Christian Science organization." I prayed for the spirit of Jesus to be with me.

After the Sunday morning service of the Christian Scientists I asked for the privilege of meeting with the members only. I recounted to them the recent experiences which had come to me with the seeking for the truth concerning the baptism with the Holy Spirit, and for this baptism, if it be God's best for me. I told them that I had felt about me a circle of marvelous light, peace, joy, and glory, where the only certainties were that Jesus lived and taught rightly, that the Good Spirit was leading us to go the way He went, the way of perfect love and utter sincerity. I told them I had no revelation concerning Christian Science, whether it would be found in whole or in part within the circle, or whether it would be left on the outside. I had the feeling that part would be found within, which has been confirmed by subsequent revelations and experiences. At that time it seems to have been the purpose of the Spirit to centralize my whole attention upon Jesus, His way of love and utter sincerity, and for me to know nothing as absolute, but Jesus and His good spirit and way of life.

In the realm of light and glory overshadowing and encircling me, I became able to know the highest certainty. Socrates, Plato, Buddha, Confucius, Fox, Emerson, Mrs. Eddy, and all others who had made contributions, were more loved than ever. But, like Moses and Elias on the Mount of Transfiguration, after having made their contribution, all others were obscured by the superlative light and glory of Jesus. Like the disciples, I saw Jesus only.

The experience of leaving the Christian Scientists was very similar to that of leaving Mercer College. But the glory and conscious presence of the Spirit was in far greater evidence. Happily I was enabled with each group to enter into a deeper fellowship than I had known while bound by formal obligations, when I needed to move on to obey the leading of the Spirit. In the light of subsequent unfoldment, I am very grateful that the Great Teacher and Educator permitted me to have the schooling and benefits of all the groups with which I have been associated.

CHAPTER V

BAPTISM WITH INEFFABLE UNION

‹‹‹‹‹‹‹‹‹‹‹‹‹‹‹‹‹‹‹‹‹‹‹‹‹‹‹‹‹‹›››››››››››››››››››››››

After I left the Christian Science movement, the Holy Spirit was upon my body in increasing power and control. My sense of light and joy and of freedom increased greatly. While I was walking in the street that day, with the power especially upon my shoulders, I became aware that it was left to me whether or not I would yield to the Holy Spirit. "The spirit of the prophet is subject to the prophet." God does not force His power, control, and glory upon us. As He is yielded to, He and His power work according to His will and wisdom and according to ours, also, as ours becomes His and His becomes ours.

That afternoon I went to the Pentecostal Holiness meeting in Moore's Hall. I tried to tell the friends there of the precious way the Lord was dealing with me. It was then that a brother from Atlanta said to me, "You will have to become more orthodox before God will baptize you." I replied, "The promise is not to the orthodox, but to those who hunger and thirst and ask."

Monday afternoon, March 21, I attended a party arranged by the Pentecostal friends for J. H. King. The meeting seemed very dry to me. I was looking for a gathering in which the presence and glory of the Lord would be much in evidence. As I walked away a new working of the Holy Spirit was upon my body. Apart from my conscious thought and volition, the Spirit moved upon my shoulders, putting them in perfect position, and I was made aware that the Spirit can move upon and control the body and the visible universe as readily as we can direct the voluntary functions of our bodies and that God is far more concerned that the body be perfect than are we.

During the entire week that I made it my chief concern to seek for God's best and for the baptism of the Spirit, if it be His best for me, my dislike of receiving money for things above monetary value reached the point where I refused to cash any cheque I received from any to whom I had rendered spiritual services. As much as I needed money later, the cheques were destroyed to obviate any possibility that they would ever be cashed. Yet I gave the minister more than a Pentecostal minister usually receives in response to a public appeal.

The night of March 21 a well-meaning brother asked for the privilege of making an appeal for a collection for the minister. He suggested "that Brother Scott and Brother Moseley pass the hat." I was embarrassed and replied, "I am sorry but I am looking for a place to worship where money is not mentioned." Of course I meant where money is not mentioned in the way the brother had done. No public collection was taken.

For several days prior to that meeting I had felt it would be easy enough to yield to the Spirit and go by Jesus' way of love, but the feeling that I had brought embarrassment to the brother and to the meeting and financial loss to the minister caused me to condemn myself and to suffer keenly. I found myself in two fires, the fire of Heaven and the other fire. I told myself I would be happy to give more than the entire group would have given, had a collection been taken. I was brought to the place of realizing the need of Jesus within if I were to go the way of perfect love and utter sincerity. I prayed directly to Him, for the first time in my life I believe, saying, "Jesus, if it is possible, come and live within me and be in me the life and principle of Your own good life and teaching that will enable me to go Your way."

The meeting adjourned about ten o'clock. I remained alone in the hall, praying until it was said to me with authority, "Stop seeking, and practice in love." The light was clear. I must start at the bottom of human need, visiting in love, the sick, the imprisoned, and the condemned. I was not only to go in love, but without any responsibility for external results. That responsibility would be His, not mine. I was made keenly conscious that the highest judgment of values is not in terms of miracles or seen achievements, but in terms of love. I dedicated my life to moving among the needy, seeking to be loving and brotherly. I also agreed to begin telling people that I had only a few certainties, but those the most precious, the certainties that Jesus lived and taught as the Good Spirit led Him and that the Spirit is also leading us. The clear leading to me, was to stop looking for the best religion, and to give myself to seeking and doing the will of God.

It must have been eleven o'clock when I reached the Old Dannenberg residence, 309 Georgia Avenue, where I was living. I retired almost at once. All the members of the household, Professor and Mrs. E. L. Martin and a nephew of Mrs. Martin's, were out of the city. The Lord and myself had the whole house that night. Then, too, there was no residence close by, so no one who desired to sleep need listen. All this was so important the Lord must have provided for it.

I slept for several hours. I awoke between three and four o'clock with some insight which I felt would be of help to the friend who prayed silently behind me at the meeting in Moore's Hall a few hours before, when I was undergoing the deepest death I had experienced up to that time. This friend had been led by the Spirit to come to Macon from South Georgia the previous afternoon, feeling that I was passing through a crisis and that she could be used to help me.

I soon found myself in what philosophers call cosmic consciousness. I was given the greatest clarification, understanding, happiness, and bliss, and put in an almost unbelievable light, revelation, and glory. So much was given that I did not think of asking for anything. Before I desired consciously, or asked, everything I could desire to know, and more, became transparent. I entered into a realm above all conflict, where everything was reconciled, fulfilled, harmonized in love. It was given me to feel and to see something of the wonder of the realm Jesus entered after His incarnation, crucifixion, and resurrection, the realm that has been named in my understanding the fourth empire or the human-divine, beyond the realm of the incarnation which is the realm of the divine-human.

I had not then read Ibsen's *Emperor and Galilean*, and knew of it only by a brief reference in Royce's *Spirit of Modern Philosophy*. However, this reference informed me that Ibsen had glimpsed more of the realm I was sensing than any other modern writer known to me. Later when I read and studied Ibsen's *Caesar's Apostacy*, and *Emperor Julian*, I was sure that he was feeling for the realm the Lord's grace had enabled me to approach near enough to see in its surpassing satisfactions and glories. But this realm is not what Ibsen called the third empire, but the fourth empire, the empire that Jesus entered after His ascension and from which He is giving the Holy Spirit through which He reveals and manifests Himself; eventually He will do so in visible victory. Ibsen saw only three empires, according to the words put into the mouth of Maximus when he addressed Julian: "First, the empire which was founded on the tree of knowledge; then that which was founded on the tree of the cross. The third is the empire of the great mystery; that empire which shall be founded on the tree of knowledge and the tree of the cross together, because it hates and loves them both and because it has its living sources under Adam's grove and under Golgotha."

In the fourth empire, the human-divine realm, into which Jesus has entered and from which He is ministering and manifesting Himself in the Spirit, there is no conflict between the tree under Adam's grove and the tree under Golgotha. The first is redeemed and glorified by the second and the second is glorified by the fourth. In the fourth realm all these trees are loved immeasurably and there is no longer a battle over which to choose.

In the later play of Ibsen, *The Emperor Julian,* Maximus is made to say that in the third empire the jarring elements between the natural and the spiritual will be harmonized, that God will reign in the natural realm and Caesar (man) will reign on the throne of God. This is great insight and is much nearer to what I have glimpsed as the fourth empire than any report since the days of the apostles.

As we receive Jesus from the human-divine realm, which I have designated as the fourth empire, and enter and abide and grow up in Him He becomes victorious and glorified in us and we in Him. Creation itself is to be brought to His realm and the glorious liberty of the sons of God through this two-sided union, victory of Jesus glorified in us and we in Him. This human-divine realm, when brought to full achievement, is to be concrete, visible, tangible perfection, in us as in Jesus, and in the creation as in us.

It is easy enough to speak of the fourth empire, and to describe it as the realization of God's original purpose for all things in which all conflicts are reconciled, in which man, through complete identification with the ascended Jesus, enters into God as God entered into man in the third empire of the Incarnation. It is another thing, however, to understand it and know how to approach it, because it implies a resurrected man with a wholly new mode of thinking which our academic philosophy and theology do not provide. This approach is twofold: the first part is its actualization in *spirit* and in the individual lives of those who have dedicated themselves to it; the second part is its spiritual and *physical* actualization in every realm of human and natural life. This latter part involves the promised transfiguration of the whole created universe: "And I saw a new heaven and a new earth: for the first heaven and the first earth were passed away. . . ." Many have been inclined to dismiss this promise as a far-fetched dream, for the significant reason that almost all our thinking on the subject has been done in terms which simply will not embrace the idea. Just as color cannot be described in terms of shape, the fourth empire cannot be realized in terms of our ordinary ways of living and resultant thinking. Therefore the achievement of this vision is apt to seem fantastic and even naïve while we think of it according to the old principles of philosophy. For logic, as we understand it, works with three dimensions. To understand the fourth empire we need another dimension to our logic.

In the world as we see it now nature is at war with itself— "red in tooth and claw"—and spirit is at war with nature in the historic conflict between natural and spiritual man, between the lusts of the flesh and the demands of the spirit. The fourth empire does not require the destruction and disappearance of the natural realm; it requires its transformation and sanctification, so that nothing which is beautiful and worthwhile in nature is lost. Now when the third empire is introduced into the first (nature) and the second (spirit) there is a violent upheaval. As St. Paul explains in his epistles to the Romans and Galatians, the old Jewish Law represented for him this struggle between nature and spirit which cannot possibly be resolved in its own terms. The Law was an attempt to *force* an issue through man's own strength, and this act of violence only increased the conflict. St. Paul saw that it was necessary to replace the Law by the redeeming power of Christ.

Christ's coming into the world instituted the third empire, and here there is at first opposition, conflict, and warfare. He comes unto His own, and His own receives Him not. He is misunderstood, falsely accused, reviled, and crucified. But when the best gives Himself to the worst and is crucified by the worst on behalf of the worst, the day begins to break. For there comes the possibility and the fact of resurrection, ascension, entry into the Holy of Holies and finally Pentecost, the gift of the Holy Spirit. The oyster of the world fights a new element introduced into it and produces a pearl.

Pentecost, or the Baptism of the Holy Spirit, is an actual experience which makes it possible for those who receive it to partake of the fourth empire in the spirit here and now. It institutes a ministry of those who have begun to inherit its tremendous possibilities and who cannot rest until they have seen it realized in the whole of life. In their inmost being, they are already in the fourth empire, and are thus ministering spirits and angels of mercy to all other empires. This ministry continues until all realms of life are redeemed, fulfilled and brought to completion, glory and perfection in the fourth. Furthermore, those who have this gift are unable to contain themselves for the very reason that the gift of the Holy Spirit can never be kept to oneself alone. That gift is of all things the most alive, but, like all living things, to remain alive it must be circulated, passed on to others and shared, and above all cannot be made the basis of any monopolistic claim to spiritual superiority. The fourth empire and the gift of the Spirit can no more be the exclusive property of any individual or group than the wind and stars.

In attempting to describe the fourth empire in the written word we must perforce use current modes of thought and expression, but, as I have tried to show, the old meanings of these terms are inadequate. We have to begin to think of a new theology and a new philosophy. Where the old theology has attempted a reconciliation of nature and the spirit it has achieved little more than compromise, for no true reconciliation is possible in the old mode of thought. In other words, it is impossible to conceive a union of nature and the spirit in which one or the other does not sacrifice something of its essential character. Obviously any attempt to arrive at a union on these terms must arouse the contentions that accompany any approach to compromise. This same problem is at the root of most of the historical conflicts of Christianity—Caesar against God, State against Church,

Science against Religion, Fate against Freewill. Hence the dominant characteristic of theology has been conflict in all realms lower than the fourth empire—a conflict due to incompleteness and partiality. This conflict cannot be removed short of the realm of the ascended Jesus, the realm of "perfect everything" where all partialities are brought into fulfillment in relation to the perfect whole and every factor thereof.

This conflict is still more apparent in philosophy. Elsewhere I speak of my philosophical outlook as that of a "totalist," which means that I endeavor through the gift of the Spirit to take a point of view in which conflicts are overcome, not through compromise, but through fulfillment and transfiguration of conflicting factors. It is as if the conflicting factors were taken up into a realm where they manifest themselves as complements rather than opposites. But this is beyond ordinary logic, which is hopelessly involved in the dialectic of "either . . . or" and can never fully grasp "both . . . and." Ordinary logic has this limitation because of a certain inability to see things whole (and therefore holy). Philosophy and science alike try to explain things by analysis, by taking them to pieces. As a result they discover many conflicting parts whose meaning cannot possibly be understood unless they are seen in relation to the whole. But this demands intuition and revelation rather than logic, synthesis rather than analysis, for intuition is that poetic quality which grasps instantly the basic meaning of things by seeing them whole and alive instead of dissected and dead.

In the fourth empire philosophy reverts to its divine and original meaning—the love of wisdom, for it becomes an act of insight and contemplation rather than a process of reasoning. Instead of being a matter of opinion and counter opinion, it becomes the act of seeing and loving the self-evident processes and laws of life and thought, enabling and necessitating the joyous approval and perpetual celebration of the ways of God and of life. Philosophy becomes the understanding and self-evident explanation of ultimate reality.

What of ethics and political philosophy? Ethics becomes the law by which we live as much as the law by which flowers bloom, and disappears as something *separate* from normal life; it loses its artificiality, and ethical living becomes as natural and inconspicuous as normal breathing. So too government disappears as something distinct from the community itself, because law is derived from inward, spiritual directions, not from external compulsion. In this you may see the utter difference of the "totalist" and totalitarian approach to life. For the former produces the reconciliation of all realms by loving all; thus it produces true union. The latter seeks to effect it by violent compulsion, and so achieves only uniformity—the solid, inorganic and lifeless condition of original chaos!

So much for the philosophical implications of the fourth empire. But all this remains fundamentally unintelligible without a change, not merely of thinking, but of inner being. No man can simply *think* himself into this total attitude because thought will not move his whole being. I have said that we achieve it by loving all, and this means the most absolute and complete giving of oneself to God, to His way of life as expressed in Jesus and to the service of His whole created universe. Love is giving oneself completely away, so that he arrives at the condition described by St. Paul as "having nothing but possessing all things." So long as there is one atom of self that has not been given away and dedicated to God there is a tiny but strong fetter keeping us out of the fourth realm. For whole self-giving produces instantly that whole vision whereby the great secret of God's creation is revealed, namely, that all things are brought into being and nourished by love, and love alone.

Even in glimpsing such a realm, I was superlatively satisfied, so satisfied that I asked for nothing. I rejoiced in the whole purpose of God and in all of His works as I was permitted to see them through "such different and such healing eyes." The consummation and all the experiences leading to it were seen together in eternity as a single glorious consummation. To use a happy phrasing of Tennyson, the whole process moving on was seen only "as toil coöperative to an end." All of our hardships on the way are "to educe the man," to bring us to victory and glory. Even to glimpse God's hand and purpose causes us to rejoice in all His works, "good and very good." In this realm prayer becomes thanksgiving, the giving of thanks for everything. The spirit of God within us proclaims superlative "satisfaction in His own works; prayer becomes the soliloquy of a jubilant and beholding soul," as Emerson has nobly said.

I saw that Heaven longs greatly to come to earth, that everything there, short of bodily glorification, longs for a body like that of the ascended Jesus and wants us to hasten to prepare ourselves and the earth for the consummation, the marriage of the bride to her Lord, the appearance of Jesus, and transformation into His dominion, even into His bodily likeness. We claim that we want to go to Heaven. What we really want is to become heavenly, so that Heaven may come fully in us and in the whole earth. We do not want to be just spirits and spiritual; we want to be like Jesus, divine-human and human-divine personalities, with love and power to do and to enjoy the whole will of God to the highest possible reaches of perfection.

In this realm of the human-divine, as in the divine-human, the body is to have limitless possibilities and will have every human and divine sense in every part. Eyes, ears, and all the senses are to be in every part of the body, functioning as one. The body will enjoy Heaven as well as the spirit, mind, and soul.

In such revelation, bliss, and glory, I had no memory that I had asked Jesus to come within. It also passed out of my immediate consciousness that I had any need for the baptism of the Holy Spirit. But at some time in my search for the baptism, I had asked the Lord to give me the baptism without the tongues if that were best, but if not, with the tongues. I had asked, too, for Him to reveal the meaning of the Cross, His blood and His Atonement. In the hours of divine cosmic consciousness, with a touch of His compassion I was drawn through the "strait and narrow gate," through the Cross, and covered with His blood in a deep spiritual sense and admitted into the realm of Heaven, permitted to see through the eyes of Heaven how very glorious it is to live on the earth preparing all for the coming realm, the realm Jesus has entered and is to establish on the earth. To use a great profundity Shelley put in the mouth of Prometheus, "It repents me that I ever willed ill or worked a single injury to a single living thing." I was being prepared for the ministry of cosmic intercession which came a little later.

I was seated in a chair with a tablet and pencil, trying to report as much as I could of the things made known to me. Suddenly, unasked and unexpected, the divine glory, power, and fire, acting as one, came over me and ran through me, taking free possession of me. The greatest glory and bliss was upon my tongue and face—I infer they felt as the body in its entirety will feel in glorification—where the Presence was singing:

> "Jesus, Jesus, how I love You;
> Interposed His precious blood."

It seemed as if my body were being played upon by a harmony of Heaven, and the voice sang upon my lips (not as mine, for I cannot sing a note)—a paean of love to Jesus, whose melody was magnificent beyond imagination. The singing was so loud and the nature of the music so glorious that some passing person must have heard it. In the midst of the glory and the praise in song, I heard the doorbell ring. Even hearing it caused a little loosening of the glory and the control. So I told myself, I have an engagement with Heaven and no time to listen to the world.

I shall never cease to give thanks that I refused to listen to other voices while He was speaking and that He had brought me to the place where I welcomed with great joy the fullest control and revelation that I was capable of receiving. Even such blessed men as Finney and Moody drew back from the glory that the Lord put upon them when they made the dedication to do His will, because of the feeling that no flesh could stand such glory. My whole being welcomed the glory, the control, and the revelation.

The power, the control, the wonder of the singing upon my lips and the music upon my whole body, increased and the Presence moved upon and within me and by my happy consent and yielding lifted me as on the cross. My arms were outstretched and my body perfectly upright. In this position I became aware of a glorious Presence standing immediately before me in the tangible form of a man, imparting the sense of barely concealed powers and immense sanctity. He made Himself known as Jesus and infused Himself within me. The way He came was the reverse of the way human personalities leave the body with the going of the breath.

I fell upon my face at His feet, as one dead and yet more alive than I dreamed it possible ever to be. I knew at once that He was in me and I in Him, as the Father was in Him and He in the Father.

That which occurred in my experience was like the occurrence, according to scriptual record, on the first night after His resurrection, when Jesus stood among the eleven and said to them, "Peace be unto you, as My Father has sent Me, even so I send you." And when He had said this, He breathed on them and said unto them, "Receive ye the Holy Ghost." Feror Fenton rendered "breathed on them," "infused Himself within them." This exactly describes what I experienced. Jesus from the realm of glory and the fourth empire stood before me and infused Himself within me.

Even when I was on my face at His feet the testings began. In the light of the witness of the Spirit and subsequent confirmations, the all important tests were, by His enabling, met in His will. Those I did not answer aright held me in God's school in the wilderness until I gave the correct answers.

This question had first of all to be answered:

Is this manifestation and in-breathing of Jesus that has just been granted the coming of Jesus that the apostles looked forward to? I answered, No, it is the preparation for His visible appearing and reigning on earth. I also said I prefer for Him to come in all, for me to be His servant and friend, and the servant and friend of all, to anything else. This saved me from the special temptation of our time, to set oneself up as another Messiah or Christ, or as God.

I was invited to ask what I would. I thank God I asked for the redemption and the best possible for each and all on earth and everywhere. As I would ask for laws, prophecies, sacred books, to be changed if need be to make this possible, it seemed as though, somewhat in terms of Hegel's categories, great, apparently impossible chasms would be bridged, mountains would be joined together to make bases for still higher mountains that would in turn be surmounted, and on and on until all things are reconciled and harmonized in Jesus.

I say Jesus advisedly, because in common with most Christian liberals I have known, Christ—as the divine word as the *logos,* as the way, the truth, and the life, as the "light that lighteth every light that cometh into the world"—had had a place of honor above that of Jesus, the divine-human and the human-divine One, Who is the highest manifestation of all. In the light of the wonder and preciousness revealed, I saw that Jesus, Who suffered and went to the cross in behalf of all, was the most beloved of all and in the highest realm. I wanted to have written all over the creation the name of Jesus as the most precious name of all and in the largest letters.

Before I left the room, the call came to go and give to the people at the top of privilege and opportunity the good news that Jesus is alive, longing to baptize with the Holy Spirit, to manifest Himself, to come within, to draw all unto Himself and into an ineffable, fruit-bearing union with Him, so that He may be revealed and glorified in each of us and so that each of us may be revealed and glorified in Him. He wanted and He wants each who enters this ineffable union to reach the few who can reach the many, as well as minister to all who are at the bottom of human need.

That afternoon when I went to the Christian Science reading room to give my friends there this witness, Mrs. Preston, one of the gentlest and friendliest souls I ever knew, said to me as I entered, "Tell us something good." I replied, "Jesus is the most precious being of all, for He is God on the plane of our suffering and need."

The last becomes first. The body and the visible creation are of no value apart from being used and transformed by the Spirit into the highest achievement in full overcoming, redemption and glorification. The universe is not to be like the invisible Spirit, but to be like the visible, glorified Jesus.

CHAPTER VI

THROUGH THE WILDERNESS

‹‹‹‹‹‹‹‹‹‹‹‹‹‹‹‹‹‹‹‹‹‹‹‹‹‹‹‹‹››››››››››››››››››››››

The first eight hours after the manifestation of Jesus and His incoming were so extraordinary that I have to be in the Spirit to be able to remember the wonder of some of the things that occurred. After the break of day I drove out to Lakeside, about four miles from the city, to give my friends there a report of what had happened. On the way I overtook a man walking to the railroad station about half a mile beyond the house of my friends. As much as I wanted to see them, the love of Jesus constrained me to take the man to the station, notwithstanding his insistence that I should not do so. Jesus would be pleased, I felt, and He was so real and precious that I was impelled to do His errand.

When I saw my friends and began to tell them of the things that had recently occurred there was, as it were, a supernatural writing of them upon the mind. Once while I was speaking it seemed to them as though it was no longer Moseley, but Jesus, who was doing the talking.

Later I had the consciousness that Jesus within me and speaking through me, had all the power and could call me and the universe to an ascension like his own in which heaven and earth were joined; then I actually felt myself, in the spirit, ascending to such a union. I felt that if I had given myself to it completely I should actually have reached it. But something restrained me, and for hours afterwards I could feel myself descending again.

Jesus met all the tests of the wilderness within forty days and came out to use all the power and gifts of God in utter unselfishness and perfect love. Moses stayed in the wilderness forty years because of his own rashness and forty more because of the lack of faith and obedience on the part of most of the company he was seeking to lead into the promised land. Every human, especially if as human as I, after a great invasion from Heaven needs sufficient time for right adjustment and for the purification of desires and purposes, so that he will choose to use the light and the power—gifts entrusted to him in the will and wisdom of God—to the good of each and all and not to further a single carnal or selfish end.

No one is out of his schooling in the wilderness and capable of being the channel of a pure revelation until this has been achieved. Only a small amount of revelation gets through without being colored by the medium of its communication. Then, too, when one is in high ecstasy there is such a new beauty and wonder over all things, that it is easy to confuse the lighted human with the divine and holy. In Jesus there was such an at-one-ment between the human and the divine that He could give an uncolored revelation.

Even before being purified sufficiently for the light to get through undimmed, I was in such glory that my unredeemed human longings seemed glorified. Because of a great love-friendship on my part (there was only a fine friendship on her part) which had been carried over into the new realm, it was easy for me to infer that it was God's will, and that it would ultimately be hers, for us to be one in an even better paradise than the one at the beginning. In the realm of such glory I was unaware that so long as there was any one ready to listen, there are talking serpents even in Eden, and in this instance it was the man, Adam, and not the woman, Eve, who listened. And for me, though I apparently did my best to defeat God's loving purpose for me, it was best to be, as Jesus advised for those and only those ready to receive it, a celibate for the Kingdom of Heaven's sake.

It cost me much—more than it is well to attempt to tell—

to make me ready to accept happily His superlative, not only for me, but also for the one I loved. I died hardly and ungraciously. But after the death, I found I had lost nothing but what had caused the suffering and the death, and kept me out of Paradise where all things on ever higher levels are mine and yours and everyone's. After all, it was perhaps in letting go that I prevented myself from the actual loss of her. I would have been a poor husband, and a loss of marriage is little compared with a loss of such a friendship.

This sudden inflowing of a wholly new world, combined with the struggle I have just described, made it seem advisable to relatives for me to rest for a while in a private sanatorium, in order to make my readjustments.

I was out of this external wilderness in thirteen days, but not out of my spiritual wilderness and ready to begin my work of purely unselfish, cosmic intercession and service of pure love and good will, until I was glad to let go once and for all every imagination and expectation of a paradise where I would be loved after the manner of even the most perfect of human lovers. For me to make this choice gladly— the only sacrifices acceptable to God are those made gladly— required all the deeper death because those I loved were so very lovable and because I had glimpsed such wonders in the marriage relationship where both husband and wife, with redeemed spirits, minds, souls, and bodies, were first of all married to Jesus, and by divine creation, education, and by selection, intended for each other. But by the help of remarkable women, each at the right time and in the right way, I was brought step by step to the place where I could choose with joy what I somehow knew, even as a boy, would be God's best for me.

Most fortunately, my discipline in the wilderness left no unhealed wounds. All has been turned to good. My schooling in the wilderness has enabled me to help keep others from needing to go. As badly as I blundered in the wilderness, the memory of this blundering has served as a beneficent thorn in the flesh to keep me in the attitude of lowly listening for guidance to be kept from further blundering. The kind of education that God gives is cheap at any cost.

As Saint Paul advised, it is better to remain in the state in which one is called. Yet if one is called unmarried, if he marry in God, he has done well, but not as well as to remain as called, if he is happy. As the great apostle also advised, if after marriage either husband or wife becomes a disciple of Jesus and sanctified through faith and because of union with Him, this one is not to leave the unbeliever, though the unbeliever is left free to leave the believer if he choose. If the unbeliever chooses to remain and the believer becomes heavenly enough, the promise is that by remaining, even the unsanctified unbeliever will be given a change of heart.

I know a family in Philadelphia, the Goetlieb Schmidt family, where the husband decided that his wife was so heavenly he could not stand to remain and told her so. The oldest daughter also said, "It's too much for me, and I am going with papa." Mrs. Schmidt replied, "Wait until I can fix you up well for the journey." The husband replied, "Since you are that good, I am not going to leave." Both he and the daughter remained where they belonged and by remaining have become more and more like the wonderful wife and mother. Nothing is so contagious as Heaven, if you have enough of it.

The thirteen days at Dr. Allen's sanatorium not only taught me much that I needed to know but gave me the opportunity to put his pecan trees in good shape. He and Mrs. Allen and the children were wonderful to me. I visited much in their home and took many of my meals with them.

The first day I was at Dr. Allen's, Sunday, March 27, 1910, I fell into such a deep sleep that it was hard to awaken me. When awakened I saw Jesus in the face of the kind servant sent to awaken me. I was in such a realm of glory that I was not certain whether I had been awakened from profound human sleep, or resurrected from death. Everything had a halo of light and glory around it. Even the cattle and the chickens, to use a fine line of Browning's, "had learned the new law," so surpassing were they in form, movement, grace, and beauty.

This new realm of the divine-human and the human-divine, as glimpsed and entered into, gives a joy that nothing can conquer. Only about a year ago, I was told by a learned student in the field of religion, "You are the happiest of the mystics," and by "mystic," he meant those who come to know the Lord by immediate revelation, fellowship, and guidance. He went on to say, "You have no periods of depression as did Luther, Madame Guyon, and others." There are no ups and downs, no "blues," in the fourth empire, and, besides, everyone who enters receives not only of the victory and joy of Jesus, but also the accumulated spiritual riches of all the overcomers. This is the reverse of the human order, where those who enter the feast last find the barest table.

When I became aware that I needed God-control to bring me unfailing self-control, I prayed to the Father. The answer came from depths beyond and behind the manifestations of the Spirit and the conscious presence of Jesus. The assurance that my prayer had been answered was complete, and since then I have been able to pass through many kinds of storms and tempests, undisturbed and unafraid. I have been able to laugh and say, "God bless you," whenever spiritual brickbats were being thrown at me and some of them were even hitting me.

A friend in the Spirit, praying for me while I was at Dr. Allen's, heard the following words spoken and understood that they were being applied to me, although originally spoken concerning Joseph:

"The archers have sorely grieved him and shot at him and hated him: but his bow abode in strength and the arms of his hands were made strong by the hands of the mighty God of Jacob."

The enemies who assail us are not flesh and blood, not human beings, but the forces of spiritual wickedness in unseen realms. Our battle is against evil suggestions and urges and never against any human here or anywhere. And even the demons deserve our compassion; they are the victims of themselves, needing release. As to Joseph, he had more of the spirit and of the achievements of what is to be in the divine-human realm than any other ancient ruler. He was the embodied prophecy and type of a kind of ruler so much needed now, combining great practical abilities with the Heavenly Spirit.

After coming back to Macon, I felt I had many problems. I had only one, to put first the expression of union with Jesus. The making of a living had already been provided for by the planting of a few acres in pecan and plum trees three years before. I had had the privilege of sending my brother Millard through college, with the understanding that he was to make and furnish the necessary amount for sending our younger brother, Windfield, through college. Windfield, in his turn, was to send Maude, the baby of the family.

But when Millard came to Byron, Georgia, to teach school, he fell in love and wanted to get married. He asked to be released of his obligation to send Windfield to college. He made the request when I was in a receptive mood and I happily granted it. Although relieved of the obligation to help Windfield, he helped him considerably nevertheless. Millard and his wife, Effie, were so grateful to me that they gave me ten acres of land to plant in trees. Brother also helped me, as he does now, in caring for them. The working in the trees furnished the finest kind of recreation for me, and the returns financially have been surprising.

Then I thought I had to live down the reputation of having been in even a private sanatorium, but God turned this to my good and to the good of others. Indeed, he has turned and is forever turning everything to good that He is allowed to by our act in turning everything over to Him.

Mrs. Walter Lamar gave me my first opportunity to speak to a Macon group. A week after I returned from the sanatorium, she arranged for me to give a talk on Maurice Maeterlinck at her home on Georgia Avenue. The good-hearted aristocrats of the city attended. Of the friendly company who so cheered and encouraged me, "Uncle Nat" Winship, Minter Wimberly, Mrs. Emory Winship, and Mrs. James H. Blount have "put out to sea." The rest, so far as I know, still live. I feel toward them as Emerson felt toward those who saw to it that the home of his that had been reduced to ashes was rebuilt in time for his return from a trip to Europe. He told the neighbors who did this that he would like to have a list of their names that he might read it daily.

I did some work among the trees during the summer of 1910. In the autumn I picked cotton and made a fairly good picker, too. Moreover, I drove my brother's team of mules and took my cotton to the gins. I began to hold an occasional meeting with the colored people and during the autumn months spent the week-ends in Macon and attended meetings with friends who met at Lakeside.

As I look back upon those days, I see that this hard work in the open gave me health and self-respect. The combining of heavenly and so-called human activities have made up much of life for me, I trust in preparation for that ever-increasing interchange, interaction, and integration of the Heavenly Kingdom and the earthly kingdom that is to go on until the two have become one. Just this morning, May 22, 1939, before starting to revise this manuscript, my tongue was taken, and this was spoken:

"I give you Heaven in the least of all things. I give you Heaven everywhere."

Upon the whole, I have failed in devotion and faithfulness to both of my commissions, the commission to minister to those at the bottom of human need, and the commission to witness to those at the top of human privilege. I realize that only God would have held me, encouraging me, and never turning on the light except to light the path. It is not because of abilities or virtues that He gave and continues to give such a revelation of Himself and His way of life, but because of His great love and of my great need.

Even the cross experience was a revelation of the law of His life, the law of love, that works by interchange, interaction, and integration. He shows me by my cross experience that when He went to the cross in my behalf He went to a literal cruel cross of shame and suffering and death, but that when I went to the cross, it was to a cross of life, and bliss, and glory. He came out of glory into shame, out of life into death. I went up out of the realm of shame and suffering and death into His realm of life and glory and honor. When He went to the cross He was deserted by His disciples and seemingly by the Father. When I went to the cross I was surrounded by the heavenly host and by my friends, and He Himself manifested Himself and came within. When He went to the cross He gave up the divine breath. When I went to the cross I received the breath of the Holy Spirit. This union with Jesus which begins in such marvelous interchange moves on into interaction and integration, whereby we become one with Him in Spirit and in services of love.

What Jesus did as a historical fact at Calvary, He is forever doing in the Spirit. He is forever taking our imperfections and giving us His perfection and this continues until He achieves in us perfect grace and perfect giving and receiving of His manifold perfection. He is initiating us in His own ministry of doing for others and with others what He did and continues to do for and with us. By becoming partakers of His nature and life, we become partakers of Him and His ministry, finishing all that is lacking to make us become like Him. We are redeemed by the Redeemer to become redeemers, we are saved by the Saviour to become saviours, we are transformed by the Transformer to be transformers, we are glorified by the Glorified One to bring others to glory.

CHAPTER VII

MANIFESTATIONS OF THE SPIRIT

‹‹‹‹‹‹‹‹‹‹‹‹‹‹‹‹‹‹‹‹‹‹‹‹‹‹‹‹‹‹‹‹‹‹›››››››››››››››››››››››››››

All the spiritual as well as natural gifts of God to men are greatly profitable in the spirit, love, and wisdom of Jesus; all of them apart from His love and wisdom are subject to misuse and abuse. As the wise Emerson puts it, the devil nestles comfortably in bibles, covenants, creeds, constitutions and in the best governments and movements. He gets in and perverts everything but the spirit of Jesus; if he were to get in this spirit he would cease to be the devil. He can remain the devil and get in and largely run everything else. This, I take it, is why Jesus refused to perform any miracles except those of love and why Saint Paul puts a much higher estimate upon the fruit than he does the gifts of the Spirit. Yet the gifts and manifestations of the Spirit in the wisdom and grace of love have high value and should be in evidence in the whole Church of Christ. To quote Saint Paul, "make love your quest," "be eager for spiritual gifts," and be eager most of all for the greater gifts—the word of wisdom, prophecy, and faith that works by love. But do not despise and resist any of the gifts and workings of the Spirit. Only insist that everything be done in the wisdom and grace of love, and be wisely and graciously loving even in your insistence on putting love first. If the tongues of men and of angels without love are as sounding brass and tinkling cymbals, what should be said of the lack of them along with the lack of love?

The experiences reported in this chapter may appear to some as extraordinary and unheard-of since the time of the early Church. But the phenomena reported here have been present in great revivals from then until now, though they rarely come to the attention of the general public. Neither, for that matter, did the doings of Jesus, for they escaped the notice of secular historians of the period.*

From Tuesday morning, March 22, to Sunday afternoon, November 20, 1910, all the words spoken through me under the inspiration and control of the Spirit were in English. I had asked for this, if it were possible. If any asked me if I had received the baptism, I reported as best I could what God had given me, the way He gave it, and the way He continued to manifest Himself and to use me. I had asked for His best and for the baptism if this was His best for me. I had felt the need of Jesus within to enable me to go His way of perfect love in utter sincerity. The answer to this desire, seeking and asking, was beyond human conception and the highest point of His giving was after I stopped seeking and dedicated myself to go His way of perfect love and sincerity.

On the afternoon of November 20, nearly eight months after my great experience, I was talking to a returned missionary from China who had been sent to China by Georgia Baptists. While in China she received the baptism with the Holy Spirit, and the Chinese group she had ministered to got together enough money to send her back to the United States as a missionary to us. This double missionary surprised me when she said to me, "The same Spirit speaking through you in English is speaking through us, the Pentecostal people, in tongues." She went on to say, "Your tongue is attuned just as much to supernatural control when you speak in English as are the tongues of us Pentecostal people speaking in other tongues." But as I understood that the

* See Goethe's tract on the gift of tongues, *Concerning Important but Up-to-date Undiscussed Sections of the Bible* (1773),—an answer to the question "What is it to speak with tongues?" which he explains as a speech of the Spirit. Another work of modern interest in this connection is Stanley Frodsham's *With Signs Following*.

Pentecostal groups generally held that the initial evidence of the baptism is "speaking in tongues as the Spirit gives the utterance," her remark came as a surprise to me. The deepest work of the Holy Spirit is, of course, to bring one into vital union with Jesus and to make the body His temple.

I realized that the missionary friend was about to offer me a fellowship on the basis of my having received the baptism with the Spirit, as had others of the Pentecostal group. I asked her not to regard me as one of their group until I could explain to her my larger desire, longing, and hope; that, to use the words of Tennyson, "Not one life would be destroyed or cast as rubbish to the void when God has made His pile complete." To my surprise, she replied, "This larger hope does not frighten me any longer." She gave me to understand that she shared this hope. I replied, "We will be persecuted not only by the churches, but also by the Pentecostal people."

As I said we would be persecuted by the Pentecostal people as well as by the churches, a new and very precious, but seemingly less glorious, control of the Spirit came upon my lips and tongue, evidently seeking to use them. I invited the Blessed Presence, taking control, to have His way. The word, "rivers," was formed on my lips and I had nothing to do with the formation except to lend my lips to the Spirit. I felt intuitively that this referred to the promise made by Jesus to those who believed in Him—that out of their inmost parts would flow "rivers of living water" and that this referred to the Spirit He would give to them after He was glorified. As I continued to offer myself and my lips to the control of the Spirit, the word "lib" was formed. So far as I know this was the first word of an unknown tongue the Spirit formed on my lips or spoke through me. The next word formed on my lips was the German "lieb," meaning dearly beloved.

Shortly after this, I was thinking how lovingly I had been led, so that I had had only love feasts in leaving the groups which I was led to leave in order to be true to the light that drew me forward. As I sat thinking, the Spirit came upon me and spoke the word *rara* several times. I knew that this meant "rare." Then the word *rata* came several times, and later *rara* and *rata* were thrown together again and again. When I looked up the meaning of *rata*, I found it to be "rate, share, or portion." I had the double witness that the Spirit of Jesus and His way of love were the rare portion.

Since then the Spirit has spoken through me in English and in other languages. When I am speaking before various groups I seek to leave it to His will and wisdom as to the way He manifests His presence and control. And, of course, He makes no mistakes. The speaking in tongues, especially when there is someone in the audience in whose native tongue the Spirit speaks, or when there is someone present with the gift of interpretation, gives a wonderful sense of the presence of God. Where there is no one who understands, it is more edifying for the Spirit to speak in English.

There have been a few times when the Spirit has taken my tongue and spoken words and phrases in the languages of people present. Once when I was speaking in Atlanta, the Spirit took my tongue and spoke in a language of which I was entirely ignorant. The pastor, who had in him a strain of Indian blood and knew the Cherokee dialect, told me after the service that the words spoken were in that dialect and meant, "My God knows me." At another time, at a different place in Atlanta, the Spirit again spoke through me words whose meaning was unknown to me. After the meeting a brother born in Lithuania, I believe, came to me and said that the words spoken in tongues were in his native language and meant, "It is so," and "He saith it."

Not long after the Spirit began to speak through me these words and phrases in many tongues, I met a Frenchman who had been interpreter for the French government. At the country home below Dublin, Georgia, where we were together for hours and shared a room for the night, the

Spirit used my tongue a great deal and spoke words and phrases that the Frenchman told me were in every tongue that he knew. Words were also spoken in tongues that he did not know. My knowledge of Latin, Greek, French, and German is very restricted, but words are often spoken in these languages that are known to me, as well as others whose meaning I do not know. Whenever there is a speaking in English which seems to be an interpretation of what has been spoken in foreign words and phrases, it comes as a result of waiting upon the Spirit for clarification of what has been spoken in tongues.

For the tongue to be used by the Spirit in any language gives a wonderful sense of the reality of God and His nearness.

Every touch of the Spirit gives life to the whole being. It was the Spirit that raised Jesus bodily from the dead. In my experience, both before and after the descent of the Holy Spirit upon me, all the healings and marked achievements have been clearly the acts of the Spirit. It is the Spirit which reveals Jesus; it is through the Spirit that He makes us His habitation and that we enter into Jesus and abide in Him, have fellowship with Him, and are made like Him; it is the Spirit which guides into all the truth; it is the Spirit which makes intercession for us and within us according to the perfect will of God. It is the Spirit which seals us as God's very own. It is the Spirit which shows us things to come.

To use still more fine insights and phrasings of Emerson, "The Spirit must come as an entire possession." The Spirit is given to "the lowly and the simple; it comes to whosoever will put off that which is foreign and proud; it comes as insight; it comes as serenity and grandeur. When we see those whom it inhabits, we are appraised of new degrees of greatness. From that inspiration the man comes back with a changed tone. He does not talk with men with an eye to their opinions; he tries them. It requires us to be plain and true. . . . The soul that ascends to worship the true God is plain and true."

To receive the inflow and control of the Spirit requires no particular technique. The greatest inflows have come upon me unexpectedly, but there are times when I consciously invite and express the need for guidance. At such times I consciously ask, "Is there anything you'd like to say to me?" but for an answer to be made requires no specific mold of thought; it may come at any time and in any activity, when riding in a car or pruning my trees or gathering the nuts, in the midst of a crowd or alone in privacy.

As the Spirit is yielded to and welcomed to take control of the body as well as the Spirit, both soul and body are brought into God in a supernatural way, and the work is begun of making the body in the likeness of the resurrected and ascended Jesus. The Spirit in possession brings Heavenly control and use not only of the tongue but of the whole being. Not only the baptism but the continuous control and use of the Spirit is what the church must have to give it life and authority and victory. The baptism, life, fruit, guidance, and transforming glory of the Spirit are all for everyone who believes in Jesus and is willing to obey Him.

Long before we come under the conscious control, baptism, and use of the Spirit, we are taught by luminous thought, by the pressure of circumstances, by the pleadings and wooings of love, to be always loving, merciful, and forgiving, and by signal after signal of God. We are also taught by the hindrance of God which theologians call "prevenient Grace." Socrates said that his guide intervened only when he was in danger of making some error of action or speech. Emerson said that whenever he proposed a journey or enterprise of any kind and found signals or obstacles against it, he respected the obstacles, and that while he did not call these obstacles as much as a commandment, he called them a grain of mustard seed, as it were, and "respected them above the combined opinion of all mankind."

Evelyn Underhill speaks of "the pressure of God in favor or against the choices we must make," and says that "the early Friends [Quakers] were accustomed to trust implicitly in the indications of this kind and were usually justified. When there is no such pressure (and God leaves us free to do what love inspires and indicates), then our conduct should be decided by charity and common sense; qualities that are given to us by God in order that they may be used."

There is guidance, all manner of guidance both ethical and factual, from the clear revelation and speaking of the Holy Spirit, to the light of the inner monitor. As we become more Christlike we are guided less by symbolic dreams and visions, and more by spiritual intuition and direct insight. But visions may continue to come if the Spirit finds their language effective for imparting factual knowledge.

There is no difficulty about being rightly guided if we are willing to follow the guidance. I have found invariably that where God seemingly left me alone to make decisions, whenever I chose that which was most loving to all, I had really chosen His best and was under His guidance in making the decision. And the sublimest revelation of the highest right that has been done on this planet was when Jesus, seemingly forsaken by all and even by God Himself, did God's highest will of love. It is always the will of God to go the way of perfect love, and as you go in His good Spirit and love, His presence and approval go with you.

At this time I wrote something of my experience to Professor James Hyslop of Columbia University, whom I had known rather intimately, in connection with his venturesome experiments in the field of psychic phenomena and religious experience. He replied that "the world is not yet ready for your experience, but will welcome it later."

In the spring of 1911, all of the contributing factors for making the new Peabody College at Nashville had been brought together, and representative alumni were invited to come to the college at the commencement season to make known to the new Peabody board what they had in mind for the new college, particularly as to its relationship to Vanderbilt University.

At the public meeting held at the college chapel on the evening of June 6, Professor T. J. Woofter, of the University of Georgia, and myself were the principal speakers. We sought to make clear that the alumni effort was to the end of giving a new and adequate body to the wonderful soul of the old Peabody. I repeated what Professor W. H. Kilpatrick and I had written previously: that we wanted "coördinate coöperation" between Peabody and Vanderbilt so that each would enrich the other, rather than that the rich life of either should be sacrificed in any way to the glory of the other.

Vanderbilt, as it was pointed out, held a high place in the field of traditional classical learning, while Peabody was pioneering in the democratic social service ideal of life and education; therefore, the preservation and development of the latter seemed to us more important than the former. What the alumni wanted of the new board and the President and faculty of the new Peabody was, as I quoted from Wycliffe Rose, "to appreciate their assets and make the best use of them."

On the night following our alumni meeting another public meeting was held and at this meeting the President of the new Peabody board, the Honorable J. G. Bradford, said that what the alumni desired and asked for was, "coördinate coöperation with Vanderbilt" and that my phrase exactly expressed their wishes and purposes. This has continued to be the desire of the new Peabody board and the college administration, as well as of the alumni.

In 1911 the young plum trees planted as fillers among the pecan trees gave their first crop. They netted me enough to pay expenses for a year and netted the man who bought them enough to form a co-partnership with me on the basis that he would prune and spray, gather and market the plums, which I would only be required to cultivate. This was a very happy and profitable arrangement for me, as well as for him. No trade is a good trade unless it is good for all parties. I made a wonderful cotton crop for the acreage planted. Everything my hands touched seemed to have the blessing of the Lord upon it.

In the late winter or early spring of 1911, Miss Carro Davis, a niece of Mrs. W. A. Scott and a former principal of one of the Macon schools, a very gifted young lady both naturally and spiritually, returned from Chicago where she had sought and received the baptism with the Holy Spirit, more in the way it was received at Pentecost than I have known it to be received by any other. To quote from a statement made by Miss Davis that was published in the *Macon News*, December 20, 1911, "In the summer of 1910 I went into a Pentecostal mission in Chicago, and although the service seemed strange . . . I knew beyond a shadow of doubt that these were God's people and this was God's power."

The statement continued, "A short time after this the Lord put such a hunger and thirst in my soul that I prayed night and day for the Holy Spirit to come and take up His abode within, no matter what the result should be. If ye ask for bread He will not give you a stone. After praying for weeks, and having become ashamed of ever having been ashamed, the Holy Spirit of God came in to abide forever, according to Acts 2:4; speaking through me in four languages, Persian, Chinese, Scandinavian, and Russian, which were understood by the foreigners present."

Miss Davis before leaving Chicago had been asked if she would be willing to return to Macon and preach to the colored people. She replied, "Lord, you can make me willing." And before leaving Macon for Chicago she had said to the Lord, "I am unwilling to go your way, but You can make me willing." After this the hunger became so great for the Lord and His Spirit that she resigned her position as the principal of the Bellevue School in order to be free to seek to do His work. The work among the colored people was remarkable in Spirit and in the early Christian "signs" that followed. Not only were the colored people baptized with the Holy Spirit in great numbers, but many of them were healed of severe infirmities without even asking, or expecting the Lord to heal them.

In December of 1911, the street meetings started which were so largely attended and so unusual in their character that they made history for the Kingdom of God and also for the city of Macon. A great deal has appeared in the papers about these meetings and I describe them more fully in a later chapter. We had great zeal in those days and most of it I feel was according to the wisdom and in the excellent Spirit of Heaven.

Mrs. Scott and Miss Carro Davis in their boldness and in initiative so eclipsed the rest of us that we did well to stand with them. Miss Davis was given a supernatural gift of singing and her wonderful voice could be heard for blocks.

In articles that appeared in the *Macon Telegraph and News,* in December, 1911, I said among other things: "I am not a leader of any sect and never intend to be a particularist in religion any more than in politics, sociology, or philosophy. In the narrow sectarian sense I hate all sectarian names; in the broad catholic and generous sense I love them all, or rather the good that has been sought after and given and done in these names. I like especially well the name given us by the Holy Spirit, namely, "Children of God." "The Spirit beareth witness with our spirits that we are children of God," and if children, then heirs, heirs of God and joint heirs with Christ, if so be that we suffer with Him that we be also glorified together.

"We should not name or limit ourselves by any gift or experience or truth, but seek the whole of God's truth and provisions of love for us. In philosophy I am a totalist; seeking the whole of truth and good and eschewing that which seems to be error from every source; in religion I am a child of God, seeking to be led by the Spirit of truth into all that God has for me."

In the winter of 1911-1912, I spoke of these things to all the pastors and religious workers of Macon, both white and colored, including the priest in charge of the Catholic church. My experience with him was of great interest. In common with nearly all of the pastors and religious workers to whom I spoke, he was a good listener. He said, "Mr. Moseley, those are beautiful ideas and if you live by them you will go to Heaven, but God, knowing that only a few would live that way, has provided the ritual and the services of the church by which man may also be saved."

I remember also John Bunting, the rector of Christ Episcopal Church, for a particular kindness. I had many visits at the rectory and spent one night as the guest of Mr. and Mrs. Bunting. Some years later when he was rector of the Church of the Ascension in Saint Louis and I told him about some of the recent acts of the Holy Spirit in my life, he was finely responsive. A little later he took me to the altar of his church and laid his hands upon me and gave me the blessing of the church.

About Christmas time, 1911, my friend Professor George Herbert Clarke, poet and scholar, came to Macon. He let me knew that he came principally to see me. We spent hours and hours talking over the things that had made history in my life. At first he wanted me to tone down, but before he left Macon he paid, not to me personally but to the Spirit of Him within me, this remarkable compliment: "There is a greatness there that you (meaning the friend to whom he was talking) and I can hardly begin to understand." To me it is both a mystery and an open secret. The mystery is that God, the author of this stupendous universe, can enter into such intimate fellowship with such tiny creatures as ourselves, and achieve such grace, wisdom, and boldness in such stuff as we are. For me, the open secret is that there is no secret to be learned, by the human processes of learning. It is not he who knows that loves; it is he who loves that knows. So far from being the kind of secret which has to be acquired in the pride of knowledge, it is something *given* to all, learned and unlearned, by the love and grace of God. He is so eager for us to have it; He is perpetually pressing it upon us, in order to win our consent to receive Himself and His secret. In the words of Emerson, "At times it seems that it is impossible by any possible human ingenuity to escape His blessed purpose concerning us, but He would that our will and endeavour were more active parties."

More and more doors were opened for me to witness to the humble people and to the lowly, as well as to people of marked ability. Very early it was made known to me that I was to centralize upon Jesus, union with Him and His way of love. While I was to help all groups, I was not to be the party to starting a new sect or of ever making a division among the children of God anywhere. I was assured that if I would be faithful to Him, I would never need to build or buy a church for myself, because He would open the churches of others to my witness or report, so that I might be a channel for His love.

All required of the channel is connection with the fountain of God and the right downward slant for the water to reach the desert of human need. The full flow of water, the heavenly water, cleanses and keeps the channel clean. All the thirsty desire is clean fresh water and if thirsty enough will receive the water without considering the size or appearance of the conduit.

CHAPTER VIII

GO IN LOVE

‹‹‹‹‹‹‹‹‹‹‹‹‹‹‹‹‹‹‹‹‹‹‹‹‹‹‹‹‹‹›››››››››››››››››››››››››››

The First World War and its aftermath of pestilence and famine, with all of its prodigious folly, madness, and unnecessary suffering called for universal sympathy and compassion, and for every possible service of light-bearing and loving kindness. Before and during the war, as well as afterward, I sought to put as strongly as possible the superlatively excellent way of Jesus for the group, the nation, and the nations, as well as for the individual.

At the time of our entrance into the war I said in the columns of the *Macon Telegraph* that the perfectly loving and altogether beneficent attitude of Jesus, which will not strive nor contend about human rights and possessions, which resists not evil with evil, which turns the other cheek, which will not go to law or to war, nor go on any mission except one of love and good will, is the attitude that is to win against all others, because it is worthiest of all to win. All men and all things, as I said, will yield to this attitude and only to this, in freedom and in joy. In our hearts by fine necessity of our being, we never really surrender on any other terms. There is no real loyalty except the free loyalty of love.

I said then, as I continue to say, that one should not be a pacifist in a neutral, negative sense, that there is such a thing as being too low-down to fight, as well as being above the zone of carnal warfare. Everyone is called to do his best against all the influences and forces that degrade and destroy life, and in behalf of every force making for the good of each and all. The children of this world fight with carnal weapons. The children of light fight with the weapons of Heaven, the weapons of light and love.

In answer to the question, cannot one draw the sword as did Peter and yet be a true disciple of the Prince of Peace? I said, Yes, he can be as good a disciple as was Peter at that time, but such a one is not so near the bosom of Jesus as was the beloved disciple who drew no sword in His defense and yet followed Him without denial in the hour of supreme shame.

In reply to the contention that a nation composed of people too Christ-like to fight with carnal weapons would be defenseless and invite invasion by the selfish and the ruthless, I answered in the wise words of the sage of Concord: "If you have a nation of men who have risen to that height of moral cultivation that they will not declare war, or carry arms, for they have not so much madness left in their brains, you have a nation of lovers, of benefactors, of true, great, and noble men. Let me know more of that nation. I shall not find them defenseless, with idle hands swinging at their sides. I shall find them men of love, of honor, and truth; men of an immense industry; men whose influence is felt to the ends of the earth; men whose very look and voice carry the sentence of honor and shame, and all forces yield to their energy and persuasion. When you see the doctrine of peace embraced by a nation, we may be assured it will not be one that invites injury, but one on the contrary which has a friend in the bottom of the heart of every man, even of the violent and the base; one against which no weapon can prosper; one which is looked upon as the asylum of the human race and has the tears and blessings of mankind."

Just as the Christ-like individual wins converts to Christ and His love spirit and way of life, so would the Christ-like nation, and the winning would go on and on until the kingdoms of this world and the whole earth become His.

Our entrance into the First World War and the bringing

of many soldiers to Camp Wheeler, near Macon, gave an appealing opportunity to touch helpfully all the soldiers we possibly could. Mr. and Mrs. W. A. Scott and Miss Carro and Miss Susie Davis held meetings with me on the streets of Macon, where the soldiers congregated, on the Camp Wheeler road, and at the home of Mr. and Mrs. Scott. The thing that was uppermost in my mind in witnessing to the soldiers was this; if they dedicated themselves to God to do His full will, their lives would be safe until all the work they came here to do was finished. A man who loses his purpose in life is already dead.

"Thus man," Emerson said, "is made equal to every event. He can face danger for the right. A poor, tender, painful body, he can run into flame, or pestilence, with duty his guide. He feels the insurance of just employment. I am not afraid of accidents as long as I am in my place. . . . Every man's task [in the will of God] is his life preserver. The conviction that his work is dear to God and cannot be spared defends him. . . . A high aim reacts on the means, on the days, and on the organs of the body. A high aim is curative."

You are safe anywhere that those in authority over you may put you, as long as you are dedicated to do God's best and all that you are put here to do. This is just as true as its companion truth, that to put and to keep first the Kingdom of God not only makes His highest of all sure for you, but also makes sure that all you need in the way of means to do God's will and work will be added.

On March 26, 1917, a few days before our entrance into the war, I had the privilege of meeting and witnessing to Plato Durham, dean of the School of Religion of Emory University. He became famous early because of his unusual gifts and his unconventional freedom and boldness. When presiding elder in the Winston-Salem district in North Carolina, he preached from the courthouse steps in that city. He was too big to be cramped by any traditional molds of thought or procedure.

He came to Macon to give an address at the first sessions of the Chautauqua of the South. I followed him to the depot and asked for the privilege of sharing with him some of the things that had been given to me with the authority of certainty. I had said only a few words to him as to the revelation of Jesus and the workings of the Holy Spirit and the way of life as love before he replied, "I have been expecting fresh revelation during my time and I expect it now more than ever."

He asked me if I was holy. I replied that I had not come to him to tell about myself, but about the revelation that Jesus was making of Himself and of His way of life. He replied, "I am glad to see that you will be able to handle yourself."

A most stimulating friendship continued until his sudden going. He invited me to come to Emory every time I had opportunity and to report to him the things that were being given me. During one of these visits he said, "Something is coming, I am watching you; it may be through you." This something wants to come through all of us, and will come to the degree of our yielding and responsiveness.

Durham urged me not to be limited by the records of what God did and said in the past, but to be wide open for what He desired to do and to say now. The accents and acts of the Holy Spirit should not only continue, but increase with the ever-increasing need of men for God and His way of life.

The last time I visited him at Emory he gave me part of his class period to witness to his class that was studying the new movements in the contemporary religious world.

In January, 1914, when I was at Valdosta, Georgia, visiting Professor W. J. Bradley and his family, there was much discussion there concerning a little bright-faced colored man who was in the Valdosta jail, because he was calling himself "God." After a short visit with him, I asked him if he was not denying his name and history and identity that he might make God all and in all. He replied, "You understand me better than anyone else." I inquired if there was anything I could do for him. He replied that he did not accept money, but that I might send bread for him to share with his fellow prisoners.

At my request, an old Mercer College friend, J. B. Copeland, who was practicing law in Valdosta, took steps to get this unusual man out of jail. Not long after that, the little colored man and a small company of his followers appeared at Lakeside looking for me. He had with him the colored woman who was later known as Faithful Mary, and introduced two of his disciples as Gabriel and Michael. When Mrs. Scott offered him a dollar, he declined it with grace, saying, "Money has been the trouble." He left a message at Lakeside requesting me to attend a meeting on Pleasant Hill the following Sunday afternoon. When I went to the place specified, I found his friends holding a meeting, but was informed that "God" had gone out for a walk.

Some time after that, I had a letter from one of our state institutions telling me about having an unusual man who said he knew me. I wrote the superintendent the things I knew about the man. In a few days he was set free and came to Macon to see me. He told me that he had to give some human name in order to be released from the institution and that he gave the name John. Since then I have thought of him and called him, Friend John.

I went with him to the station where he boarded a train for Americus, Georgia. A few days afterward I received a postcard from him. After that I knew nothing of his whereabouts until a few years ago, when it occurred to me that the one I had known as Friend John might be the same person who was becoming famous as Father Divine. I am not allowed to call any one on earth "leader" or "reverend," much less "father" in a religious sense. To me the best we can be is friends and servants of Him and of each other.

On the first trip we made to New York from Philadelphia to see if the one who had become famous in Harlem was my Friend John, the Philadelphia friend who accompanied

me made the mistake of telling Friend John's secretary that
I had befriended him years before in Georgia. His secretary
protested that statement with emphasis, saying, "You are
not certain that the one Mr. Moseley knew in Georgia is
father, and if the same one, it was father who befriended
Mr. Moseley, and not Mr. Moseley who befriended father."
I explained I was not certain that the one I knew in Georgia
was the leader of their group, but that I would like to be
informed if he had been in Georgia twenty years before and
if he did know a Mr. Moseley of Macon. I received no letter
giving the information. Later when another friend drove
me to New York, we called at the headquarters of the group.
The secretary was all smiles and said, "Father is at the
phone now, but wants to see you."

We were ushered into his reception room and a little later
he came in and greeted us warmly. He not only gave me
the free opportunity to witness to him, but soon called in
his inner circle. Later he took us through his building and
urged me to return, after I filled an appointment at another
place in New York, and speak to his group. While in his
reception room I explained to him that I could call no one
on earth "father," the One Who is our Father is in Heaven.
He replied, "I am not on earth."

A short time before my visit a Brooklyn minister had
challenged him, saying that if he were God he should prove
it by killing him. I sought particularly to drive home the
truth to him, that to the degree one has the Spirit of God,
he desires to resurrect an enemy and do him all possible
good, having neither desire nor power to hurt or kill. He
welcomed this heartily, and at the night meeting made a
fine statement of it to his group. In the afternoon interview
in his reception room he said to me, in effect, that what he
meant to convey was something like this: God is seeking to
get Himself successfully incarnated in all of us; if we yield
to Him sufficiently we shall all be what His disciples say
He is. (We would not be God but His victorious sons.) I
said, "Well, if any one should out-surrender you, he would

'beat you to it'." He smiled and said, "Yes." I hoped that at
the night meeting he would make this point to his group,
but in speaking to them he did not go as far as he had
with me.

At the night meeting I not only gave my testimony as the
manifestation and in-breathing of Jesus and of His revelations to me concerning Himself and His way of life, but I
also told him and them that the whole leading of the Spirit
with me, as it had been with Peter and John and Paul, was
to refuse every semblance of worship and to turn all to the
worship of Him. One of his disciples said, after I took my
seat, "That fellow (referring to me) has got all of that wisdom from 'Father,' and does not give him any credit for it."
Friend John handled himself rather brilliantly. He said,
in effect, that his old Georgia friend had lived with Jesus
until he was in the realm of Jesus, that is, in the realm of
sonship, but that he himself had gone on to the realm of
the Father.

Of course Jesus as the divine-human and the human-
divine is in the highest realm of all, sharing the throne with
the Father.

The ending of the First World War, with the seeming
victory of the Allies and the fine vision of President Wilson
and other forward-looking men of good will, raised high
hopes for a new kind of peace and for a pull together for
a new kind of world order. I saw clearly the appealing opportunity for rich America to have the principal part in
helping the needy peoples of the world to get on their feet
and make a new crop. This applied to hungry Germans
and Austrians, as well as to persecuted Armenians, Jews,
and the Chinese famine sufferers.

When Germany called for bread, I was at Byron, Georgia,
where my brother lives, and where I spend some of my time
working with the pecan trees. The mayor of Byron, at my
suggestion, sent this telegram to President Wilson: "Shoot
the hungry Germans with biscuits harder and faster than
we have been shooting their soldiers with bullets."

Some time later I wrote a lengthy appeal in the form of a letter to the *Telegraph*, in behalf of the hungry Austrian children. When I handed it to W. T. Anderson, editor-in-chief, he said he would use it the following Sunday. Sunday morning, to my surprise, the letter with a few changes appeared as the leading editorial. Mr. Anderson requested me to prepare a detailed study of the covenant of the League of Nations, which he ran later in parallel columns when he published the whole covenant in the *Telegraph*.

While I was doing this work, I wrote several articles that appeared as editorials. A little later he asked me to write three editorials weekly. I suggested that he leave me perfectly free to write whenever and whatever seemed good to me, he being equally free as to the disposition of it. He sought to pay me for this editorial writing and put money in the bank to my credit, but I did not feel free to use it for myself and told him I preferred to do my writing without monetary consideration, so long as I could get along without it. Happily the need for receiving money for the writing of things I would gladly pay for the privilege of getting before the public has never arisen.

During the time that Nelson Shipp was responsible for the editorial page of the *Telegraph*, I often dictated to him all the editorials due to appear the following day. At other times, I did work among the trees, or was busy with something else and would not dictate anything. Through the generous attitude of Mr. Anderson, I have been saved the need of having a paper of my own, and he has helped more than any other man in furnishing for me a channel to share the things that I have been under a high necessity to make known in every way open to me.

In these post-war days I joined heartily in all the efforts to meet the desperate needs of the victims of the First World War. The Jews awarded me a humanitarian medal for services in their campaign to raise funds to meet the needs of their brethren in Northern and Central Europe. Through the coöperation of R. F. Burden, who acted as treasurer, we conducted a newspaper campaign to aid the Chinese famine sufferers. There was generous response to the appeal.

I also took up the work of writing letters to leading editors, such as the editor of the *Saturday Evening Post*, the editor of the *Outlook*, and to the leading public men in all walks of life, urging a pull together to induce rich America, made very rich by the war, to help the impoverished victims of the war everywhere.

The editors of the *Saturday Evening Post* and the *Outlook* made fine responses. The *Outlook* published my letter, together with an editorial inspired by it. Having been informed that President Wilson's private secretary, Mr. Tumulty, allowed appeals such as mine to reach the President, I wrote him to urge President Wilson, who was then attending the Peace Conference, to ask the Congress of the United States for an appropriation to aid the needy peoples of Europe. Mr. Tumulty replied that he had just cabled the contents of my letter to the President. A few days later, the President made his appeal to Congress for an appropriation to the amount of thirty million dollars for the aid of Europe. I am certain that the goodness of the President's own heart, in common with the urges of a multitude of people of good will, prompted him to make this appeal to Congress.

The keynote of our work in those days was expressed for me by John R. Mott when he came to Macon with his stirring appeal for all Christians and all people of good sense and good will to strike while the world was plastic, in the interests of a new kind of world, based upon an ever-increasing measure of the Spirit of Jesus. He said he would prefer to be alive then and be permitted to live and work for the following twenty-five years, than to have had the privilege of living through any previous century.

After his address I went to the *Telegraph* and wrote something for publication on the increasing wonder of being in Jesus and the increasing danger of being outside of

Him, saying, "It will be better and better in Jesus and worse and worse outside of Him." As I wrote these words, my right hand that was doing the writing was almost under conscious divine control. A little later when I went out to the home of the Bradley family to spend the night, as I walked on College Street between Forsyth Street and Appleton Avenue, there was a supernatural lightness in my body and such a weight and pull of glory upon my shoulders, I felt it would have been easy to yield to the upward pull.

For two or three summers during these post-war years, Byron peach growers sent me to New York to be an observer and an influence when their peaches were sold on the New York market. That was the easiest work I ever did and was paid for. I was free most of the time to attend meetings, all kinds of meetings at all kinds of places. A young man from Baltimore who knew religious New York exceptionally well, made it a good part of his work to arrange places for me to witness.

In an afternoon meeting in Brooklyn, where the Free Methodists and the Nazarenes were celebrating the fiftieth anniversary of the public ministry of a very sweet-spirited man, I was asked to talk. One of the Nazarene ministers came under the control of the Spirit while I was witnessing and laughed and rejoiced. After I finished my testimony, or report, the dear old man who presided and whose fiftieth anniversary was being celebrated, said that I reminded him of a visit he had recently made to a place in New York where they have specimens of many kinds of fish and while there he saw one the like of which he had never seen before, "but it was a fish all right." If there are unusual fish, there are also unusual Christians. The Nazarene who had laughed under the power of the Spirit said, "I want it understood I was not laughing at Mr. Moseley," and he explained that when he was previously in the Spirit, he saw into Heaven and they were doing up there what I was doing down here.

The weeks I spent in New York not only gave me an opportunity for witnessing to various groups, but to meet and to witness to people from different parts of the world who were at the top of human privilege and opportunity.

One afternoon I was privileged to witness to Mrs. Augusta Stetson, who was at that time the most discussed and written about of all living Christian Scientists. She received my testimony with joy and said that the kind of union with Jesus I had been telling her about should bring victory over every enemy, including victory over death.

On the same afternoon I met, for the first time, Joseph Fort Newton, who was then pastor of the Church of the Divine Paternity. During the latter part of the First World War he preached in City Temple, London, as ambassador of good will. He also lectured widely in England. At the time I met him, the *Atlantic Monthly* was publishing a series of his articles on preaching in England. When I witnessed to him and spoke of the need of the union of first-hand vital Christian experience and the charitable spirit, he gave the heartiest assent. He encouraged me greatly and since then has meant much to me.

The summer of 1920 when I was in New York being paid for the privilege of being at the peach market for an hour every day and of spending the rest of the time getting my testimony to all kinds of people from almost everywhere, I had two or three hours with J. B. Gambrell, the former president of Mercer, George Truett, generally regarded as the greatest Baptist preacher of today, and President E. Y. Mullins of the Southern Baptist Theological Seminary at Louisville, Kentucky, the day before their departure on their Baptist world mission.

Gambrell unconsciously paid himself about the highest tribute I ever heard a man pay himself, when he said he had reached the place where he could not look into the face of anyone without feeling a sense of compassion and without praying for him. After I gave my testimony to George Truett, he said, "These experiences you have been telling me about are of God. They could not have come from any other source, but most people would think that anyone who had such experiences must be insane." Sanity has become so rare that it may seem insanity when we meet it.

During the three summers I spent in New York, I joined many groups in their street meetings and I especially liked to work with the band from the Glad Tidings Mission on West Forty-second Street, where Robert Brown and his gifted wife were joint pastors. A little later they bought a church building near the new Pennsylvania Railroad Station, which is today the most generous church in its missionary giving of the whole group of churches associated together as the Assemblies of God.

In February, 1921, the *Telegraph* asked me to prepare, in the form of an interview, the net results of the first twenty-one years of my quest, from the time I left Mercer until then. I went to Byron to attempt to put my material into satisfactory form.

I wrote much, but realized that I had failed utterly. I stopped writing and went to work among the trees, something I could do. Then the light began to come. The next day I went six miles out of Macon to prune the young pecan trees of Holmes Mason. While I pruned the trees, so much light was given me that if I had had an expert stenographer I could have dictated the report of my quest even while I was pruning trees.

I went to the street meeting that afternoon in great joy. The next morning I attempted to dictate to Nelson Shipp, at that time the editorial writer of the *Telegraph*. I found it impossible to say the right thing. I inferred that this meant I was not to write or report my quest. I told God that if attempting to report put me out of His inspiration and the Kingdom of Heaven, as it seemed to have done that morning, I would give myself to those things which were clearly pleasing to Him, namely to witnessing and ministering personally to people in deepest need.

I went to Lakeside that night and retired early. I slept until about one o'clock in the morning. When I awoke one sentence was given to me that was good enough to record. As I wrote the sentence, sentence after sentence came, and when daylight came, I was writing as rapidly as I could move my hand and apparently under a higher wisdom and volition than my own.

All the other writing and dictation on the report of the quest was done with the same ease and joy. This report of the quest was published in the March 27 edition of the *Telegraph* and opened up a new world of freedom and opportunity to me. I was put in more glory and revelation through this experience of writing and dictating than I had known for years.

We sent clippings to people we hoped would take the time to read the report. Charles Eliot, President Emeritus of Harvard University, wrote me later that he liked my ethics, the ethics of love, but drew back from all forms of mysticism. Editor E. S. Martin, occupant of *Harper's* "Easy Chair," wrote me that he had read the whole of my report of my quest and agreed with all of it. Bishop Ainsworth, Bascom Anthony, and other friends were generous. Bishop Ainsworth felt at that time that I ought to be associated with some religious group, as he put it in a letter written from Texas. Herbert Hoover, then Secretary of Commerce, wrote me that he had read the quest and liked it. Joseph Fort Newton wrote that I was going the way that people who have known God in a first-hand way had gone before me and was succeeding in saying things almost impossible to say, about as well as any one could hope to say them.

As I have already stated, I had no ability to speak, except when I was under the anointing and almost under the control of the Spirit who can take anyone who will yield and cause to be said the things that should be said, the things that cannot be said apart from Him and His anointing. Jesus can take unlearned fishermen and by His anointing make them equal to the writing of the Gospel, while the most learned have no words of life, or truth, or power, or beauty apart from Him and His anointing.

In the winter of 1922-1923 a very interesting man came

from Saint Louis to Macon, with the testimony that for twenty-eight years he had not suffered from even a cold; that during that period he had once fasted for forty-two days and that for the last four days of the fast there was an angel dressed in gray with him, making revelations of the things that are at hand, and that "within the veil," within the most holy place, within the ascended Jesus, there is a place where one can be preserved "blameless unto the final revelation of Jesus."

I asked for the truth about this teaching and if this experience be God's best. The answer was that God has made Jesus wisdom, righteousness, sanctification, and redemption to us, and that the way for His redemption for the whole being to become real in our experience, is first of all to take Jesus as our wisdom and be led by Him. As we are so led, He becomes in our experience our righteousness, our sanctification, our redemption, and our everything.

I felt the urge to confess to the utmost the desires and thoughts that did not please the best within me. The first effort I made at confession brought the answer that I had not told the full truth. The second effort gave the answer, "Now as you have told the truth to Me, tell it to others only as you can help them by telling it." I was put in great joy and peace and in fellowship with Heaven.

About a week later I was in such glory that I could see flashes of light out of the invisible Kingdom. This place of such great blessedness "within the veil," within Jesus, within the Kingdom of Heaven, was so exceedingly precious that I resolved I would let everything go that stood in the way of abiding in it. I went to Mr. Anderson and told him that I was in such a happy place I would not lose it for every newspaper in the universe and that I might not be free to write or dictate another editorial.

That night at the residence of Mr. and Mrs. Ben Durden near Lakeside, I went down flat on my face to enquire what I needed to give up and what I needed to do in order to be in Him and under His anointing all of the time.

The answer came through the use of my vocal organs, but clearly from Him.

"My Presence shall go with thee and give thee rest. Go in love and I shall always be with thee."

I knew this was the secret. If we abide in His love and always go in love, feeling and willing and giving out nothing but love and all possible love to all men and all things, we will always be in Him and under His anointing. It was made known to me that I could write editorials and do everything else that can be done in the loving Spirit of Jesus. I could even be in Heavenly places while plowing with a mule, pruning trees, in courtrooms, in death cells, in all places of need, provided all was done in the Spirit of love. It was also clear that one may give all his time to so-called religious work and yet, unless this work is done in the Spirit of Jesus, he will be outside of the Kingdom of God.

It is not what we are doing, but the spirit and motive in which it is done that counts with God. I was made glad and free almost beyond belief. God had simplified everything to me and made sure that Heaven can and will be everywhere as we go in His love, manifesting His love and nothing but His love. The master key of the Kingdom of Heaven, of abiding union with Jesus, had been given me.

CHAPTER IX

"YOUR ONLY RESPONSIBILITY"

◄◄►►►►►►►►►►►►►►►►►►►►►►►►►►►►►►►

In the latter part of January, 1923, the Spirit impressed these words upon me: "My presence shall go with thee and give thee rest. Go in love and I will always be with thee." Friends in Saint Louis, soon after, urged me to come there for a time. I made arrangements to make the journey with a friend who was teaching the redemption of the body as a present experience. The friend of such daring faith felt that he had the assurance that apart from possible injury or death by accident, he would be preserved until the coming of the Kingdom of Heaven.

We left Macon on the "Dixie Flyer" on February 26. A few miles below Calhoun, Georgia, the train moving at high speed jumped the track. I was seated by my friend. I closed my eyes and threw myself as best I could upon the bosom of the unseen Companion, as a little child in time of danger throws itself upon the bosom of a parent. A friend who kept his eyes open told me afterward that I was bounced like a ball. When I felt the coach slowing up, I opened my eyes. I found myself perched upon the strong wood and steel bar between the fragile glass windows of the car. It furnished a safe place for me. As I looked through the windows of the car (it was perched up some distance from the ground), I saw one man who had fallen through glass. He was badly wounded and bleeding. I also saw the body of my Saint Louis friend, the head severed from it and not in sight. When the undertaker came and brought out my friend's head on a platter, it reminded me of the experience of

John the Baptist, who prophecied of the Kingdom nigh at hand that he failed to enter while in the flesh.

There were so many people injured that the hotel at Calhoun the night following was virtually a hospital. The next morning a special train was provided to carry us and the body of my friend to a point up the road where we could board the southern train that would take us to Chattanooga, a junction point for trains to Nashville, Evansville, and Saint Louis. Before our train reached Saint Louis the next morning I was warned by the Spirit not to allow the friends in Saint Louis to look upon me as their leader in any way.

When I entered the room in the Moise home at 2829 Washington Avenue where the unusual man had been ministering, Mrs. Moise sought to put me in the chair he had occupied, saying, "We have been praying that you have a double portion of the Spirit." I replied, "I have heard from Heaven about that. He is to have no successor. We are all to be taught of the Lord and led by His Spirit."

Prior to the visit of the Saint Louis friend to Macon, four very unusual men from northern Maine, Moody Wright, Charles Flewelling, Clifford Crabtree, and Gideon D. Merchant, visited Macon and joined in the street meetings and in other group work.

Moody Wright, as a boy, had sought and waited for the baptism of the Holy Spirit. He became discouraged before receiving it, but dedicated himself to do God's will as well as he could without the baptism. Then God baptised him, and also healed him of consumption of the lungs. He felt God's call to go as a missionary to Africa, but before going he fell in love with a Miss Flewelling, a sister of Charles Flewelling, and for a time almost forgot God's call. Children came in rapid succession. Wright felt he could never have God's best, which would have been service as a missionary in Africa, so he would work with his hands part of the time in order to support his family and give the rest to the work of the ministry.

He returned to Macon and brought Mrs. Wright and some of their children there in November, 1924. He reached Macon sick and deeply discouraged. A tubercular condition had developed in very sensitive parts of the body. Soon after reaching us he felt that the end was near. He expressed one major regret, that he had failed to go to Africa as a missionary, and one minor regret, that he had bought a little Star car on credit. He consented to allow the greatly kind Dr. C. C. Harrold to drain the pus from the affected organ. Doctor Harrold felt that a major operation was necessary and, of course, was glad to perform it as a service of love. A friend put up the money to pay the hospital bill, but for some reason the operation was not performed at that time.

Later, when Doctor Harrold was getting ready to operate, Wright said that as his people believed in divine healing, their faith might be shocked if he underwent an operation and that as he had failed the Lord by not going to Africa as a missionary, his life was not worth much and that he would not undergo the operation, even though refusing it meant the death of his body.

The Spirit made it clear to me that Wright could yet go to Africa as a missionary and fulfill God's highest call and will. When I told him this, it awakened faith in him. This faith opened him in a new way to the healing touch of Heaven. He dared to start back to Maine and to drive the little Star car. He made the trip with ease, and after each day's drive found himself more nearly well. By the time he reached Maine he was healed.

He let it be known that he wanted to go as a missionary to Africa. The money necessary to provide for the family, who were to remain in northern Maine and to enable him to make the journey to Africa, as well as the eleven hundred dollars required of him upon landing in South Africa, soon came in. It was only a short time before he was on his way.

A few weeks later I had a letter from him saying that he was preaching to the natives and that he had an interpreter who seemed to be able to look down into his throat and know what he wanted to say and to say it for him. Wright soon became the assistant superintendent of the work of the Apostolic Faith in a large area of South Africa.

In February, 1924, I received an urgent request from friends in Saint Louis to come there as early as possible. These friends believed that the Lord was ready to form a church that would be immediately under His guidance and government, and that I was to have part in it.

I did not share their faith, as I realized that God is no more a respecter of places than of persons, but realizing that since they desired my presence for a time, it seemed the most loving thing to do. On my way I saw that I was facing a difficult situation. I wanted to be sincere and at the same time I did not want to discourage their hopes.

While crossing the Ohio River near Henderson, Kentucky, and Evansville, Indiana, these words were written upon my mind:

"Your only responsibility is the responsibility of being in union with Me."

This put me in deep accord with the Spirit and with the Spirit's revelation and knowledge of Him and the things of Him, and kept me there for seven weeks, which was the longest time of continuous Heaven on earth I had yet known. Even after this, I realized I had been given one of the greatest truths, namely that life in Jesus is gloriously easy and has but one responsibility, the responsibility of remaining in the union, while all realms outside of Jesus are weighed down with responsibilities.

The Lord had been seeking to teach me this truth for a long time, but I had been too dull to see it. I would load myself with burdens that were too heavy for me to bear. Then I would turn to the Lord and He would deliver me from the burdens and make me glad and free. I would load myself again, and again He would deliver me. Thus I lived in a round of being burdened outside of Him, with seasons of glorious release in Him. This continued until it became a reality to me that I had but one responsibility, to be in union with Him all the time and that I was under but one compulsion, to give His love alone, continuously to all life. If you are giving out God's love all the time, you will be in God all the time, for you are always a part of what you are giving out.

The weeks spent in Saint Louis in March and April, 1924, were happy and fruitful. After that, I found that the quality of my editorial writing and of all my work improved surprisingly. During those weeks, it was made clearly known to me that we enter into union with Jesus by yielding to His Spirit, by manifesting His qualities, and by obeying His teachings as recorded in the New Testament and as immediately given as one is dedicated to walk in His love and to be taught by Him alone.

The teachings of Jesus took on new meaning. It became self-evident that everything must be done not only in the Spirit of love, but also in its technique. If a brother is offended or feels that he has a grievance, we are to cease all other activities, even the making of religious offerings, and go and be reconciled to him, as Jesus urges. And if anyone has sinned, we are not to say anything about it to anyone else, but go to him alone and do our best to win him. If this should fail, we are to take with us one or two or three, and see if this little company cannot win him. If the two or three or four fail, then we should seek the help of the whole church.

One Sunday morning in 1924 while I was in Saint Louis and things of the Spirit were becoming unusually clear to me, it was put in my mind that the highest revelation of all is where everything, the thoughts, the words, the images, the illustrations, are given by the Spirit. This was the order of revelation given by Jesus. But everyone, in the degree that he yields to the Spirit of Jesus, receives revelation, although it may be colored and limited according to the finite limitations of the receiver. The more universal one's love, the more universal the revelation that can be made by Him. Narrow people receive narrow revelations until they are ready for broader ones. God reveals Himself as fast as we can endure His light and the extent to which we are channels of revelation depends upon our willingness to humble ourselves and to yield and respond to Him.

That afternoon, while I was resting there came upon me a vivid sense, almost a vision, of a beautiful serpent close at hand. If I thought of striking at it, it would come nearer. If I felt friendly toward it, it would get further away from me. A little later a friend invited me to go with him to one of my favorite restaurants.

On the way to the restaurant while he was seeking to make me wise as to a certain situation, he became, as it were, a serpent in human form. When I called his attention to it, he received it pleasantly. While we were having our meal together, the very movement of my friend seemed to be that of a wise and friendly serpent. As I told him, I did not know what it meant for a certainty, but I had the feeling that after the serpent's spirit in him had been fully Christianized, he would have beneficent control of serpents' spirits and even over serpents themselves. I felt he would be "wise as a serpent and gentle as a dove."

That was the beginning of the understanding that the judgments of the Lord are working to bring light, love, and victory to all. The next morning he came to my room, while I was in bed and found that I had no intention of doing anything but love back where a certain opposition had developed; he looked into my eyes and said, "You are a fox." None of the animal types prior to their redemption has a worse reputation than the fox. In redemption, in the victorious judgment of love and mercy, even the fox is given the opportunity to become a spiritual diplomat in the interest of everybody's highest good.

Later, John Bunting, rector of the Church of the Ascension in Saint Louis, said to me that he saw me as an eagle. The same person may have manifested in him many different spirits. In redemption, every spirit that is discerned is an object of love.

Sometimes, I suspect the Spirit of a divine and subtle sense of humor.

In one of the meetings in Saint Louis, when we were much in the Spirit, a friend said, "I don't know whether it is pleurisy or pneumonia in one of my lungs, but I want you to pray for its healing." It seemed that the Lord Himself, almost, spoke the words through me, "If any one believes in Jesus, if he drinks even a poisonous thing, it shall not hurt him, and he who believes in Me shall not be hurt by pneumonia or pleurisy germs." The friend said at once she felt the healing touch and the trouble in the lung disappeared.

After my return to Macon, a friend complained of chills and fever and that the chills came upon her at regular times. I told her about the healing of the woman in Saint Louis and the Lord Himself appeared to make known to her that any one believing in Him should not be hurt by the germs of malaria. She rejoiced and said she had the assurance that she would not have another chill; she did not. She was set free from malaria at that very moment.

In January, 1923, or 1924, a very gifted man came to Macon from Detroit. He was a graduate of Wake Forest College and of the Southern Baptist Theological Seminary. He invited me to come to Detroit to teach his people. I told him I was not allowed to be called a teacher, but that I would gladly come to Detroit for the purpose of witnessing or reporting. When I went to a convention held in Detroit in the summer of 1925, I received a great welcome.

He then advised his people to follow me about to get the insights that were likely to be voiced at any time. But I had not been at the convention long before he and I, in the friendliest kind of way, found ourselves at opposite poles. Our only unity was in the unity of the good spirit. He and those associated with him felt that the Kingdom of Heaven on earth had already come to Detroit, and that all nations, if they were to receive God's best, must come to Detroit through their representatives.

As I told him, the Kingdom could be localized in Detroit, but not monopolized. He smiled and admitted this to be true. Whenever he would stress the externals of the Kingdom, I would stress the spiritual and the ethical requirements of the Kingdom, saying if the Kingdom could come externally as power and authority, before it came as perfect love, purity, and sincerity, those who had the power of the Kingdom apart from its Spirit would at best be hypocrites and at worst, anti-Christs. I also told these friends that instead of seeking a personal following and allowing themselves to scatter the flock of God, their whole purpose, our whole purpose, must be to bring all under the leadership of Jesus.

At the meeting in Detroit, a pleasant Welshman appeared one morning in the glow of the Spirit and said, "That fellow Moseley's praising of the Lord crucified me so greatly that I felt it surely could not be of the Lord, but when I went alone and prayed, the Lord put me in a vision, and in the vision I saw Moseley praising the Lord and the praises framed and kept him in an enveloping wall of fire."

There was a young man of unusual natural and spiritual gifts in the work in Detroit who interested me greatly. One night he said that some time before a shining Being had appeared to him telling him to baptise for the dead, as some of the brethren at Corinth were doing at the time Saint Paul wrote his first epistles to them.

As the reader will observe by careful reading of this epistle (see chapter 15:29) Saint Paul neither commends nor condemns baptising for the dead, but argues that if the dead did not arise, it would be perfectly meaningless. At the conclusion of the young man's discourse, he invited those who desired to do so to prepare themselves to be baptised in behalf of any dead friend or relative, or for any one of special concern.

I have a way of going to all altars and trying everything that has no harm in it, but gives promise of good. While the baptising was going on, I presented myself to be baptised first of all in behalf of Adam and others of his progeny, like Plato, to whom I owe special debt for the inspiration of his precepts.

In February, 1925, I attended the semi-centennial celebration of Peabody College and had the opportunity to testify to some of the leading people of the time. I was especially impressed with the British Ambassador, Sir Esme Howard, who, as Justice Sanford said, was much more than an Ambassador from England to the United States, since he was an "ambassador of understanding and good will." Speaking of George Peabody and his contribution to the betterment of England as well as the United States, the Ambassador said, "The great justification of great wealth, and perhaps the only justification for it, is to be found in great service to country and to fellow man." He also said that if England had not been so afraid of the word "socialism," she might have had a great deal more of it in the best sense and have helped the world to escape so much of it in the worst sense.

Late in the summer of 1925, I received a gracious letter from Dean Brown of the School of Religion in Vanderbilt, suggesting that I attend and report the Vanderbilt centennial celebration that was to occur from October 13 to 18. He also sent me an article of his own that had recently appeared in the *Southern Methodist Review*, or *Quarterly*, containing this rare thing about the excellent spirit of Mr. Moody:

"Moody and Drummond liked each other heartily and Moody invited Drummond to speak at Northfield. This raised a storm of protest from some of Moody's associates. Moody told them he would pray about it. When he returned from prayer he told these protesting friends that the Lord said that 'Drummond was a better man than Moody and that Drummond would speak at Northfield.'"

The Vanderbilt celebration brought together a group of eminent men in various walks of life. They agreed in their speeches that our greatest need is true religion, not a philosophy, a theology, or a creed, but the religion of the Spirit, the religion of love, the religion of Jesus.

In a lengthy editorial that appeared in the *Macon Telegraph*, October 19, I sought to give not only a report of the best things I heard during the days spent at the celebration, but also an interpretation of the contribution of Vanderbilt to our cultural life. Later Chancellor Kirkland wrote me that of all the material written about Vanderbilt in connection with the centennial celebration, he liked the editorial in the *Telegraph* best of all, and selected it to read to the student body at the chapel exercise reviewing the celebration.

This was another witness to me that the more we are in the love, the victory and glory of Jesus, the more efficient we become in dealing with practical affairs and the more successful in adapting ourselves everywhere, when our motive is to win people to His Spirit and way of life.

CHAPTER X

I GIVE YOU THE KEYS

‹‹‹‹‹‹‹‹‹‹‹‹‹‹‹‹‹‹‹‹‹‹‹‹‹‹‹‹‹‹‹›››››››››››››››››››››››››

Beginning with the crime waves that came with and out of the First World War and extended into the thirties, our work among prisoners, especially those under the death penalty, was both extended and intensified. We helped in obtaining commutation of sentences for some of them. Remarkable conversions and baptisms with the Holy Spirit occurred among those who were under the death penalty. Some of them faced death in fearless love, great joy, and much glory.

During the year 1926, I did the hardest physical work of my whole life; I also did some of my best writing. Best of all, it was during this year that Jesus gave me visions of Himself as glorified man and also gave increasingly the keys of abiding union with Him.

During the latter part of January, 1926, Bishop William Pierce preached for a week or more at the Free Methodist Church in Macon. On the morning of January 22, he preached on what it means to be wholly sanctified, saying, "It means to abide in the holy place and to have upon you the holy fire and to have with you the Holy Presence all the time."

At the conclusion of the sermon, he invited those desiring entire sanctification to come to the altar. I arose and said, "I want first of all to give thanks for the baptism with the Holy Spirit and to Jesus for manifesting Himself and coming within, and for His precious presence that goes with me, but if there is an experience of sanctification that keeps one in the holy place and Holy Presence and holy burning all the time, I want it, and with this understanding I go to the altar." I was joined by one of the Methodist ministers of the Macon district and I soon found myself praying for him, with my right arm around him. The Lord greatly inspired me with words of boldness, wisdom, and grace, and took charge of the meeting through the use He made of me.

As I was standing and talking with my external eyes closed, I was granted visions of the face of Jesus. The face as shown me was that of perfect, glorified, universal man. He looked as I feel Plato might have conceived the ideal human archetype—but glorified through union with Jesus. Jesus, of course, has the power to appear in any form that is most helpful. After the resurrection, He appeared as a gardener, as a stranger, as the good fisherman. But He never appeared as a *professional* preacher. He appeared to Saint Paul as Glorified Lord; He appeared to me as glorified man.

Saturday, March 23, the day following the vision of Jesus as glorified man, I dictated an editorial, or rather it was dictated through me, "Burbank on Religion," in which was said among other things, "True religion is such a living thing that all old, static religions are necessarily dead things. Not true religion, but these static forms for religion, are petrified. And when a man like Burbank says all of them are petrified, he is as ignorant in the field where Jesus lived as many of the saints have been in the field where Burbank lived."

As Emerson said, in effect, the older these static religions are, the deader they are, but there is no religion so dead that it does not resent being told it is dead and the deader it is, the more it resents it. But because water gets scum on it when it becomes stagnant is no argument against the reality and worth of water, only a reminder that the natural state of water is running, flowing, serving. All the symbolisms of water used in true religion, especially by Jesus, point to the fact that water, to be living water, must be flowing, that it must form springs, wells, rivers, not ponds where tadpoles gather and mosquitoes breed. There is no better evidence of the transcendental worth of religion than that it is so living that it refuses to be encased in the mold and formulæ of death. You may dam it up and try to make ponds of it, but it will break over and, in the end, sweep the dams away and become purified by becoming free and flowing.

This editorial appeared in the *Telegraph* Sunday morning, March 24. Professor and Mrs. Charles Beard, greatly enlightened social historians, were in Macon that Sunday morning. They read the editorial. There was something about it that so appealed to them that they decided they were going to find the person who wrote it before they left Macon. Mr. Aaron Bernd, who had studied under Professor Beard while he was on the faculty of Columbia University, brought the Beards to our Sunday afternoon street meeting.

Professor Beard told me that it was the first religious service he had attended for a long time, but graciously added, "If we lived in the same town, it would be different." Of course the thing that interested him in the editorial was a quality of insight and reality that came from the revelation of Jesus and that put me enough in the Spirit to heighten greatly my powers to see and to report. As we go in union with Jesus and in living His life of love, no matter how dull we have been and still are, we shall become super-intelligent. Enough of the spirit and mind of Jesus will make even the insane both sane and super-sane.

On Saturday evening, January 23, Professor Carl Van Doren had given a brilliant lecture on "Revolt against Dullness" which moved me to dictate an editorial dealing with the dullness of the revolt itself, saying in effect that no matter how brilliant one may be, as in the case of Professor Van Doren, one has to dwell in the realm of the great affirmations to be alive and to escape dullness.

This editorial and the one dealing with Burbank's state-

ment that religions are petrified were both dictated when
I was in unusually close accord with the Spirit, for when
one is enough in the Spirit, things are done without effort.
They seem to do themselves.

In the spring of 1926, I made another visit to Saint
Louis, reaching there the first day of May. On the following
Thursday, May 6, while in prayer at the Moise home, I
asked the Lord if He had anything He would like to say
to me. I commenced laughing at myself for my stupidity in
not asking this before. I realized how ridiculous it would
be to have an hour with, let us say, the President of the
United States, and monopolize the conversation, then ask
him as you said good-bye if he had anything to say. How
much more stupid to monopolize the conversation in prayer,
in communion with God. As soon as I was ready to listen,
these words came through me:

"I want you in Me all the time and I give you the keys."

I had realized, since Jesus manifested Himself and came
within me and I had come out of the marvelous enveloping
glory, that my great need was to take up my abode in
Jesus and abide in Him without ever going out any more,
just as He had taken up His abode in me to abide forever.
We need to be in Him perpetually, as we need Him to be in
us everlastingly. It is in the double union of Him in us and
us in Him, and in the bearing of the fruit of the union,
that we become like Him and joint heirs with Him in the
services and in the inheritance of time and eternity. His full
revelation in us and our full revelation in Him is our full
salvation, redemption, and glorification.

I inferred rightly that His gift of the keys to me meant
that He was giving me the secret of entering into and
abiding in Him and in the Kingdom of Heaven, not that
He was giving me authority over the church of God. We do
not want power over man in the human sense of power and
authority. In Jesus and through Him we only want power
to be a channel and an organ of unlimited good and
blessing.

From May 6 until the following Sunday afternoon I was especially concerned in helping a friend to take the steps advised by Jesus to get back in fellowship with some estranged brethren. At a meeting that afternoon I said, "The Kingdom of Heaven or blessed union with Jesus is at hand. All that one has to do to enter it is to leave on the outside everything that is keeping him on the outside, everything that opposes his going in, and that will not and cannot go in itself—if it were to go in, Heaven would not be Heaven. Nothing has to be left on the outside that will have any value on the inside and nothing can go in that would keep Heaven from being Heaven."

I went on to say that all the revelator saw outside of the holy city, the murderers, the adulterers, the liars, the unbelievers, and the workers of harm and injury, were on the outside precisely for the reason that the traits and practices that made them such were antagonistic to Jesus and to the heavenly life and the Kingdom. They were on the outside because if they were on the inside, the city would not be heavenly.

It was also seen that the gate or door into Jesus and into the Holy Place is the perfect condition and qualities required for entrance. If the door were wider, some evil would get in that would keep Heaven from being Heaven. If it were any smaller some good would be left on the outside.

It was next revealed that after consenting to leave off and to leave outside all that keeps you out of Jesus and the Kingdom of Heaven, you are to humble yourself as a little child at His feet. The humbler you are and smaller you are, the easier it is to enter. It is easy for the child-like, the meek, the lowly, and the poor in spirit to enter—it is easier for harlots and outcasts to enter—than it is for the self-righteous and self-important. All enter into Jesus and into His Kingdom at His feet. No matter where you belong in His body you only find your entrance into Him at His feet. All must enter at the one door which is at His feet. Even if you are to go to the top, you will never get to it except by being tremendously glad to have a place at the bottom.

I was even pulled down on my face at the feet of Jesus by the Spirit. It was while there that it was made known to me that the key to the door which is Jesus and to all doors, is love. Even the popular proverb says, "Love laughs at locksmiths." Love is the condition and the bond of the union with Jesus. The only way you can be in the person and Kingdom of love is to be loving. If you love, you have everything. If you miss love, you miss everything. For in God love *is* everything.

I was so overshadowed and enveloped in glory that afternoon while ministering and while a friend was driving me about Saint Louis, that it seemed to me if I ever got back to Macon someone would have to drive me who would not be offended or frightened by so much glory. I told the friend so. But that night it was made known to me that these transfiguration experiences are the very preparations for the work to be done down in the valley of human need and that He would make me increasingly adaptable to all environments where I was needed to minister.

The next morning, Monday, May 10, when I went to the meeting in the Moise home, the gift of the discerning of spirits was so in evidence that it seemed that everyone in the meeting represented some kind of an animal spirit, as did the sons of Jacob. When I told the friends this, they themselves began to discern what manner of animal spirits they were. A wealthy woman with a good heart, who loaded herself with the burdens of others, said she knew she had the spirit of a mule, the spirit of the burden bearer. I reminded her that the mule was the only animal humble enough to carry Jesus.

Once Reedy said that it was because he had no ancestry to boast about and no descendants to worry over, the mule was free to serve. Later, when Ben Pemberton was ministering in the Spirit, I looked up at him, and saw in him the spirit of the bull dog. When I told him this, he rejoiced

in the Spirit and picked me up and swung me around in the
air. As I told him later, to fulfill his calling, he must use all
of his strength to guard the sheep, that he must not be a
"dumb dog" nor a "greedy dog," but a good shepherd,
never failing to bark and never failing to guard whenever
there was danger threatening the sheep.

Later in the day, when I was in the room of a friend
of great strength and ability, being sorely tempted in the
wilderness, I asked the Lord to make known to us the kind
of a spirit his was. I looked into his face and the wolf appeared and when I told him so, he replied that he knew it
was a true discernment. He had seen before that he was of
the tribe of Benjamin and that Benjamin was a wolf. "Benjamin shall raven as a wolf: in the morning he shall devour
the prey, and at night he shall divide the spoil." (Genesis
49:29)

A few mornings later my friend who had formerly been
discerned as the wise serpent in human form was lying in
bed a few feet west of where I was lying and between our
beds he appeared in vision as a golden serpent seated on a
throne of gold, and beneath him was seen a golden ocean
in which were swimming all kinds of golden serpents. This,
as I told him, was a confirmation of the victorious judgment of love and mercy that had been given me for him;
namely, he was to be the beneficent king in the realm of
the tribe of Dan, who, as a serpent, was to judge his people
(see Genesis 47:17). This man is a remarkable character.
He fought in the open battlefields of France for a period of
sixty-six days and had no protection except the Lord and his
own ability to dig in with the simplest kind of tools. While
others fell all around him, he did not receive the least bit
of injury. For years he held a position in the Federal Reserve
Bank. He is unusually generous and has apparently the most
powerful will of anyone I have ever known.

For years prior to the discerning of spirits it had been
spoken through me to go to the kings, to the kings of the
most unusual names spoken in tongues unknown to me.

But my feeling all the time was that I was to go to the strong ruling spirits in the religious world. In the loving providence of God, it appears that my many trips to Saint Louis were to bring me into close touch with a kind of colony of kings.

Later in the week, the Spirit spoke through me, saying, "Go to my holy kings." And that day all the spirits discerned were of lions and lionesses. Still later the command was to go to "the Kings of the Cocos," which I understood to mean the kings of big business and the leaders in our highly organized life.

After I returned to Macon a few weeks later, I told Walter Anthony, at that time pastor of the Mulberry Methodist Church of Macon, about this discerning of spirits while in Saint Louis. He smiled and said, "Haven't you seen that—— (a certain famous Methodist bishop) is a bull dog?" After he called my attention to it, it was so apparent that I realized I had been quite dull in not having seen it before. That evening while having dinner as his guest at the Macon Cafeteria I saw Anthony as a lion in the guise of a man. And that night his uncle, Bascom Anthony, was seen striding around as a lion.

I found that this discerning of the animal spirits of different individuals was something people have as a natural gift or instinct. With me, it never occurs except when I am much in the Spirit. Some time after the beginning of the working of the spiritual gift, I found that George Fox, among others, had had this gift. Jacob and Moses and most of the Old Testament patriarchs seem to have had it. The blessed thing about the gift with me is that there is never any condemnation of the person or the animal spirit manifested, only a judgment of enlightenment. Even as loving a man as George Fox said severe things to those in whom he discerned the serpent spirit.

On my way from Saint Louis to Nashville in the latter part of May, where I was to have conferences with leading educators and heads of Southern Methodist and Baptist activities, I said to the Lord, "What is the truth about evolution?" I knew that some of the educators I expected to witness to in Nashville were evolutionists and having seen so many animal spirits in human form, I had the feeling that there were close connections between humans and animals, perhaps closer than I had previously suspected.

The answer came quickly, "Evolution is not true, but seems to be true, and is truer than popular conceptions of it." This was spoken in English. Next the Spirit took control of my tongue and spoke words in an unknown language, which were interpreted by the Spirit as meaning, "I created the things above the earth, the things upon the earth, and the things beneath the earth." Following this, it was spoken through me, in English, "I even created the tempter in the garden. Man did not have to fall, but it was contemplated that he would fall. Hence the provision made for his redemption. When he gets back he does not have to stay, but it is presumed that he will stay."

Next came this unfoldment and statement: "It does appear to the natural mind that the higher forms of life have come up out of the lower forms, but when My work is finished, it will be seen that all has come from Me." The explanation given to my understanding was that the animal forms and spirits I had been seeing in humans meant that man, made to have beneficent dominion over the animals, had yielded to the animal spirits and that they were presented for redemption.

I understand these things to mean that the development of man from his animal kinship to his high predestination is not as we see it humanly—as a development of the higher out of the lower. The higher (as well as the lower) comes immediately from God; it is only because of our finite and limited view of time and of history that we misinterpret the divine process as a temporal and mechanical affair. The whole creating and developing process is to God eternally *present*; "before Abraham was, I *am*." Jesus as a young man was not only older than Abraham, but older than Adam.

Now with regard to the words spoken concerning the Fall and return of Man, I hesitate very much to intrude my own views on this profound subject. However, since it is often an unnecessary stumbling-block to sincere souls, I believe there are some who might find my own private thinking on this subject of help. Perhaps it is best explained by comparison with the parable of the Prodigal Son, which is cosmic as well as personal in its implications. You can *make* things by pattern, but they have to *grow* freely into freedom. This involved his freedom to go away from home, to fall from his innocence, and experiment with good and evil until he found that the love and pure good in which he had originally been created was the only home for him. Returning he discovered the meaning and value of sonship, whereas before he had taken it for granted and esteemed it so lightly that he was ready to exchange it for "wasting his substance in riotous living." For man to grow into the likeness of God, requires that he should be as free as God, and yet the love of God would call for a universe which rescued the wanderer before he got too far from home, that would have a whale prepared for every fleeing Jonah—ready to spew him out on dry ground as soon as he came to himself. The presumability of the Fall was the certainty of the Atonement.

After I saw a number of the Vanderbilt University friends and testified to them, Dean Brown of the School of Religion suggested it might be worthwhile for me to listen to a certain editor of a liberal Christian weekly who was to speak at the Vanderbilt Chapel service that morning. I inferred from what this editor said, that he did not believe in the virgin birth of Jesus. My spirit suffered, not so much because of his unbelief, but because of his seeming lack of sincerity. For a time I tried to lose myself by looking out upon the beautiful trees and thus escaping the painful experience of having to listen to what did not ring true. But there was no escape except in prayer and when I asked Jesus about the truth of His birth, the answer came, "I was born of a virgin, but I welcome those who do not see it." How like Jesus! Certainly it was in this spirit that He dealt with Thomas and in this same spirit he deals with everyone, not cutting any off, but giving all the proof necessary to enable belief.

When I told Dean Brown the answer that came when I asked for the truth as to the birth of Jesus, it impressed him so much that later he told me he had shared it with his class.

While in Saint Louis, when so much precious light was given, both in March, 1924, and in May, 1926, I sought to carry the report of it to as many as I could, both by personal witness and by letter. In 1924 I wrote to the leading bishops and influential key men of different groups. I even wrote to the Pope.

In May, 1926, I succeeded in getting the ear of Archbishop Glennon of the Saint Louis diocese. He gave me the most courteous attention for half an hour and told me that he would pass on to the Pope the things I had shared with him, in a brief written statement and by oral report. I told him among other things that if the Catholic Church in common with all other churches, would humble itself at the feet of Jesus for His immediate control and use, it would come forth new and alive and that this would be done in such a way that it would take time even to begin to realize what had happened.

The Second Baptist Church of Saint Louis, as well as the wonderful Catholic Cathedral, were kept open so that anyone could enter for meditation and prayer. In both I had precious manifestations of His presence.

After I returned to Macon, with Mr. Anderson's generous approval, I sent some of the things that were being given me, rather widely over the world, and from far-off India came a postal card from Gandhi. It was dictated, but con-

tained his signature. At this time of special anointing and
revelation, I attended the Georgia Methodist Pastors' School,
and I have continued to do so from then until now. It has
brought me in touch with many leading people of today and
has opened many doors for me to witness. It has also helped
to keep me in touch with the currents of thought in contemporary religious life, a valuable function.

From June 20 to the latter part of August, 1926, I budded
pecan trees in a nursery that brother and I owned jointly
near Byron, Georgia. I would sometimes be at work before
sunrise and, with a short recess, for mid-day lunch, I would
work as late as daylight permitted. It was the most exacting
labor, but through all this combining of things at seemingly
opposite poles of the spiritual and the natural, I was being
taught that Jesus and His Spirit are to be revealed and
glorified in the whole of life and work, and that the whole
of life and work are to be lifted up and glorified in Him, so
that all things that have been separated are united in Him,
to the marvelous fulfillment, enrichment, and perfection
of each and of all.

CHAPTER XI

DELIGHTING TO DO HIS WILL

◄◄◄◄◄◄◄◄◄◄◄◄◄◄◄◄◄◄◄◄◄◄◄◄◄◄◄◄◄◄►►►►►►►►►►►►►►►►►►►►►►►►►►

Late in the summer of 1927 I went to Philadelphia, where I met new friends and had many open doors before me. From Philadelphia I went to Saint Louis. I was there at the time the tornado tore its destructive path through the city. We were only a few blocks from the path, but the meeting was so overshadowed by God's presence that we paid little attention to what was going on outside.

In October my friend in Saint Louis whom the Spirit had discerned as king of the wolf tribe, the tribe of Benjamin, asked me to go with him to visit a group in a certain city where it appeared that most of the group were especially subject to his mind and spirit. I told him I would go with the understanding that I went to get the group out of his mind and from under his control, into the mind of Jesus and the liberty He gives. The friend was glad for me to go on these terms, saying, "Get ready to go with me tomorrow."

We left Saint Louis on Monday and the following Wednesday evening after the meeting had started, I remained in a little park and prayed. I realized that with the wonderful call and gifts of my friend how much it should mean to him, and to the groups which almost worshipped him, if they were brought with him into the mind and under the immediate guidance of Jesus. A short time after I entered the meeting, he said, "I want all of you in and under the mind of Jesus and not in and under my mind." He went on to explain that if all the group were in the mind of Jesus and he, or any of them, should stumble and fall, the rest need not stumble but would be used to help the stumbling ones get up and walk. There was great rejoicing and victory in the meeting after that.

Before I reached Macon in the latter part of October, 1927, Robert Jones, of whom more later, had confessed to the killing of an old man, and had received the death sentence. Soon after this, he received the baptism with the Holy Spirit and entered into the most vital ministry I have ever witnessed in any prisoner. I gave the best of my time to this wonderful colored boy until his execution June 30, 1928.

In the winter of 1928-1929, Homer Simpson, former chief of police of Cleveland, Tennessee, and Bascom Morrow, another World War veteran, also a man of remarkable parts, were brought from Brunswick to Macon and kept in the jail until their execution in September, 1929. I spent much time with them and after starting on my summer trip and getting as far as Greensboro, North Carolina, I returned to Macon to be with them until the end. They reached unusual moral and spiritual elevation before their execution. For about two years I was thrown constantly with people under the death sentence. Two or three of them received commutations to life imprisonment. All who had to pay the extreme penalty faced death in victory.

About this time I had a dream of such beauty and human appeal that it tended to divert my mind from being centered on Jesus and the rather difficult situation I was soon to face. Suddenly something awoke me from my pleasant day-dreaming and I found myself saying, "I choose to think about Jesus"; instantly I felt His quickening presence and by that experience I was taught that no matter what may be my temptations and problems, turning to Jesus and the conscious choosing to think about Him, please Him, and do His will, will always set me free from temptation and bring the consciousness of His transforming presence with just the help needed.

Early in June, 1930, the session in Macon of the Georgia Pastors' School at the old Wesleyan College, and the meeting at Mercer of the Baptists for a week of study, gave me an opportunity to meet people who have meant increasingly more to me from then until now. One morning I first attended the Georgia Pastors' School and was asked by Edmund F. Cook, who was teaching a class dealing with the machinery and the finances of the Methodist Church if I had any contribution to make to their discussion. I replied that I was not a member of any religious group or organization, but if I were, I would seek first of all to fill the denominational ditches full of water and in addition seek a downpour that would cause a flood that would hide all the ditches.

As to finances, I reminded them that you may feed a cow so poorly and milk her so strenuously and get her udders so sore that she feels like kicking even at the sight of the milker or the bucket, or you may feed her so well and milk her so gently that it is a relief to her to be milked.

Later when I went to Mercer to see and hear for the first time Walter N. Johnson, the Sage of Mars Hill, and the Socrates of Southern Baptists, I found the Baptists were also discussing financing their work and I had the opportunity to tell them the same things that I had previously told the Methodists.

Johnson opened wide to me and later asked me to join him and E. M. Poteat, who were meeting for two weeks every summer at Mars Hill College, North Carolina, for conversations and meditations concerning the Christian way. These friends, a few years prior to this, had agreed to meet for these conversations and meditations as long as they lived. Others were welcome to join them and very rare groups did join them from year to year. Poteat was a genius of the purest water, vital, brilliant, and profoundly interesting.

The Mars Hill retreats have brought great enrichment to many. It is one of the best places to go on earth. Through these retreats and the friends I met there, churches and groups almost beyond belief have opened wide for my testimony. In the summer of 1937, Poteat was forced to give up his work at Mars Hill and the particular type of work he was doing was taken up by O. T. Binkley, a remarkable combination of intelligence, excellent spirit, scholarship, and first hand Christian experience.

The last time I saw Poteat was late in July, 1937, at the Duke University Hospital. At that time he was almost all soul; his body had become only a shadow. I was allowed to see him with the understanding that he was not to talk, but all of us combined could not keep him from talking. I had just come from the Mars Hill retreat, the first one he had been denied the privilege of attending, and he said time and again, "Tell me more about Mars Hill." Finally he looked up in my face and said, "Moseley, I love you." With the exception of the words of my father, spoken to me when I was leaving the old country home in western North Carolina to go to Peabody College, "Rufus, I know nothing about the world you are to be in; I have no advice to give; I trust you," these words of my friend Poteat mean more to me than anything that has ever been spoken to me by any human.

In September, 1930, Shepherd, a minister from England, preached at the Pentecostal Gospel Tabernacle in Macon. In his sermon he said, "If we are not every bit whole, there is a reason for it and if we will ask the Lord, He will let us know what is required to enable us to become every whit whole." That night before retiring I thanked the Lord for such good health as He had given me and asked Him what was necessary to enable me to be every whit whole. The reply came at once, "Be wholly sanctified." I knew that this was the right answer, that entire consecration or devotedness would bring one into the everything of God. Even the seeing of this and the reaching out for it brought me great spiritual blessings and even new life for the body.

In December, 1930, I was given a little book written by S. D. Gordon, containing the gold story. The next morning, as I was to go early to direct and to aid in the transplanting of some pecan trees, I took the little book along with me. When not busy, I read it. It contained the astounding story of a miracle of multiplication. When Gordon heard of this miracle, it impressed him so profoundly that he made the journey to Finland to make a first-hand investigation and became fully convinced of its truth.

The circumstances surrounding the miracle were these: A very intelligent, well-balanced, good-hearted Christian, who was postmistress in a Finnish village, decided that her neighborhood must have a chapel for community worship. She gave and raised more than enough money to pay for the material necessary to build the chapel, but the contractor who had agreed to furnish the material at certain prices fraudulently added so much to the bill that the postmistress had nothing like enough to pay for the material.

The Lord impressed her strongly that she must not resist him who was evil, but instead go cheerfully the second mile. She seemed under compulsion to write to the contractor, telling him to deliver the material, and to trust the Lord for the additional money required to pay for it. The Lord also put and kept before her mind His miracles of multiplication of bread and fishes while He was on earth.

Under the Lord's leading, she took her money and carefully counted it and prayed for its multiplication so that she might meet the fraudulently raised bill. She realized that something was happening to the coins. When she counted them again, she found them increased and that she had enough and more to pay for the material that had been fraudulently overcharged.

The great lesson that the postmistress received from the miracle was this: that she must turn to the Holy Spirit to shape her desires and to direct her prayers. Up to the time Gordon saw her, the Spirit had never again led her to pray for another miracle of multiplication, but had led her to pray for just the things that she and others most needed and were made ready to receive.

I was profoundly impressed with the wisdom and necessity, if we would have His best, to turn to the Holy Spirit wholly to redeem our desires, and to direct our prayers.

Years before then I had seen that we must seek for the redemption of our desires, but never before had I seen that we should always look to the Holy Spirit to direct our desires and prayers.

I attended a prayer meeting that night at the home of Mr. and Mrs. M. L. McDaniel on Applewood Street. I told them about what I had read during the day in Gordon's book, and suggested that after we prayed for a sister in special need of help, we ask for the Holy Spirit to direct our prayers. We knew it was His will to pray for her, but needed his guidance as how best to pray for her. I soon found myself praying to enter into Jesus and into the Kingdom of Heaven so deeply that I would never come out any more.

Then, as at other times of unusual clarifications of the Spirit, I laughed at myself for having been so dull as not to have seen the wisdom and the necessity of turning always to the Holy Spirit to direct my desire in every particular and my asking for His best for me and for all others. For much of my life I had been longing for the experience of being always consciously in Jesus and in the Kingdom of Heaven, and yet had never specifically prayed for this very thing until I definitely turned to the Holy Spirit to direct my praying.

Nothing is more clearly and gloriously His will than for us to enter into Him and abide in Him forever. If we ask anything according to His will and everything is according to His will that is best for us and all others, He hears us and answers in terms of experience as soon as we are made ready for His answer.

Sunday morning in a meeting in an upstairs hall on Main Street, East Macon, I requested again that all join me in asking the Holy Spirit to direct our prayers. I soon found myself praying for everything to be burned that diverts the mind from being on Him and the heart centering on Him. I was made aware in a new way that we will always be in great peace and the renewing of the Holy Spirit and in fellowship with Jesus, as we keep our thoughts and affections centered upon Him.

Later, with great clearness and authority it was made known that we should ask God to write His own nature and love and will so deeply upon our minds and hearts that it will become the happiest thing of all to think His thoughts, to speak His word, and to do His will. I was made aware that the Holy Spirit had led to the asking for the deepest need and the greatest secret of all, the new covenant relationship where one delights in the Lord and in His will and wisdom, so that His will becomes spontaneous, happy preference instead of a duty. In this new covenant relationship, our wills become one with His and we do as we please, because what we please He pleases. And until the miracle of the redemption of our desires occurs in us, so we desire in Him, it is not possible to be always in heavenly places with Him. But after this miracle occurs there is no occasion for any more breaks in the blessed fellowship and companionship with Him.

Puppies go to barking, not because they receive special instructions on the duties of barking and how to bark, but because they are born of dogs and have the dog nature, the dog inheritance with its longings, urgings and instincts. They need only to have the proper food and exercise and they go to barking spontaneously.

In like manner, calves that get plenty of milk and grass and sunshine go to frisking and kicking up their heels, not because they are taught to do so in any didactic way, but because they belong to their species. Pigs go to the mud hole and to the other things that the hog species has been going to instinctively from the beginning. Even if you take a pig away from all hogs and give it conditions for health and growth, it goes to the things that pigs and hogs have been doing as long as there have been such. Birds grow feathers and take to the air. Children likewise jabber and talk and play.

So through new birth and by new divine nature, more than by conscious educational processes, we do the will of the Father and of our Elder Brother. When spontaneous living in the Spirit becomes as natural for us as the unself-conscious behavior of animals, only then can there be full accord with the Divine Will. For so long as we think of *ourselves* in doing His will, there is still too much of *ourselves* and not enough of the will. In the new nature, in the new covenant relationship is the key to the very thing that all of us are most in need of and that I had been seeking for so long, without having had intelligence enough to ask for it.

The Spirit knows what we really want, which is God's best for us and His best in relationship to all. He alone can lead us until we are brought to the place where we become one with Him, desiring together, praying together, working together, each of us doing what we like best and can do better and happier than anyone else.

Some time after these revelations that came through turning to the Holy Spirit to transform and shape desires and to direct our praying, I was in the Bibb County Jail talking with a young white man who had been sentenced to serve in one of our Georgia chain gang squads. He told me that while he had sinned, he didn't belong in a Georgia chain gang and couldn't afford to go there. I asked him if he knew any good people who would take him into their home, give him work, and be a good influence to him. He said, yes, that the good people who had reared him after the death of his father and mother would be glad to do this. He explained that they had done a wonderful service to him, although they were quite poor people. He thought he could make his way in the world, but under temptation he fell.

When I put the matter before the solicitor and the judge they were pleased for the boy to be paroled to his foster parents. I arranged a date for them to come and get the boy. Their plans miscarried and they failed to come. The solicitor and the judge gave me an extension of time to see if they would still come, and have the boy paroled to them and take him to their home. They agreed to come the following Saturday. They arrived very early and were happy almost beyond belief that they could take the boy back home with them. While I was in Judge Matthews' courtroom talking with these fine country folks and waiting for the judge and Solicitor Garrett to prepare and sign the necessary papers for the boy's release, I found myself singing and singing seemingly under the inspiration and control of the Spirit, "I am in Him and He is in me, forevermore, forevermore."

I said to myself, I hope this singing is inspired by the Holy Spirit. It is just what I have needed and longed for. It was too good not to be true. I dedicated myself in a new way to make it true in my experience. This experience came to me on Saturday, January 31, 1931. From then until now there has been an overshadowing and a warning under temptation and a conscious guarding that I had never been aware of before. I have lived in the consciousness that to have Jesus in me and for me to abide in Him is of such infinite worth that nothing must be allowed to break, even for an instant, this ineffable union.

Since then the subtlest kind of temptations have come, but I have always been warned and made aware that this heavenly fellowship so far surpasses everything else that one can say "no" happily to everything that would break it, and say "yes" to everything that keeps and increases it.

Three or four years ago, when S. D. Gordon gave several addresses in Macon, I had the privilege of telling him how the Lord had used his little book to cause me to turn to the Holy Spirit to direct my desires and prayers and how this had enabled the Holy Spirit to bring me to the place where I had been guarded and kept in a new way.

He seemed deeply impressed by what I told him, and said, "Guarded, did you say?"

Yes, guarded and sealed in a new way. Of course I live as yet around the outer edges, as it were, of the glory and blessedness He has for all of us in union with Him, but it is far better to be least and nearest the outer edges of this inner Kingdom, than it is to have the best and all there is on the outside of it.

CHAPTER XII

EXPRESSING HIS LOVE

‹‹‹‹‹‹‹‹‹‹‹‹‹‹‹‹‹‹‹‹‹‹‹‹‹‹‹‹‹‹›››››››››››››››››››››››

The main reason for putting in book form the story of the quest for continuous fruit-bearing ineffable union with Jesus has been accomplished, to give the keys to the secrets of this union. For me it required a long time, with many outgoings and returnings before the witness of the Spirit came: "I am in Him and He is in me forevermore, forevermore!"

Since then two unfoldments of great significance have begun:

First, the request and commandment to give His love to everybody and everything and to be doing this all the time.

Second, the revelation that He is perfect everything, giving, enabling, and calling for perfect everything on the part of each and all of us.

With these unfoldments, commandments, and enablings have come enrichments of every kind, in fellowship with Him, in services, in joy, in peace, and in transforming glory. During these last years of the quest I have found more readiness on the part of the rulers of this world to listen to appeals, to show mercy to the imprisoned and condemned, more doors open for witnessing, more of the renewing and transforming power of His presence. These last years have also enabled me to have more contacts with men of the first order of ability and gifts, such as Kagawa, E. Stanley Jones, William T. Ellis, Rufus Jones, George Buttrick, and W. A. Smart. I have become increasingly aware that perfect everything is for me and for all.

Soon after E. Stanley Jones' *Christ of the Indian Road* appeared and became a best seller, a well-known bishop made a criticism of it in the *Atlanta Journal* to the effect that we had just as well have a Christ of the Dixie Highway as a Christ of the Indian Road.

In an editorial in the *Telegraph* under the heading, "The Christ of Every Road," I said that Christ is not only the Christ of the Indian Road, but the Christ of Every Road. I sent Mr. Jones a copy of the editorial and the title of his next book was, *The Christ of Every Road*, although of course he may have selected this title entirely independently of my editorial.

When Mr. Jones visited Atlanta, I had the privilege of hearing him on many occasions. One morning after he had spoken on union with Christ, I told him about the supernatural writing upon my mind, "Your only responsibility is the responsibility of being in union with Me." He asked me to repeat it to him.

I also had the privilege of hearing Rufus Jones and George Buttrick at the preaching mission, September, 1936. Mr. Buttrick gave a course on preaching, and concluded with these words: "If you have the mind of Christ, you may violate all these rules I have given you and be a good preacher. Yet it you have not the mind of Christ and obey them all, you may still be a poor one." When Kagawa was in Atlanta for a number of addresses in January, 1937, Louie D. Newton, who invited him to preach in his church the Sunday morning he was in Atlanta, arranged for me to have a brief interview with this remarkable man. When I told him about the ineffable union with Jesus, he said, "That is great."

The commandment and the great blessedness that came with it, to give the love of God to everybody and to the whole of life, came under these circumstances:

One Saturday in January, 1932, while I was much in the Spirit and in especially great joy, I received a letter to which I was tempted to react with inner complainings, rather than with thanksgiving. The man who wrote it was using scripture to do a rather wholesale business of getting money and the other things he wanted.

It appears that he stopped farming and went to writing letters making known his wants. In the letters he would quote the words of Jesus, "Give to every man that asketh of thee." He wrote so many letters and received so many that the United States postal authorities made an investigation. He read some of my articles and began to put his desires to me with long-drawn-out regularity.

On that Saturday when my spiritual thermometer was registering very high, another of these letters came. I realized my first inner reaction toward the letter was causing my heavenly thermometer to start down. I began to pray for it to get back as high as it was before I read the letter. I attended a prayer meeting that night in Bellevue, a suburb of Macon, and told friends there of my need and asked them to pray. During the night when I was awakened, I found myself praying to Jesus to restore to me the great joy of His salvation. I had reached the place where I could not live, save in the free overflow of Heaven.

The next morning early while I was at a very humble task, I said, "Jesus, it seems that it does not please You to give me that keen, great joy I had before receiving the letter, but is there anything I can do for You?"

Instantly my tongue was taken under control and this was spoken, "Give My love to everybody." I then found myself in an even more precious place than I had been before receiving the letter. I told Mr. and Mrs. Robert White, who had entertained me as their guest for the night, about the message to "give His love to everybody." It gave them much joy and increased mine.

From then on during the day wherever I saw individuals or little groups, I sought to tell them how greatly the Lord loves them and that He told me to give them His love. Jails, Sunday Schools, churches, street meetings—all these places were among those where I sought to share this joyous understanding, for no joy is complete unless passed on into living circulation.

Sunday night I decided to go to the church where there would likely be the largest congregation in the city, so I selected Mulberry Street Methodist Church, where Walter Anthony was pastor. While he preached, I prayed for the Lord to make a way for me to give His love to the large congregation.

Just before the benediction Friend Anthony said, "Moseley, come down here in front and pray for us." As I remember, he was so finely affectionate that he put his hand upon my head. I looked up to him and asked for the privilege of saying a few words. The request was granted graciously and heartily. When I told the large congregation the things that had led up to the Lord's request for me to give His love to everybody and while in His name I was giving the congregation His love, there was a spiritual, inexpressible atmosphere in the church. A newspaper man who was there that night told me he had never seen or felt anything like it before. Before I slept that night, I had been enabled to pass on the love of God to a surprisingly large number of people.

Following the request, "Give My love to everybody," my tongue would be taken under control and the Spirit would say through me, "Give My love to everybody and everything. Give My love to the whole creation." From then until now, this "giving His love" to each and all has been the superlative urge of the Spirit.

In my article in the combined issue of the *Telegraph* and *News* the following Sunday morning, January 24, 1932, I stated among other things that the commission and the will to obey it, to give His love to everybody and everything had the immediate, blessed effect of causing me whenever I even thought of anyone, as well as when I saw anyone, to bring me to the feeling that "God loves you." As I quoted Canon Raven, "Everything that we say or do in love is an eternal possession." And everything that is of the highest good, every longing and prayer for the highest good of anyone or anything, is also an eternal possession.

The giving of His love to all and the giving of ourselves in services of love to all, at all times and in all ways, are the very conditions for abiding in Jesus and increasing in Him and in His realm of love, joy, and peace. We cannot be in heavenly places in Jesus all the time, except in this freely continuous outflow of His love to all people and to the whole of life. Whatever we give, we are. If we give the Lord's love all the time, we are in the Lord's love, in the Lord's Spirit, in the Lord's Kingdom or realm, and in the Lord Himself, all the time. If we give out hell any of the time, we are in hell all the time we are giving it out. If we give out Heaven all the time, we are in Heaven all the time. "The mind is its own place," says Milton, "and of itself can make a heaven of hell, a hell of heaven." If we are manifesting Jesus and His good Spirit all the time we are in blessed fellowship and union with Him all the time. If we give out any other spirit any of the time, we are in that spirit that we are giving out. It could not be otherwise.

This perfect law that we are in and that we are whatever we are giving out, is the Lord's way of teaching us by all experience the wisdom and the necessity of manifesting and perpetuating Him and the things that are His to everybody and to everything, and to give out nothing contrary to Him and to the things that are of Him.

If we could give out that which is harmful and destructive and therefore hellish, and yet be in Heavenly joy and peace ourselves, there would be no sure way to teach us the blessedness of giving out the Lord and His good Spirit and only these. The very fact that we get whatever we give out and get more than we give, whether it be good or evil, puts us under the necessity of giving out all possible good to everyone and to the whole of life and to refuse to become a channel for any ill will or evil to anyone.

I seek to drive this truth home in all possible ways, because it is all important and as the understanding is opened to see it, it is as simple and self-evident as the multiplication table. In my understanding, His gift to me of His keys and His command to give His keys to all, is, by His enabling, the opening of the understanding to all to the beautiful, shining and self-evident conditions of union with Him, and by His enabling, the way to enter and abide in His Kingdom.

These laws are so perfect that they could not be otherwise, and as we see them more clearly, we would not have them otherwise if we could. Moreover, the conditions of ineffable union with Jesus are so simple, so satisfying, so perfect, that we marvel we were ever so spiritually obtuse as to have failed to recognize them always. When once seen clearly they are essentially self-operative.

Emerson said that the light of Heaven comes to us through obedience and that obedience comes through joyous perception. When we see with great joy the truth, the wonder, and the beauty of the Lord's way and the laws of life, it is easy to obey them. As we obey them we are given ever more light and increasing joy in walking in it.

We are brought to the clear perception of the perfect law of life and of being, that giving is necessary to receiving, that forgiving is necessary to receive forgiveness, that giving out freely is necessary to receiving freely, and that it is even better to give than it is to receive, to forgive than it is to be forgiven, and to have Heaven flow out through us, than to flow into us.

The way to be a good in-breather, even physically, is to be a good out-breather. The way to receive increasingly is to give increasingly, the way to be flooded with joy is to out-flow with joy, the way to be filled with love is to let love out-flow perpetually and freely from us, like a river. There is no possible way to be loving except to love, to love everybody and to minister lovingly to the whole of life. The only way for water to keep fresh is to keep flowing. The only way that we can be perpetually and increasingly heavenly is to be perpetually desiring, praying for, and giving out the heavenly to all.

In recent years it appears that I have been used more to minister in the Spirit and to be present in the Spirit in places of need, than I have in the customary ways of rendering services.

Saint Paul was consciously present in the Spirit with the churches he sought to help. I have no awareness of the uses the Lord is making of me when he uses me in the Spirit in His own ministry of release and benediction. The best explanation understandable to me is that as we allow Jesus to use our spirits, souls, minds, and bodies, He in turn manifests Himself in terms of us and renders services as us. I believe this is to go on and on until He is fully revealed and manifested in terms of us and the creation, and until we and the creation are manifested in terms of Him. The relationship between Him and us and Him and the creation is to be after the manner of His relationship to the Father and the Father's relationship to Him.

About a year ago, a group of us prayed for a friend in East Macon. There was no apparent answer to our prayers. The friend was greatly depressed because of gall bladder poisoning and had reached the place where she could not even pray. A little later in the evening I yielded to the Spirit and began to rejoice and to dance under the power. The power and the glory upon me seemed to the friend to leap from me to her, and starting with her head passed through her body, setting her free from mental depression and healing her affliction. Her release and healing was clearly the work of the Spirit. I had nothing to do with it, except to act as if I were a conductor of the heavenly lightning.

Another Macon friend, in the summer of 1937, was very much depressed and suffering in body and spirit. She believed she heard my voice just above her head saying, "Thank Him for your blessings." She acted upon this and commenced praising the Lord, and thus became released in spirit and comfortable in body.

Still another Macon friend was struggling some years ago to get her breath because of a serious heart trouble. It seemed to her that I appeared in the room and said, "You are always healed when you look to the Lord and praise Him." She looked to Him and praised Him and His miracle of release came to her.

Some years ago when a group of us met in East Macon and I began rejoicing in Spirit, the glory of the Lord came upon me and that glory passed over me and to the feet of one of the friends present, from the feet to the heart, and the friend felt for the first time in her life, "the love of Christ which passeth knowledge." When she opened her eyes and saw one of her friends, she had a love for her that she had not previously felt for anyone. It was the love of God.

The first time I went to Edgewood, Illinois, about six years ago, Mrs. Florence Lauder told me that she had seen me before. She went on to say that some time before when she was apparently in a dying condition, Jesus with six angels from Heaven and six persons living on earth appeared in the room. She thought it was for the purpose of conveying her soul to Heaven, but Jesus told her, "I am the resurrection and the life and I have come to heal you." He then placed three of the six people who were living upon the earth, on each side of her. While these six lifted her up, the Lord healed her. Mrs. Lauder said that I was one of the six and that it was in connection with the Lord's raising her up that she had seen me before.

A Bethlehem, Pennsylvania, friend had this vision at the time she received the baptism of the Holy Spirit. She saw Jesus standing upon the sea and giving His love in tears to all as the man of sorrow. Later the vision changed and where He had stood, one looking like myself was standing and giving his love to all in great joy. This is the privilege of all in union with Him, to give in great joy where He gave in sorrow and in tears.

A little girl of Russian parentage, living in Philadelphia, had a vision of three lands. The best land was where Jesus was ministering; the intermediate land was where a very likeable and gifted friend was ministering; the other land was the land of confusion. In the vision I was seen to be with Jesus in the best land, part of the time, and the other part ministering in the land of confusion. When I was in the best land with Jesus He gave me His words of release for those in the land of confusion and sent His angels with me as I went giving these words. If the words were received, Jesus Himself appeared and set the people in confusion free.

This is in entire accordance with the revelation made to me in March, 1924, while crossing the Ohio River, that my only responsibility was the responsibility of being in union with Him. We have a responsibility and the responsibility is to let go of and die to everything that prevents vital and fruitful union with Jesus, and to yield joyously, respond to Him, delight to do His will and to choose happily above all else to be and to increase in union and fellowship with Him. This is the only responsibility.

Mrs. Grace Munsey, the Florida friend to whom I dictated the first draft of this chapter, had this experience: Years ago when she was seemingly in deep muddy waters someone appeared to her and led her into the realm of light and freedom. For a time he appeared to be me. She feared he would leave her, until he said, "I will never leave thee nor forsake thee." Then she saw it was the Lord.

Jesus appearing as a gardener, or an ignorant stranger, or a good fisherman and cook, or as you, or as me, should not frighten anyone, nor should the revelation that it is not the gardener, nor the ignorant stranger, nor the good fisherman and cook, nor you, nor me, but Jesus Himself assuming a humble guise to render His eternal services of love, mercy, healing, and transformation.

I believe that as we enter into union with Jesus all of us will be astounded by the ways He will manifest Himself and in the ways He will appear and work as us. If He is allowed to be glorified in us, we will also be glorified in Him. If He is allowed free use of us in manifesting Himself, He will go to the fullest limits of divine possibilities in manifesting and using us in terms of Himself.

CHAPTER XIII

PERFECT EVERYTHING

‹‹‹‹‹‹‹‹‹‹‹‹‹‹‹‹‹‹‹‹‹‹‹‹‹‹‹‹‹‹‹‹›››››››››››››››››››››››››››

This chapter brings the report of the mountain top accents and acts of the Holy Spirit in God's quest for me and my quest for Him up to date, that is, to June 9, 1939. Early in March, 1936, the Spirit spoke through me, saying, "I am perfect everything. I give you perfect everything." The morning after finishing the first draft of this book, I awoke saying, "I am perfect and complete in Jesus. Everything is perfect and complete in Him." Everything outside Him is imperfect and incomplete.

The perfect everything that Jesus has entered into through His perfect self-giving, resurrection and ascension and is giving and leading us into, is the perfection of the Son of Man in His glory that I have designated as the fourth empire, or the realm of the human-divine, which perfectly harmonizes and brings to glorious fulfillment the empires of (1) the natural, (2) the spiritual, (3) the divine-human, or God-with-us.

The perfection He is in and refers to now is of the fourth realm, and is away beyond the perfection of the second realm, that of the ideal, the logos or the Word, prior to His successful incarnation, self-offering, resurrection, and glorification. Even to dwell upon the perfection of the ideal, behind the seeming, as did Plato and as does every school of metaphysical healing of the present day is healing and transforming up to a certain point. But to be in union with Jesus in His present and eternal realm of fourth dimension timeless perfection, one must pass in the spirit through Gethsemane and Calvary to enter with Jesus into the realm of resurrection and ascension. Just as the treatments given by these schools of metaphysical healing affirm the perfection of the ideal and deny the discords of the seeming actual to prove their unreality, so those who are in touch with this fourth realm apply the "Jesus-treatment" to the whole order of three dimensional experience and by this means transform it actually to the fourth.

Even those who knew Jesus after the flesh, as the divine-human, as did John and Peter and the Marys, had ultimately to know Him as the human-divine. Even in the realm of the divine-human, Jesus did perfectly all the things that are being done comparatively imperfectly by modern schools of healing, which are seeking to project bridges over a chasm between the ideal and the seeming actual— a chasm which has already been bridged by the triumph of Jesus. So many are trying to build bridges of their own rather than accept graciously and humbly the bridge which He has already made; after all, this gracious acceptance of divine guidance through humility is itself the bridge; we pass over it by utter receptivity and response to His love.

During the days when that remarkable man, George Bernard Foster, was one of the teachers of the Divinity School of the University of Chicago, I had the privilege of an evening with him in his own home. He said something that caused me to ask him if God is not enriched by all experience, not only all of His experiences, but also by all of ours. Mr. Foster felt this to be true in all probability.

But whether it be true, as Emerson says, "that only the finite has wrought and suffered, the Infinite lies in smiling repose," it is certain that Jesus on the plane of His resurrection, ascension, glorification, and on the highest throne as the Son of Man, is both the everlasting victory and is in and through His people in all of their sorrows and afflictions, their joys and victories, and will continue to be in and with them until the consummation.

In His own body, Jesus is above the whole struggle in

the realm of victory. In His people He is in all of their experience, forever leading them forward and upward, healing their wounds, washing their feet, rendering every service of His as perfect love and as perfect everything, forever taking upon Himself the imperfections of His people and the creation, and giving as fast as He can make them ready and they make themselves ready to receive His own perfect everything.

As perfect love and perfect wisdom and perfect power, He is the solution and the solver of all problems. Even when we do not know how He will solve our problems, we are aware that in and by and through Him and His way of love, there is the best possible solution for every one of them.

Jesus will not fail nor be discouraged until He has brought forth His victorious judgment of enlightenment and love; He brings forth and must succeed in bringing forth in us and in the creation, not only perfect spirit, mind, and body, but perfect harmony and blessedness with the relation to everybody and everything.

His ministry was, is, and shall be the ministry of love, light, redemption, and transformation of the individual and of the social order, and of the whole of life. So is ours. His gospel is individual, social, and cosmic. So is ours.

The self-disclosure of Jesus is perfect everything: it gives, enables, requires and achieves it. It is the fulfillment of all that the Spirit has said of Him. This carries us as far as human conception and language can go. Here we have the fulfillment of all former disclosures concerning Him and His perfect way of life for Himself and for us. Here Jesus is seen as perfect God and perfect man in one, as the all-loving, all-powerful, and all-intelligent One, using the all-power of God in terms of perfect wisdom and perfect love. As Fairbairn has observed, absolute power would corrupt anyone except the Absolute Good.

He is seen as perfect person, law, and principle, working together in sublime unity; as perfect light and light-giver, truth and teacher, way and way-shower, health and healer, redemption and redeemer, resurrection and life; as the one who listens and answers all of our prayers good enough to be answered, and even answers with goodness the poorest prayer, but not always in the way expected. He meets all of our needs, and at the same time is the answer to every true desire and prayer and the supplier of every need.

If it were possible for Him to minister anything but the highest, He Himself would not be that highest. Everything is what it ministers. The way we who are imperfect put off our imperfections and resultant mortality is by yielding to Him and His perfect everything, manifesting Him and His perfect everything.

As long as imperfection is ministered by anyone, he remains imperfect. We cannot escape the means we use and should not escape them until we repent of them. They who take the sword must perish by the sword, unless they disarm and put on the armor of the Spirit. There can be no entering into the Kingdom of Heaven except in terms of yielding and responding to the nature and Spirit of the Kingdom, the Spirit, love, sincerity, purity and the perfect everything of Jesus.

Jesus would like to save everyone immediately and deliver from all unnecessary suffering, tragedy, and catastrophe, but, to quote N. C. McPherson, Jr., "There is no dodging the process, no jumping of the steps." Salvation, redemption, perfection, and all of the things of God are living, dynamic, and can only be received in terms of happy yielding, responding, and manifesting. When our giving equals our receiving, there will be perfect growth and should be perpetual youth. Decrepit old age is the hardening and poisoning resulting from the failure to give out perfectly and perpetually, as well as failure to receive perfectly and perpetually from God. Perfect receiving and perfect giving are one. In the fourth realm man is made a whole being, having the faith of childhood, the vitality of youth, the maturity of middle life and the wisdom of age. Here there is neither ignorance nor decay.

Sometime after the clear revelation of Jesus as perfect everything on the highest plane and realm of achievement, the realm of the human-divine, a book, *The Spiritual Life*, by Evelyn Underhill, was put in my hands by O. T. Binkley. This book gave me a beautiful statement of things that had been revealed to me by the Spirit.

"Creation is the activity of an artist possessed by the vision of perfection, who by means of the raw material with which He works, tries to give more and more expression to His idea, His inspiration, or His love. From this point of view, each human spirit is an unfinished product, on which the Creative Spirit is always at work.

"The moment in which, in one way or another, we become aware of this creative action of God and are therefore able to respond or resist is the moment in which our conscious spiritual life begins.

"We know that perfect goodness, perfect beauty, and perfect truth exist in the life of God; and our hearts will never rest in less than these. All creation has a purpose. It looks towards perfection. In the volume of this book it is written of me that I should fulfill Thy will, Oh God. Not in some mysterious spiritual world that I know nothing about, but here and now, where I find myself, as a human creature of spirit and sense, immersed in the modern world, subject to time with all of its vicissitudes, and yet penetrated by the Eternal, finding reality not in one but in both. To acknowledge and take up that double obligation to the seen and the Unseen, in however homely and practical a way, is to enter consciously upon the spiritual life. That will mean time and attention given to it; a deliberate drawing-in from the circumference to the center, that setting of life in order for which Saint Thomas Aquinas prayed."

I have friends in East Macon who find that when they are enough in the Spirit, even the washing of dirty clothes becomes an act of worship. As one of them puts it, "When I am prayed up, when I am enough in the Spirit, I hear the sloshing of the water saying, 'Glory to God, Glory to God.' " Everything becomes as an act of worship when approached and performed in the right spirit and attitude.

A rare friend, Joe Overstreet, went to his accustomed mountain top a few years ago to shoot squirrels, as was his custom when he had a vacation. Something had happened to him beyond his conscious awareness. He knelt and prayed before commencing to hunt. The squirrels instinctively aware that there was no harm coming from anyone praying, gathered around him, joining his prayer meeting. And when Joe looked up and saw the squirrels he could not think of shooting members of his prayer meeting. He tells me that the gun has never been shot from then until now.

A sinner is only an opportunity for Jesus and for us to minister to him the transforming light and love whereby by His yielding he becomes a saint. All need in every realm simply becomes great opportunity. There is no defect that complete yielding to Jesus will not bring to normality and ultimately to perfection. We can tell the blind man with perfect assurance that in and by and through Jesus he has perfect eyes and sight, and that through faith, through his yielding to Jesus and His perfect everything, perfect eyes, sight, and all else needed will become his in the actuality of experience.

If one should be as unstable as water, as was Simon who became Peter, the Lord's highest judgment and opportunity for him is to make him so firm and supporting that he would now be given even a new name to indicate his new nature and position in and with Jesus.

While the prayer of petition and intercession will continue with us, as it did with Jesus, until all conscious needs for self and others are swallowed up in fulfillment, we will have as companion to the prayer of petition and intercession, the prayer of fellowship, of communion, affirmation, and realization of the perfect everything of Jesus, which, through union with Him, is also ours. No matter what is wrong or lacking in spirit, mind, soul, body in society and in the world order in which we live, we can not only ask for all lacks to be supplied and all wrongs to be removed and supplanted by their opposite good, but we can also know and rejoice that every hunger and thirst for righteousness and perfection and every prayer of good are approved with answers ready to be manifested as we and others affected are made ready for their manifestation in actual experience.

When we ask according to His will, according to what is best for all, He hears and answers beyond our ability to conceive. There is no lack but that He and His perfect everything are the supply. And by beholding as in a mirror the glory of His perfect everything, our imperfect everything is replaced by it. Everything below Jesus' way of affirmation and realization is shadow in comparison with such high reality.

About a year and a half ago, when my gums and teeth were giving me some trouble, I asked J. W. Culpepper, a man of unusual faith and love, to join me in asking that I might have, through union with Jesus, perfect gums and perfect teeth and perfect everything of body, as well as of mind and soul and spirit. Quickly the Spirit took my tongue and said, "Done, done, done!" Friend Culpepper said, "There is no need to pray more." This occurred on Saturday morning. The following Sunday night, when an altar call was made at the Blackburn Avenue Gospel Tabernacle and I was walking toward the altar with no conscious thought as to my gums and teeth, it was spoken through me, "I give you perfect teeth and perfect gums." I do not know when they will be perfect in manifestation, but all of the gum difficulty disappeared quickly and now the teeth are remarkably improved.

Just this morning when I was not thinking about my eyes or ears, it was spoken through me, "I give you perfect eyes and ears." Perfect everything is for us through union with Jesus and as we yield and respond to Him and hold fast to His perfect everything, it will be manifested in the whole of our being.

I have been enriched immeasurably in recent months in connection with the effort to put in accessible form a report of the accents and acts of the Holy Spirit in His quest for me and in my quest for Him. I have been aware of a greatly increased sense of dependence upon Him, and have needed His help throughout the whole work. While He is not in our imperfect perceiving and reporting, and while His perfect gifts to us are too often obscured by us, still it is true that all of our good comes from Him and that everything worth while that each of us does is inspired by Him.

At times he overrides the imperfect reporter and gives His own perfect words direct. This book centers around the few perfect things that He Himself has succeeded in making me yielded enough to become the channel for conveying:

"Go in love and I will always be with thee. Your only responsibility is the responsibility of being in union with Me. I want you in Me all the time and I give you the keys. Give My love to everybody. I am perfect everything, I give perfect everything, I give you perfect everything."

God occasionally manifested Himself to Jesus by a voice or by some special witness from above, but the greater part of the teachings and miracles of Jesus appear to have been from that perfect union between Him and the Father that made the supernatural, supernaturally natural.

Of Jesus' relationship to us, I believe He is seeking to make us as fully one with Him as He was with the Father and to bring forth in and through us as the Father did in and through Him. Yet it is better to be in union with Jesus now, for He has passed into the highest realm of victory and glory as the human-divine, than it was for Him to be in union with the Father prior to His own crucifixion, resurrection, and glorification.

While all of our work in union with Jesus is the best

possible for each and every one of us and while "every advance made by one," as Miss Underhill says, "is made for all," my work appears to be to centralize upon Jesus and His way of life as love, and through Him to give the secrets of ineffable fruit-bearing union with Him.

It is hoped this book may reach at least the few who might be used to reach the many. My work, in common with all the rest, is to make intercession in behalf of all. All are in greatest need of Jesus, His love spirit and way of life. The dictators and the war-makers are in especially great need of Him.

This reminds me that some time ago when a Saint Louis friend, Mrs. A. Pickett, was praying for the Ethiopians, she was lifted up in the Spirit and filled with such great love that she also made intercession for Mussolini. She heard the Voice say, "Now you are praying right." The more we yield to the love of Jesus, the more we will be making intercessions for His love to win in all and especially in those most in need of Jesus and His way of life. How can we fail to keep on praying and working for war and the causes of war to cease, and for righteousness, justice, good will, and brotherly love to triumph everywhere?

All of us should be seeking to get the simplicity of Jesus' way of life as vitally and widely known as possible. The Spirit often says not only, "Give My love to all," but "Give My keys to all."

All of us who know Jesus are fully aware that without Him and out of union with Him we can do nothing. This is the basis of our conscious dependence upon Him, which is humility. We know that in union with Jesus our place and work are infinitely important. I know mine is, and I know that yours is just as important as mine.

Through union with Jesus each of us becomes an all-important incarnation of His perfect everything. Each of us in His full will and achievement will be an individual glorified being in a body like His, and whose spirit will minister and bless all the rest and be ministered to and blessed by all the rest.

BOOK TWO

<<<<<<<<<<<<<<<<<<<<<<<<<<<<>>>>>>>>>>>>>>>>>>>>>>>>>>>>

THE JESUS WAY OF LIFE

Those who seek Truth apart from Love miss Truth, while those who seek Love get Love, Truth, and Everything.

CHAPTER I

THE WAY OF IMMEDIATE GUIDANCE

‹‹‹‹‹‹‹‹‹‹‹‹‹‹‹‹‹‹‹‹‹‹‹‹‹‹‹‹‹‹›››››››››››››››››››››››

First of all, the Jesus way is that of immediate guidance and fellowship. All who give themselves to be led by Jesus and by His good Spirit become like Him. This is the law: You become like the one you believe in enough to give yourself as subject and follower. Like leader, like people; like shepherd, like flock. To follow the blind long enough and far enough is to go blind yourself as well as into the ditch. Even those who follow the dry, the dull, and the dead also become dry, dull, and dead. Everywhere it takes the resurrected to resurrect the dead. The dead are expert on burying the dead, but have to become resurrected themselves before they can become channels for the abundant life of Jesus.

The tendency of all the old covenant leaders, both religious and secular, has been to enslave their followers. Jesus makes His followers freer and freer until He achieves absolute freedom in and through them. Other leaders have limited and kept under their followings, not desiring any of them to get ahead or above them, with the notable exception of John the Baptist, who told his following that he himself would decrease while Jesus would increase and that they had better leave him and become disciples of Jesus (may his kind increase). Jesus says to His followers, I have not been able to tell you everything, but I am going away to send another Helper, Teacher, and Comforter, who will be with you and within you always, and He will guide you into all the truth. Even the very things and greater things than I have done, you, through belief and union with Me, are going to do.

Moreover, the old covenant leaderships have been especially susceptible to fondness for good salaries, positions, offerings, tithes, and such. Jesus, on the other hand, loved people and not money and according to the New Testament report only took up collections for feeding the hungry multitudes.

Jesus gives to all of us who receive something of His nature, a hatred for this love of money, power and fame with which most of us have been tainted, and which has corrupted every priesthood thus far after the order of Aaron—Jewish, pagan, Catholic, and Protestant. We may give up these things slowly, but even to hate them in yourself more than in others, is progress. The going of the Jesus way of limitless love and the hatred of the things that hurt life, does not make us insecure, but secure; does not make us beggars, but benefactors; does not make us paupers, but princes.

Once I asked Jesus if He wanted me to be as poor as He was. The reply came, "I want you to be as rich as I am." Sometimes I get so busy that I forget to go to my little reserves (witnesses of my lack of faith and love), and draw out enough to meet the expenses of Saturday afternoon and Sunday. I did this very thing only the other day. I decided I would not ask for a loan or buy anything on credit, and see how it worked out. I had an invitation for breakfast, three for dinner, and one for supper. Finally, during the day, I grew in faith and gave away the one penny I had. And, with my little faith and love, by seeking to render all kinds of services without pay and some of them at considerable personal expense, and by being glad to work with my hands when there is nothing more urgent, never since I started this way have I needed to take up a collection for myself or even give hint of my need. So far as I've tried it, the Jesus way of even desiring to put first what is first and to be a giver of all possible good and only a giver of good, makes you far more secure even in the way of the supply of ordinary needs than any other way of life.

Other leaders not having power over death, make provision for carrying on by the means of written rules or laws and by the appointment of fallible successors. Jesus laid down His life in the behalf of all, and came back with all power and authority of Heaven and of earth in His hands and with the gift of Omnipresence. He is at the same time in His own body on the highest throne of Heaven and, through the Spirit, also within every one of us who will receive Him and enter into fruitful union with Him.

To His glory and praise, He seems to be with each of us even more fully and wonderfully than He could have been with even one of us had He remained on earth, as God-with-us on the plane of His incarnation. On this plane He has had no rival as a leader, teacher, revelator, healer, resurrector, redeemer, and transformer. But even a visible personal leadership as perfect as was His, needed to go away that He might send the omnipresent other Comforter, Teacher, and Guide to be with us and within us forever. Only by giving oneself completely away, as He did, can we enter the fourth realm.

Moreover, the new priesthood after the order of Melchisedec and of Jesus, where each is taught and directly led by His Spirit, does not take away our power and willingness to help one another but greatly increases them. If you are an immediate disciple of Jesus and are taught first of all by Him, then you will have real power to help me and all the rest. To be taught by Him does not make us in any sense independent of each other, but on the other hand makes us members one of another, bringing us into the same kind of union with each other that Jesus has with the Father and we have with Him. It is precisely because of the perverse tendency of the old covenant shepherds to feed themselves instead of the sheep, to divide the fold of God, and to keep their little flock away from better pastures that the prophets of God foresaw the far better days when the Lord Himself shall shepherd all of His sheep.

Here is the paradox: Those who pride themselves on being teachers, preachers, and such-like, have the persistent perversity of misleading into deserts of dryness and desolation, while those who know that only the Perfect One is worthy of the name and position of teacher, leader, reverend, and father are invariably given much to give the rest. Here is another paradox: Those who insist that if they do not lead, the sheep will become divided have been usually the very ones who have scattered and divided them, while those who knew and acted upon the knowledge that no one was wise and good enough to lead but the Perfect One and who pointed all to Him and sought to get all in union with Him, have been given, as was Saint Paul, unusual authority and power to help the rest in the brotherhood of His immediate disciples.

To illustrate, if we are all making our way on the same highway from Macon to Atlanta and there is on the highway an expert driver who keeps straight ahead, never turning off into any of the side roads, we do well to watch and follow him so long as he continues to go straight ahead. And as Saint Paul puts it, and he himself was such a one, Follow me as I follow Christ. Follow Paul or anyone else who is ahead of you so long as he is ahead of you and is following Christ, but follow no one because of reputation or rank. As Frank Buglo once put it to a group at Owensboro, Kentucky, "If you are in my mind under me, if I fall you fall with me; but if you are in the mind of Jesus (and under Him directly), if I fall you will not fall with me, but will have power to lift me up."

As Tennyson says, "He fulfills His will, or makes known His will to us," in various ways, "lest one good custom should corrupt the world." As great as were each of the teachings of Jesus as reported in the New Testament, he repeated only one of His teachings, namely that His disciples should love one another, as He loves them. He not only repeated this on the last night, but also prayed that the same kind of love that the Father had for Him might be in the disciples and that He might also be in them.

Jesus made known His will to Saul of Tarsus by speaking unto him as man speaks to man. He sometimes does this yet. I am reminded of Mrs. W. A. Scott, a sincere, intelligent, and unselfish friend who brought up her deceased brother's family of children, giving them wonderful care and love, and who at that time had a very narrow theology, not nearly so good as her heart and her life. She sought for the baptism of the Holy Spirit and after receiving this baptism continued to pray and to surrender for God's best for her. She was then granted the great grace of Jesus speaking to her in an audible voice and of being taken up in the Spirit with Him and of seeing some things unlawful to report. She was taken over all the countries of the world and the islands of the sea and saw them in worship at the feet of Jesus. Sometimes during this heavenly control and use, she was told to tell a certain well-known religious leader and preacher that while there was no condemnation for him, he was failing to lift Him (Jesus) up, and to tell him to let her preach. Mrs. Scott, never having preached nor been accustomed even to testifying in public, had no idea as to what or how to preach. In answer to her question as to what she was to preach, she was told to preach: "And I, if I be lifted up, will draw all men unto me—not some men, *all* men." Jesus still has so much to say and has such unlimited authority and ability to say it, that He yet sometimes speaks as an audible voice.

Jesus speaks most often by the influence and enlightenment of the Holy Spirit. The highest guidance is in terms of the new nature which He implants within us, which brings us to the place where the Father seeks to please the Son and the Son, the Father. Here neither is conscious of any tension. This was the normal relationship between Jesus and the Father and should be the normal relationship between us and Jesus. But in case of temptation, the Son realizing that the Father sees above the fog while He is yet in the fog, chooses the will of the Father.

He speaks through the luminous thought, through the quickening of the written Word, through the pressure of circumstances. There is, in fact, no limit to His ways of teaching and guiding and of indicating both His approval and disapproval of thoughts, desires, words, and actions.

The walk with Him and within Him has sign posts everywhere they are needed, and every side road has its danger signals.

Years ago it was made clear to me that when I was in doubt as to His highest will in any situation, if I would do the most loving thing possible, I would always be doing His will. There is no doubt that we are doing His will as we manifest His good Spirit and apply to the details of life the Spirit and the wisdom of the Sermon on the Mount. Miss Underhill speaks of His guidance through the pressure of circumstances in favor of one course rather than another. And as she so finely puts it, "When there is no conscious pressure of God in favor of the path that we should take, then our conduct should be decided by charity and common sense; qualities which are given us by God in order that they may be used." Here again the words of Emerson ring so true: "There's guidance for us all and by lowly listening we shall each hear the right word."

As O. T. Binkley puts it, he has known in the situations and crises of life what the right thing to do was, but has not always chosen to do it. And even to desire and choose to be led by the Lord is to be led by Him whether we are aware of it at the time or not. We find out later that we have been so led. Emerson was aware that if he needed anyone, that one also needed him, and if they were at opposite parts of the earth, their feet were headed toward each other.

It is clearly apparent that whenever we put ourselves in line to do the most perfect will of love, the sign posts are unmistakable. Everything helps us along.

As God gave His children in New Testament as well as in Old Testament times necessary factual knowledge for their protection, guidance, and best uses, so does He still. But, as we have seen in matters where only moral and spiritual enlightenment is required, He usually guides by spiritual intuition and insight, by the teachings and urgings of love, and by the pressure of circumstances. There is no possibility of missing the way for those who love the way.

I have found in my own experience that when I have been

ready to do the less important, not to mention the sinful, He has given me signal after signal that I was missing His best for me and my best for Him. Rather early in life when headed towards making known my affection to a very intelligent, admirable, and beautiful young lady, I was warned in a vivid dream that I should not propose marriage to her. In this dream we were already married and were both unhappy.

Even as a boy I found clarification in dreams that I had not found in waking moments. Some years ago, while debating in my mind whether I would return from Evansville by way of Louisville and Nashville to Macon, or whether I would yield to the urge of the Philadelphia friend who wanted to drive me back to Philadelphia, I had a very vivid dream of crossing a series of railroad tracks in Ohio. The next morning the preponderance of evidence pointed to accepting the friend's great kindness and going with him to Philadelphia. As we drove through Ohio I saw the same or similar railroad tracks that I had seen in the vivid dream.

Once when I wrote a letter that would have brought embarrassment to someone, I was warned in a vivid dream. As the result of the warning, I wired the postmaster to return the letter to me. Years ago a friend came to me telling me how she was imposed upon. I went to sleep praying for her and the person who was doing the imposing. During the night I had a vivid dream of crossing over the most beautiful river I had ever seen, by walking over a bridge that also appeared to be the most perfect and the most beautiful I had ever crossed. Soon afterwards I found myself crossing over the same river, swollen and agitated. All I had to walk upon were wires laid over the surface of the water and crossed without being firmly tied together. Before getting over the river I came to a high stone wall. In front of me were the crossed wires hanging over the wall. A voice spoke to me, saying, "If you can get the wires wound around your feet you will be taken over the wall." I turned my right foot to make the effort of twisting about it, then the wire grasped my feet, and I was carried over the wall. A voice then said, "The hard trials that your friend is facing, if she will welcome them, instead of resisting them, are the very things that will carry her over." I said, "That is fine, but my feet are still tied." I was told that when the tying of the feet is no longer needed, it goes. Instantly I was set free. Here the remarkable thing happened, that I was not only given the revealing clarifying dream that I needed, and the friend needed, but I was also given the interpretation of the dream in the dream itself.

There is also the guidance of immediate knowing, which in the language of the street is a "hunch." Shortly before I tendered my resignation at Mercer, a friend wrote me for consent for him to present my candidacy for a position in the University of Illinois. Somehow, I knew this was not God's will. A little later that rare man and friend, Chancellor Walter B. Hill, of the University of Georgia, wrote me to meet him in Atlanta. When we met I found that he wanted my consent to present my name for a chair in the University of Georgia, and said if I could come to the university, he would let me in a large measure choose my own work. I knew that I was not to accept this. I was headed another way, the way of the cross, and the way of ever enlarging freedom. I loved Mercer so well, and the Mercer faculty, students, trustees, and contingency had been so good to me, I could not go to another and nearby institution. Then, too, I was made aware that I would be unhappy at the university or anywhere else except in the quest for God's best in terms of highest guidance and greatest freedom.

This very clear light was given me some years ago as to the real essence of the Jesus way for us. In a dream or dream vision, I was in a meeting that seemed to be in East Macon and not far from the Ocmulgee River. I arose in the meeting and said, "Christianity is belief in Jesus, the baptism of the Holy Spirit, the life of love, and the meeting of all evil with good." There was a stranger in the meeting with a tender, intelligent, beautiful face who arose and said, "This is fine." This awoke me. More recently, when I was coming out of a dream I was saying, "Remembering the full salvation, bearing the full testimony."

In all of the various leadings and even free compulsions of the Spirit, the more we are in the Spirit, the higher the certainty and authority of the guidance and teaching. We never doubt God nor His guidance nor His providential love and care when we are in the clear consciousness of His presence.

With immediate discipleship and guidance comes joyous surrender to God and our own higher self, inspiration, revelation, and freedom. Receptivity and response to Him as it becomes perfect brings us to perfect freedom. What He wants of us is full development, use, and bliss in terms of our God-given and acquired capacities. What He wants of us is what we really want for ourselves. Thus full and complete surrender to His best for us and for all is found to be our perfection, our bliss, and our freedom. When we delight to do His will we find that He delights to do ours. The tension of wills gives place to the joy of fellowship, union, and fruit bearing.

Just recently, while reading E. Stanley Jones' *Victorious Living* from pages 100 to 119 I was brought to seek His guidance and best uses in the seemingly smallest as well as in the clearly all-important things of life. I have known for a long time that He guided in all that was all-important and in other things too when we were motivated by love. As I read *Victorious Living* I was gripped by the clear insight and fine statement of the author as he discussed the fruit of the victorious life, how one enters into it, and how by giving our all we find we have His all. The victorious life is of course a release from ourselves and our problems and an entering and abiding in vital, fruitful union with Jesus. It is a shift from being self-centered to being Jesus-centered; it is a freedom from strain and self-effort and an entrance into a joyous trusting in Him and a happy spontaneous delight in Him and in doing His will. In union with Him we are set free from sin and fear and every form of bondage. We have life and have it abundantly. It is divinely easy and natural to love Him and to love all. To quote Stanley Jones, "The mind becomes keener and more creative, the emotions become broader and more sensitive, and the will more active and decisive. The whole of life is outreaching. Lives begin to be changed, movements begin to be launched, a creative impact is made upon life." It is a life of limitless love and love is always creative.

We enter into the vital union with Jesus which is the victorious life, through love, through asking, through knocking, through becoming as a little child, and by gladly dying and saying good-bye to all that keeps one out of union with Jesus and the Kingdom fo Heaven.

As Stanley Jones sees so clearly and expresses so well, "it is not by fighting your individual sins you enter into the victorious life, for this gets the imagination upon your sins; and when there is a battle between the imagination and the will the imagination wins," especially if the sin has a "sensuous sweet appeal" and its very sinfulness is because one in his blind selfishness is seeking to obtain "the sensuous sweet" and to escape "the sensuous bitter." To quote Jones again, "The imagination must be centered on Christ. But the imagination cannot and will not be centered there unless there is complete surrender to Him. For the imagination goes where the supreme treasure is. . . . So the problem . . . is the shifting of the place of your supreme treasure, the shifting of your very life. You must surrender. . . . When the surrender takes place love springs up." And the imagination always follows your leading love. As a wise proverb puts it, "Commit your ways unto the Lord, and your thoughts shall be established." As Jones reminds us, "You don't even have to try to forget your sins or to whip up your will for a stiffer fight against them." Just shift the basis of your life from self to Jesus and then, as Jones says, you will love and trust Him and through Him have the victory. Since individual sins are "rooted in the unsurrendered self," the victory comes as we surrender and keep surrendered to Jesus; so that the center of our lives is Jesus and not self. So as Jones advises, give "all you know and all you don't know to Jesus"; then you are ready to make the venture or leap of faith. "Faith," he says, "is the adventure of acceptance," and the moment that we give all, we can with assurance reach forth and receive all. His all is forever offered to all who will give their all.

When I reached page 119, which is Jones' meditation for April 20th, where the call is made for the adventurous acceptance of His All when you give your all, I went to my knees asking for His fullest will and guidance in everything. Almost instantly it was made known to me that I had passed into perpetual and ever increasing freedom and victory and that all things were mine, and yours too. I found I had passed into a realm of clearer seeing and guidance. A new veil had been lifted, and things already seen were seen in a clearer light.

When I returned to the reading of *Victorious Living* I found on the next page, page 120, an account of the author's own experience, very similar to my own. His experience came while reading *The Christian's Secret of a Happy Life*, which caused him, under the leadership of the Spirit, to go to his knees and ask: "What shall I do?" The inner Voice replied, "Will you give me your all—your very all?" He replied, "I will," and the Voice said, "Then take my all, you are cleansed." Jones replied, "I believe it," rose from his knees and walked around the room, affirming it over and over, and pushing his hands away from him as to push away his doubt. This he did for ten minutes, when suddenly he was filled with strange refining fire that seemed to course through every portion of his being in cleansing waves. The Divine waves could be felt from the very inmost center of his being to his fingertips. His whole being was being fused into one, and through the whole there was a sense of sacredness and awe—and the most exquisite joy. The very sources of his life were being cleansed and were taken possession of by Life itself. Both his will and emotions were involved, and the whole life was on a permanently higher level.*

*From *Victorious Living*, by E. Stanley Jones, copyrighted 1936. Used by permission of Abingdon-Cokesbury Press, publishers.

CHAPTER II

THE WAY OF LIFE AS LOVE

◄◄◄◄◄◄◄◄◄◄◄◄◄◄◄◄◄◄◄◄◄◄◄◄◄◄◄◄◄◄►►►►►►►►►►►►►►►►►►►►►►►►►►►

All the teachings of the Spirit centralize around Jesus and His way of life as love, making known there is but one responsibility, the responsibility of being in union with Him, and only one commandment—to love as Jesus loved. All who have entered into union with Jesus have found that the condition and fruit of this union is perfect love.

As Saint Paul saw, love is the fulfillment of the law and the very heart of the Gospel. As Saint Peter saw, love is the highest attainment in Christian experience. As Saint John saw, "God is love," and he that loves and only he that loves knows God, is known of God, and abides in God, and has the abundant life of God, while he who neither hates nor loves is in a state of death, and he who hates is a murderer.

The great concern of Jesus is for His disciples to love one another, to love their enemies, and to do them all possible good, and to meet all evil with good.

Love is the highest impersonal reality and at times seems to be also the highest personality. As Mrs. Grace Munsey put it while I was dictating the first draft of this chapter to her, "Everything that is done in love is done by God Himself."

If you have love, you have everything. If you miss love, you miss everything. Moreover, such great things as suffering, and gifts of the Spirit only have value in the Spirit and technique of love. Those who seek truth apart from love miss the truth, while those who seek love get love, truth, and everything.

Even before we know how love will achieve its perfect end, we know that it is the solution and has the solution of everything. Even wisdom is the way that love does things. Nothing is ever won except in love. There is no real success except the success of love. Love is the greatest power of all and will finally be seen as the only power. In my own experience, I have never known it to fail. Where there is failure there has been some lack of love. Once when I was in Saint Louis talking to a group of friends about the love spirit and love way of Jesus I was asked, "What is one to do if he tries the love way and it doesn't work?" Of course the reply was, "Love never faileth." After everything else fails, love wins. The more other things fail, the more ready everything becomes for love to win.

The only time I have ever been ordered to move toward the jail, I realized that it was not purely for Christ's sake that I was being taken by the policeman, but because I had failed to be loving enough to him. When he asked me to stop a street meeting, I replied, "My work is not to stop meetings, but to help them along." This turned the laugh on him and it angered him. While we had been told by the City Council to go ahead and hold the meeting that Sunday afternoon, it is only in the love spirit that there is real value in any religious activity or any other activity. Nothing can be done for God unless it is done in love, for God is love. I realized clearly on the way to jail that there would be great glory in going to jail purely for Christ's sake, but no value in going because of the lack of the gracious spirit. So I said to the policeman, "If you love me as well as I do you, we are going to have a good time." The policeman smiled and released me.

In the years of my rather excessive zeal, I went to a business man in Macon with the hope of inducing him to be more generous in his dealings with a certain man. The Macon business man misunderstood me and became very angry, saying, "You have accused me of being dishonest. Get out of here and get out quick, or I will kick you out."

I knew if I left him without making peace, I would have to return and that it would be far easier for both of us for me to humble myself and to make peace at once. As the Pennsylvania Dutch put it, "If you have to swallow a toad, the less time you take to look it over, the easier it is to swallow it." It is great wisdom not to let the sun go down on your foolishness. So I replied to the angry business man, "I have used the wrong word. I did not mean to call you dishonest, I was only appealing to you to be more generous. I ask you to forgive me and I am not going to leave the room until you forgive me, and love me better than before this occurred."

There seemed to be a struggle in his face for a few moments, then came a sweet smile with these fine words, "I forgive you, and do love you better than ever before." He has proved it from then until now. Whenever I see him there is that wonderful friendly smile on his face, indicating his memory of the happy quick turn that a little humbling and grace achieved in a difficult situation.

In the early days of the street meetings, after we had been shifted from one place to another, and felt that we had finally been put at the right place, a business man put up a gasoline station so near there that he asked us to move. Unfortunately I did not react graciously and said the wrong word. After we went to the new place, I realized that I was of no value to the meeting until I left the meeting and went and asked forgiveness of the man who had asked us to move on. After I had humbled myself and made peace with him, I came back to work with redoubled vigor.

At one time while I was at a meeting in Charleston (West Virginia), I encountered a very likable man by the name of Martin, who had been offended at something and had separated himself from the brethren. When I first came he and the brethren had come into a renewed fellowship, until one morning the subject of baptism was mentioned in a way that offended him. He grabbed his hat and started for the door. I went to him and put my arm around him. I told him that if he left the meeting part of my joy would be taken from me and as I needed to remain, would he please remain with me. He smiled, surrendered, and stayed.

While at Charleston on the same visit I was told of a most charitable and humble woman who had come to believe that she had sinned against the Holy Spirit. Her trouble was that she had yielded to the temptation to ask the Lord to let a certain healing come as the result of her faith and prayers rather than those of others. Later the person died and this kind woman became self-hypnotized with the belief that she had committed the unpardonable sin. While talking to her the light broke upon her that anyone who is loving to God's children and does not pass by on the other side of anyone in need, goes with the sheep into life. This set her free and all the years that I have known her since, I have found her to be among the humblest and most cheerful of Christians that I have known.

In several instances law suits have been stopped by making appeals in terms of the love way of Jesus. Only a few years ago I had the happy experience of seeing a courthouse trial changed into a prayer meeting. A group of neighbors, living near a certain tabernacle, felt that the worshipers were making too much noise, and made an appeal to the city court to stop the meetings, which they claimed to be a nuisance.

This rather stiffened the spirit of the worshipers, who felt that they must stand bold for Christian liberty. While the witnesses on both sides were being sworn, as my memory serves me, I entered the courtroom, taking a seat in the rear. The presiding judge, Judge Felton Hatcher, remarked, "I see a former Mercer professor of mine in the courtroom." He said to me, "Come up here and have a seat with me and help me decide this case."

After shaking hands with the judge and taking a seat near him, I arose and asked the litigants, "How many of you are Christians, or hope to be?" All the litigants held their hands very high. I then quoted to them the verse from Saint Paul that says that it is a shame for Christians to go to law with one another. I told them they ought to be in a prayer meeting instead of in the courthouse. That put an end to the spirit that caused the law suit.

Judge Hatcher asked me to see if I could not settle the matter out of court. That was Saturday about noon. By Monday at noon a good understanding had been reached that preserved religious liberty and at the same time sought to be considerate of the neighbors. The incident appealed to a bright newspaper man, who was in the courtroom, as something unique enough for Associated Press news.

The settling of another case outside of court set in motion unusual blessings to the litigants and to the neighborhood where they lived. A party of youngsters celebrating on Hallowe'en night were too noisy for the patience of a nervous man with a sick wife. He threw a brick-bat and hit one of the boys in the party, fracturing his skull. The doctor in charge gave out the opinion that the boy might die.

When I went to the jail I found the young man who had thrown the brick-bat hysterical. I told him that he had better be giving his time and energy to praying for the injured boy to get well, explaining that if he got well his own punishment would not be severe, but if he died it was likely to be. He said he knew that. The injured boy recovered rapidly and fully. I then proposed to the young man in jail and to his family that no money be spent on a law suit, but that he give the money that usually goes to lawyers and for court expenses to the injured boy and his family. This pleased all concerned and Solicitor Garrett approved of the matter taking this course.

During the First World War period, I had the happy experience of helping to prevent a lynching. The experience taught me that I need fear no one so long as I have a good enough spirit toward him.

Out in the neighborhood of Byron, Georgia, where for

years I have spent some of my time working with pecan trees, back in the days of the First World War there were a few people who objected to the colored people either owning or driving an automobile or a truck. When a negro drove for one of the white neighbors, or bought a car, he was waited upon by masked men and threatened. The neighborhood as a whole was shocked and grieved. The thing was so unreasonable that surely nobody in those parts could be guilty of it.

On a certain Saturday night, a popular colored boy by the name of Jack drove one of the Byron merchants, who lived a few miles out from Byron, to his home. As Jack walked home by a certain store some one that Jack knew called out to him, saying, "Is that you, Jack?" Jack said, "Yes," and proceeded toward Byron.

A little later a party of men in a car dashed by him and then stopped as quickly as they could. Jack failed to take to the corn field, as he realized he should. The party of white men searched him, relieved him of his pocket knife and a little loose change, took him to Crawford County and whipped him and told him that if he told he would never live to tell again.

Jack reached Byron on Sunday afternoon and told what had happened. This caused Mr. A. J. Peavy and my brother, M. C. Moseley, to take active steps in the matter. They were, of course, backed by the best people of the county. When they reported the outrage to Judge H. A. Matthews and to the solicitor general, Judge Ross, Ross said he would prosecute vigorously if he could get the backing of the Byron people.

Jack was put in a little house back of Mr. Peavy's residence, where his grandmother lived. Mr. Peavy gave instructions that if any individual or group came for Jack, the grandmother was to make all the noise she could.

The night before Jack was to go before the grand jury of Crawford County, a party of six masked men went to the little house where Jack was being kept and asked for him.

The leader of the party represented himself as "the high sheriff of Crawford County." When the masked men insisted upon entering the house to look for Jack, the grandmother commenced sounding the alarm. Mr. Peavy grabbed a few clothes and his pistol and reached the scene of danger before the men got into the house.

With great boldness and good sense he held back the six men until he could be reinforced. My brother did not awaken me until he had dressed and was leaving his home to go to Mr. Peavy's aid. I realized that we were confronted by a situation that would make it worthwhile to do the best possible regardless of the cost. So I grabbed the best clothes I had, having enough pride to prefer to be a corpse in a decent suit and not in the old clothes that I had used while working among the trees. When I reached Mr. Peavy, he told me that he had succeeded in frightening away the six men, but asked me to go as quickly as I could to the front of his store where a car was waiting to take the six men and Jack to some place agreed upon.

When I reached the car, I struck a match and put it in front of the faces of the two men in the front seat, saying, "If you are all right you won't object to the light." They seemed very much embarrassed. The men had been telling my brother and Mr. Peavy's brother that their car was broken down, and had asked them to go and fetch a mechanic. I said to the men in the car, "Something bad is going on here tonight, and if you men are all right you will not leave until the matter is cleared up." They started the car and fled.

It was not long before the majority of the male population of the town appeared on the scene. Most of them were well armed. Friends offered me a pistol. I refused it. It was suggested that some of the men in the party were likely to be down in a certain dark wooded hollow. I asked for the privilege of going down and seeing. I preferred to go alone and went singing and praising the Lord.

I did not find anyone. When I returned one of our party

suggested that there was someone out in the open space between the house where Jack had been kept and Mr. Peavy's downtown property. I led the search party. After we had gone a few yards I saw something that looked like a man. I reached down and found that it was a man. He had a shotgun by his side, but was so drunk that he had gone to sleep on the job. After he was taken to the railroad depot he told everything. A little later the two men in the car returned with the hope of getting the man they had left behind. When I saw them I cried out, "There are the two men." They fled.

Later two trials were held. One man was convicted, but the leader of the party managed to get a mistrial.

One thing I learned from this was the difficulty of identifying strangers. Before locating the two men who were in the car, who were strangers to me, and in whose faces I had struck the match, I found I had suspected several innocent persons. We let it be known that we only wanted the old unreason to go. It was not long before even the leader of the whipping party was having a colored man drive his own truck.

I have passed by on the other side so many times that I am unworthy of the great blessing that came to me on the coldest night of winter in 1917, when God put the pressure of circumstances and His good Spirit upon me so that I did on that night what all should do whenever near extreme human need.

One day when I was downtown at Byron, I heard some of the white men talking about a jealous colored husband who had tried to kill his wife with a knife, and had also tried to set fire to the house where they lived in order to burn her up. He fled in fear, but repented and came back, and was caring for his wife as best he could. A certain white man went to the home of these colored people because of the failure of the colored woman to return the washing given her by his wife. This frightened the colored man away, and the colored woman was left alone.

When I heard about it I took steps to have her looked after, first of all building a fire for her. The colored people agreed to care for her, and I felt that I had about enough money to pay Doctor Kline to look after her cuts and burns, and asked him to take charge and look after her needs. But, being a good-hearted man, he refused to accept a cent. He gave her a purgative and attended to her wounds. The colored people agreed to stay with her by turns.

Some of them stayed with her on Saturday night, others were to look after her on Sunday night. Sunday night was the coldest of the year. I was deeply interested at that time in reading one of the volumes of Paul Wernle's great work *The Beginnings of Christianity*, but God tugged heavily upon me to leave the warm fire and the book and go to the woman's home, some distance away, to make sure that she was being cared for.

It was given me to write in the book, "It is better to do what a good book says than it is to read a good book." I closed the book and made the necessary distance to the little shack where she lived. I found her all alone and without any fire in the house. God had caught me in an unusual situation and there was nothing left for me to do but look after her, acting as fire builder and nurse.

After providing a fire and looking after her immediate needs, I returned to the home of my brother to tell him that I would spend the night looking after her needs as best I could. My brother commended me warmly and offered to go with me. But as he had a cold and I wanted to spend my time quietly in devotion, I thanked him and accepted only the rich pine and coal with which he loaded me.

I was a poor nurse that night and had a difficult patient to deal with. But I realized that two lives hung in the balance, that if she was cared for and got well, her husband would escape being lynched or electrocuted.

Sometime before day came, the Spirit gave me an understanding of the good that would come out of the night's experience. Afterwards, the colored people took good care of the woman and she recovered. I believe this work helped many of the folks in Byron, but it taught me especially how really easy and inexpensive it is to do God's will of love.

In a previous chapter I have told how I was lifted out of what seemed to be approaching death when I reacted in terms of love. Before closing this chapter, let me share the miracle of love of my friend, Mrs. W. A. Scott. Her brother, Henry Davis, father of five unusual children, had died of consumption. His wife, a deeply spiritual woman, was also near death and much troubled as to what would become of the children. Mrs. Scott, then Miss Minnie Davis, and her older sister, Carro, told her to her great comfort that they would do the best they could for the children. Carro contracted the plague and soon died. That left Miss Minnie, as she was called, with the five children. Later she too was stricken and in the opinion of the doctor was likely to pass on as well. The doctor gave orders for the children to be kept out of the room where Miss Minnie was in bed with a high fever. Yet she had such great love for the children that she realized that she could not afford to leave them; she commanded that one of the children be kept in the room as far removed from her as possible, but within her sight, to remind her that she must get well and see them through.

Her love and her will to live enabled the God of love and life to lift her up and to make her well. She did magnificently by the five children and in doing so opened the way for almost unbelievable blessings to come to her.

There are no investments like the investments of pure love and mercy. When we expect nothing in return we receive the most and best of all.

CHAPTER III

THE WAY OF VICTORY BY LOVING
JUDGMENT

<<<<<<<<<<<<<<<<<<<<<<<<<<<<<>>>>>>>>>>>>>>>>>>>>>>>>>>

One Saturday morning in May, 1939, soon after I awoke
these words came to me: "He does not turn the light on to
hurt but to help. Happily for us we are going to be enabled
to see every fault, error, and imperfection of thought, of
word, and of act until these imperfections give place to His
perfection. It would be tragic for anyone to miss the judgment of enlightenment, to miss seeing everything that is to
be repented of and forsaken, and to miss seeing everything
that is to be attained to, perfect union with Jesus and His
perfect everything."

Soon after the above appeared in the *Macon Telegraph
and News*, a man of great ability and rare insight wrote me,
quoting the above and saying, "You've said it. That is the
key, I sincerely believe, to the mystery of life's chastenings."

We must see the whole truth, learn to love it, act upon
it, and become free. Nothing could be worse than to be
permitted to drop back into unconsciousness and fail to see
the truth about ourselves, God, and all things. As I understand the loving purpose of God, no one will be permitted
to escape His truth. Happy for us if we accept it and react to
it in joy. And according to my sense of values, God's victorious judgment of enlightenment, love, and mercy illu-
minates Him and His will and work in our behalf more
than anything that I have thus far been permitted to see.

What better could be done with an enemy than to make
him a friend, and especially to make him a friend of God

and of the whole of life? As good as it is for us, it is even better for him. While it is blessed to be persecuted for righteousness sake when met in God's wisdom and love, it is tragic to persecute. Even here as everywhere He is ever seeking to turn the persecutor into a disciple, turning his blindness into his own greatest good. As we have already seen, this is precisely the way He dealt with Saul of Tarsus, the chief of sinners and persecutors, making him a chief apostle, friend, and servant.

In like manner, there is nothing so good for one who is hard-hearted as to be dealt with in such a way as to melt him down into love. While it is best of all for him, it is also good for the rest of us. There is no limit to the possibilities of God and to the possibilities of all life when seen in the light of God's desiring and effort for the best.

This view of God and of life makes it easy to love even the worst of folks and to have faith for them. It makes it impossible to hate anyone or knowingly to work an ill to anyone. It enables you to see unlimited possibilities in everyone and even in the most tragic of situations. It enables you almost to envy the opportunity that even the very worst have to turn all that has been wrong in their attitudes and experiences to unbelievable good for themselves and for others.

It was this kind of love that the Lord poured out not only to Saul of Tarsus but to everyone who would open to it. What everyone has been outside of the Will of God is going to be reversed in the Will of God. This applies to the animal realm as well as to the human. In the achievement of God, the lion becomes the friend of the lamb, and the serpent the innocent plaything and protector of little children. "The wolf shall also crouch with the lamb. The leopard's lair shall be the kid's. The lion shall eat straw like an ox. Wolf and lion shall graze side by side herded by a little child; the cow and the bear shall be friends, and their young lie down together; the infant shall play at the hole of an asp, and the baby's feet at the nest of a viper, none shall injure, none shall kill anywhere." (Isaiah, 2:6-9, Moffat's trans.)

It was while I was in the midst of the tribes of the new Israel of the Spirit, discerning the Spirit of the kings of the various tribes, that I found myself even to my own surprise administering no judgment of condemnation to anyone, but judgments of enlightenment and love. The king of the serpents was to judge according to this new judgment. The king of the wolf tribe was to become a special friend and protector of the lambs and sheep. He was first of all to protect them from himself and from themselves, and from everything outside of their highest good. He was to Christianize his wolf tribe.

My friend who was first discerned as king of the wolf tribe, Frank Buglo, was later seen as an innocent collie. And, as Stanley Jones says, the innocent, friendly, and protective dog is the wolf who turned away from his own life and associates and went to following, befriending, and guarding man as his master.

Later Frank Buglo was seen in the light of the sun. In the light of the judgments of love and mercy for him, his Saul qualities which were at first very much in evidence, were to give place to Paul-like qualities. The ruling qualities were to give place to the ministries of light and love. The king was to become a servant and friend.

He has already moved far in line with these judgments of enlightenment, love, and mercy. He puts himself out more to get open doors and ears for me than any other of my friends. He is ready to drive me to great distances and tells all the groups he ministers to, to open their doors wide to me. He seems to have almost unlimited faith in God to use me to work His best everywhere he can get an opening for me.

Since the above was written early in June, 1939, Friend Frank has had a release and entered into a victory so fresh, joyous, and contagious that he and those to whom he ministers appear to be among the happiest and most victorious of the fellowships of the Spirit it is my privilege to know. This new experience came about this way. One night while tormented by an allurement of the imagination that the best in him hates and which even in thought brings defilement, he knelt and cried unto the Lord for deliverance. The Lord made known to him that He had already heard him.

A little later came the words, "I give you the victory right now." He felt as though new and warming blood streams coursed through his body. When spiritually led to look at his body, it appeared white as marble and his mind became pure as that of an innocent child. He was made aware that the body is the temple of God and must be kept pure. Then the heavenly fire came over his head and the glory of the Lord descended to his feet. When we are desperate enough, as Emerson says, the God of fire always answers. He began leaping, dancing, and praising the Lord in the Spirit, going through the house telling everyone about it.

Those who believe that victory is for them right now, rejoice and feel the resurrecting, cleansing power of the Holy Presence. When he went to the church next morning, the same thing occurred, and has been re-occurring wherever he has spoken of it to others. He has testified to many people in many states since that day, traveling as far West as Saint Louis on his mission.

At the time of this writing (January, 1940) he, and those who first believed with him, have had over seven weeks of this experience and their conviction is that God has given them the key of continuous overcoming. It is bringing new life, great joy, and miracles of bodily healing. They feel it is the answer to every present need, and are aware that it rightly requires them to walk in the Light and choose the Highest happily in every step of the upward way. Their hope is that the knowledge and experience of this "victory right now" will spread until the whole earth knows and enters into it.

In this ministry of enlightenment, it matters not what

one has done, nor in what spirit one has been heretofore; everything is turned to good when there is receptivity and response to the Perfect One. The worse the spirit and the greater evil that one has worked, the greater his destiny and services of helpfulness as he yields to the good spirit of the Lord.

A few years ago, I published an article in the *Macon Telegraph and News* on how God longs to turn all of our self-made and human-made hells into heavens on earth. I sought to set forth how He delights to take the worst people and make the best people out of them, the most miserable and make the happiest, and those in the worst hells at hand, and transfer them into places of greatest blessedness.

A good-hearted woman of Forsyth, Georgia, took a Sunday dinner to one of the prisoners there, wrapping it with the page of the *Telegraph* containing this article. I don't know whether it was intentional or not, but in a few days I had a remarkable letter from the prisoner, a mere boy, telling me that the light in the article opened the door of hope for him and that he had experienced a transfer from hell to Heaven.

One day when I was talking to the prisoners in the Bibb County Jail about God's loving judgment and will for them, a young man with a very bright face said that had he had this view of God and of life he would not have gone wrong.

He was a member of a good family, and had been a student at one of our large universities, having had unusual advantages in many ways. By yielding to temptation he had been caught in a vicious circle. He was enabled to see that all the evil he had yielded to and was being punished for could be turned to his own and others' good. He became the friend and intelligent helper of the other prisoners. He wrote their letters for them and was the bright and efficient man of the jail, and was especially sympathetic and helpful to men under sentence of death.

He was in jail here because of an attempt to pass three small worthless cheques. He was given two years on each of these cheques and the sentences were not allowed to be served concurrently; this heavy sentence was passed because of his past record.

The Georgia Prison Commission was informed of his unusual possibilities. They sought to deal wisely and helpfully with him, and notwithstanding his yielding to the temptation to try to get away, they continued to coöperate with me with the hope that he would make good. Later one of the commissioners suggested that I and others write to the prosecuting attorney of his native state, asking if he would not waive the claims of that state and let him have an opportunity to go free as soon as the prison commission and the governor paroled him.

I made a trip to see the prosecuting attorney. Before I reached Atlanta he had wired the prison commission that the city and state he represented would not press claims against the young man, who was soon given his liberty. An unusually fine man, Wilbur Collins, gave him a position, after I explained to him the former history and the possibilities of the young man. He did his work well and was greatly liked.

One Sunday afternoon he rented a car to take a ride, with no intention of stealing it he told me later, but found the lure of the road so great that he returned to his native state and soon married a very fine girl. He then told her the wrong he had done. She advised him strongly to go at once to the authorities and surrender himself. This was in his favor. A United States marshal brought him to Macon. When I called to see him at the Bibb County Jail, he said the hardest ordeal of all was facing me.

I reminded him that he could yet make good, that while he had made it harder for himself, the victory would become all the greater even though made harder.

He told me about his fine wife and her insistence upon coming to Macon to be near him and to help him, but feeling that it would be accepting too much from her, he had advised her not to come. She came anyway. I told friends at the Macon Cafeteria about her; they gave her a position as a waitress. She soon secured a better paying position.

She impressed the United States District Judge and the assistant prosecuting attorney so favorably that they agreed with me that the young man, with her help, could yet make good. He was given a suspended sentence. Since then he has climbed and climbed and I was informed today that he is at the head of one of the departments of a big business, drawing a salary of $3,500 a year.

This understanding of God's loving judgment has been most helpful to me in dealing with people who felt that they had "crossed the dead line" and were "doomed."

About a year and half ago I was called to see a man who had fallen in the depths of despair and said he could not pray. I prevailed upon him to ask Jesus to come with him and do His best possible for and with him, and for those he loved. I succeeded in getting him to repeat the words after me.

It was only a few minutes before the powers of darkness which had laid hold upon him were being broken and he prayed the sublimest prayer that I have ever heard fall from human lips. It was more like the prayer of Jesus in Gethsemane than any other I have heard. God delivered him, of course, and within a few months his life was utterly transformed.

While he was in the depths of despair, his wife asked me to pray, and I went to the closet and closed the door. The Spirit took my tongue and said, "I will heal him." Instructions were given for him to be kept at home, though the doctors had advised treatment in a hospital and offered small hope for recovery.

About eight months ago I received a letter out of deep depression from a genius whom one of his doctors compares with Keats. He writes poetry of insight and exquisite beauty. The letter urged me to come to him as quickly as I could, although I had been to see him a short time before. It did not seem that I could make the trip again, but God kept tugging at me and put on so much pressure that I decided to go.

When I took the bus for the little city where he has been in a hospital much of the time for the past thirty years, the Lord put me in almost unbelievable joy. When I reached the hospital, the doctor in charge told me that he was glad that I had come, that my friend was in a deeper despair than he had ever seen him, that he refused to see most people, but he believed he would be glad to see me.

"Moseley," he said, "I am lost." I replied, "You are nearer salvation that I have ever seen you. Jesus came and is here in the Spirit to seek and to save the lost." The friend told me how terribly he had sinned and acted the hypocrite. He said that he hated his mouth and his tongue so greatly for having been the organs of falsehood that he could scarcely keep from doing physical violence to them. I reminded him of the words, "If we confess our sins, He is gracious and merciful to forgive us of our sins and to cleanse us from all unrighteousness." (I John, 1:9) "And," I added, "I have never heard anyone confess his sins more searchingly than you are doing." This brought a smile to his face, and he said, "Moseley, is that possible?"

I remained with him for an hour and a half to two hours, and it appeared that I had been given the right answer to all of his questions. The things that I was enabled to give him made such an appeal that he wrote many of them down, that he might have them with him if dark hours came again. By the time I left, he had become quiet and I felt sure that God had started a work in him that would never end and would bring forth in him the divine likeness.

I receive wonderful letters from him, most of which are requests for prayers for those he is seeking to help. He has moved out of the realm of self pity and condemnation into the realm of love. A grand move.

Recently, I have seen him again. He now has the freedom

of the hospital, its spacious grounds and the little city where the hospital is located. He is one of the happiest of humans and is glowing with health.

Nearly two years ago, when he reached such low depths of despair, his health was gone and he had not had a normal bowel elimination for years. Since we prayed together for Jesus to come and reign in the whole of his spirit, mind, soul, and body, including every function and cell of his body, his health, he tells me, "has become unbelievably good" and his "bowel action and elimination perfect."

When I was at Mars Hill Retreat about four years ago, the pastor of the First Baptist Church in one of the North Carolina cities told me that he had been pastor of his church so long that he felt that it should have a new pastor. I replied, "Why not become such a new man in Christ that the church would have a new pastor without having to change pastors?"

He did it, or the Lord did it for him, or they did it jointly. It became the common observation among his church members "Our church has a new pastor." Their pastor became so new in comparison with most other pastors, that he was called by the State Board of Baptist Activities to go over North Carolina seeking to make new pastors and new churches out of old ones.

CHAPTER IV

THE WAY TO PEACE

<<<<<<<<<<<<<<<<<<<<<<<<<<<<<<<>>>>>>>>>>>>>>>>>>>>>>>>>>>>>>>

The spirit and techniques of Jesus are ways of peace and peace making. Outside of Jesus we are outside of the realm of peace, and in the realm of confusion and disturbance. We cannot bring estranged individuals and groups together unless we love every one of them. We cannot be at peace with anyone until we love him. The One who loves all superlatively and has the wisdom and grace of love is the Prince of Peace and Peace Makers.

We are peace makers to the degree that we are in union with Him and are manifesting His love, wisdom, and grace. Everyone is a mischief maker to the degree that he yields to the spirit that judges, condemns, and hates. Everyone is in and of the spirit to which he yields, so long as he yields. Jesus called Peter Satan when he was yielding to Satan and voicing his spirit. He calls everyone of us His beloved as we yield to His spirit and cease to yield to every opposite spirit. As the wise Emerson says, "The devil nestles comfortably" in good laws, constitutions, and even in Bibles; in fact, in everything except the good Spirit. If he were to yield to this Spirit he wouldn't be the devil.

So long as there is will misdirected, or a grievance, or even a secret pleasure in any evil coming to anyone, there is a hindrance to the in-flow and the out-flow of the love and peace of God. Love and peace are inseparable. To have peace that is continuous we must keep our minds on what is all-important—vital union with Jesus and the bearing of fruit of this union, which is love, out of which comes joy, peace, and every good.

The Spirit that gives peace and makes one a peace maker is utterly loving, compassionate, merciful, kind, patient, and forgiving, the Spirit that knows no jealousy; the Spirit that is never glad when anyone goes wrong, but is gladdened by any light and goodness coming from or to anyone; the Spirit that is always slow to expose and eager to believe the best; the Spirit that never grumbles or complains; the Spirit that is always optimistic as to God's love and love-way triumphing and all the more because of every hindrance; the Spirit that keeps on loving and increasing in love, hope, and faith with every trial of its hope, faith, and love; the Spirit that knows no discouragement, no defeat, no failure—that is the Spirit.

As Sundar Singh, seemingly more Christ-like than any other recent disciple of Jesus, has so happily put it, "The peace of God that passeth understanding also giveth all understanding." Even on the human plane it takes the spirit and will to peace, even to begin to understand anybody or anything. You cannot understand except in good will, which is the key to the Kingdom and to the hearts of all men. The God of love and good will gives us the keys to all doors as fast as we are ready to enter them.

It would be tragic to have power beyond love, wisdom, and goodness. We need not trouble ourselves about receiving power or understanding. Both will come to us as we are ready for their right use. Understanding, peace, and power to make peace, will be ours as fast as we are made ready for them.

My experience has shown me that the following are the great principles of making peace:—

(1) Pray for the Spirit of Jesus, the Great and Perfect Peace Maker

He is our peace and we are peace makers to the degree we yield to Him. The prayer for the Spirit of Jesus is always heard and answered, and is the one thing that makes and reveals a real disciple of Jesus. If you have the Spirit of

Jesus you belong to Him; if you do not have His good Spirit, no matter how loud you say, "Lord, Lord," you do not belong to Him. One belongs always to Jesus and to Heaven when always manifesting Their Spirit. You can abide continually in Heavenly places by yielding to and manifesting the Spirit of Jesus. He gives this ability to everyone who desires it, who offers himself to be its incarnation and channel of blessing.

(2) Forgive All

As Jesus puts it: When you stand praying, or kneel, or are flat on your face, before the Lord, forgive if you have aught against any, that your Father also, which is in Heaven, may forgive you your trespasses.

God's gifts of love and forgiveness and peace are such that, for them to flow into us freely, they must flow out freely from us to all. We can have all the love, peace, joy, and everything else of God that we are willing to pass on and share. We cannot continue to receive love and give out hate. This is the deepest law of life; to have anything from God as a continuous possession, we have to become channels for its out-flow and the out-flow is even more blessed than the in-flow. We would never be educated in Jesus' way, if this were not true. It would be tragedy for us if we could be in His peace with being His peace makers.

(3) Seek the Forgiveness of All

As Jesus advises and commands, "If thou bringest thy gift to the altar and there rememberest that thy brother hath aught against you, leave there thy gift before the altar and go thy way; first be reconciled to thy brother, and then come and offer thy gift."

H. C. Morrison once expressed it in this manner while preaching in Miami: "If you have left an unpaid grocery bill or jumped your house rent in Macon, and are in the act of putting a dime in the collection plate at Miami, return to Macon and pay the debts you owe to your brothers and then come and offer your gift, and I will receive it."

The great truth is that you must render unto man what belongs to man. You have to forgive and seek forgiveness to the fullest limit of possibility to be in the peace of God and in undisturbed union with Jesus.

In all of my experience I have never found one who refused to forgive me and to be at peace with me when I desired it enough so as to be willing to go as far as the Lord led and enabled me to go. One must humble himself by seeking forgiveness and by keeping on seeking until he receives it. The person who has not forgiven us is being hurt most of all and for his sake we must be ready to humble ourselves, even if it requires going the second mile and turning the other cheek. There is no Heaven here or anywhere for the unforgiving, though one who has gone as far as God requires in seeking forgiveness may still have the forgiveness of God, although it should be refused by men. But I have never found a case of refusal. Many of the finest experiences of my life have been the victories of love when I refused to let offended persons alone until they forgave me and loved me better than before. "Love never faileth." If the quality of love you have shown has not brought victory, keep on increasing and improving it until the victory comes.

(4) Never Talk About, but Talk to, Those You Would Help

Jesus says: "If your brother shall trespass against thee, go and tell him his fault between thee and him alone; if he shall hear thee thou hast gained thy brother. But if he will not hear thee, then take with thee one or two more, that in the mouth of two or three witnesses every word may be established, and if he should neglect to hear them, tell it unto the church; but if he neglect to hear the church, let him be unto thee as an heathen man and a publican."

As I understand Jesus, after we as individuals, and as two or three united, and as the church united, fail to win a brother, we stand a better chance of winning him by

working for him as an outsider. In my own experience I
have found it wisest, most loving, and effective never even
to hint to others that anyone has missed the way until I
have done my best to get him right. When I have failed by
going alone—and it is very rarely that I have failed when
I have gone in the love and wisdom of Jesus—I have found
it most effective as well as most loving not to tell others
until in his presence. By this technique of love in dealing
with him, he is the easier won. Love is very wise, very
"foxy," and very considerate, and apart from the spirit and
and techniques of love there could be no successful peace
making.

There have been only two instances where I have found
it necessary to take matters to the church. These were cases
of unlawful love affairs. There is nothing that one holds
on to so persistently as forbidden fruit, until it becomes
bitter. By going all the way prescribed by Jesus and required
by love, victory came at last in these two cases.

You cannot be a peace maker until you get your tongue
and spirit under control, under God's control and under
self-control. The way the members of ordinary religious
groups talk about each other makes them too impotent
even to discipline a member without doing him and themselves more harm than good. So long as a church is more
in the spirit, mind, and technique of the world, than in the
mind and Spirit of Jesus, it is under seeming necessity of
letting the tares and the wheat grow together until the Lord
through his angels makes the separation. The church has to
be, "a real colony of Heaven" in order to have the wisdom
and authority of binding and releasing. The work of the
Lord cannot be done except in His spirit, love, wisdom,
and authority.

(5) You Must Be a Friend of All

The Christian fight is for the good of everybody, and is
not against anyone. It was precisely because Jesus so greatly
loved God and man that He could be used to bring them

together. Whenever anyone loves estranged parties greatly
enough he becomes God's agent to bring them together. Any
taking of sides one against another is fatal to successful
peace making. We have to take the side of the best in
everyone as against the worst. To love the sin and hate the
sinner is satanic; to love the sinner so well that you hate
the sins that blind and defile and bind him is Christ-like.

There is nothing more precious about the way of Jesus
than this, that He makes one the friend and lover of every
man, woman, and child in the whole world, and only an
enemy of their enemies. Our battle is for all flesh and
blood and against all the enemies of everyone. In this spirit
and understanding, it is easy to love and bless, even where
you are hated and persecuted. We only want the destroyer
destroyed that those who are being destroyed may be saved
and, under the Divine Savior, become saviors. As long as
one sees and fights evil as a person he cannot be in peace
himself nor be a peace maker.

(6) Make No Arbitrary Commands

The teachings of the Spirit and of Jesus are not arbitrary
commands, but revelations of the Spirit and laws of life.
They were true before announced and if all the Bibles that
have recorded them should be destroyed, they would still
be true. Happily, every teaching of Jesus and of the Spirit
for the time being focuses the whole of REALITY. When
you really comprehend any word of Heavenly light, the
Heavenly Kingdom has been implanted. The Cross is the
symbol of the whole of God. The sword is the symbol of
the whole of Satan. Jesus is love and works by love. The
weapon of love is the Cross.

(7) Be Ready Always to Go the Second Mile; Never Contend Over Such Trifles as Money

Do not contend over the many things that people quarrel
and go to war over. Remember the wisdom of Robert E. Lee

voiced to his estranged generals, Stonewall Jackson and A. P. Hill, "The one who is least in error will take the first step towards reconciliation."

The Kingdom of Heaven is of such infinite value that we can happily let go everything that keeps us on the outside of it. To be in peace and love with a neighbor or an enemy is of such high worth that one should not allow such things as houses, or lands, or position ever to become matters of contention. If we are wise, we will give two dollars where only one is demanded, be glad to go two miles where only one is asked, and happily meet all requirements of God to be in His peace and to be at peace with one another.

(8) Get Everything and Lose Nothing of Value

By going Jesus' way, we have only to give up our enemies and we get everything. Instead of having a hard time in His way, we have an easy time. In going with Jesus we give up nothing worth keeping and become heirs to all. Next to the blessedness of full overcoming, are the blessings of the overcoming life. We have so much Heaven going to Heaven, or rather in coöperating with Jesus to bring Heaven on earth, that we are already in Heaven while being used to bring Heaven.

If people persecute you because you are going Jesus' way and have His presence and the gifts of the Spirit, then you can rejoice and be all the more in the Kingdom of Heaven. But be sure what you call your persecutions are purely for His sake and not for the pride of making yourself a martyr.

(9) Confess for Yourself Only

Never explain a failure where you are in any way responsible for it in terms of the failure of others. Confess freely your own faults and talk all you will about how you could and should have done better; but don't talk of other people's failures. For others to get good rather than evil out

of their past failures, they have to do the confessing themselves. Never throw up benefits, nor fail to be grateful for
any benefit that has come to you from anyone.

(10) Watch the Spiritual Thermometer

Every time I have desired and sought above all else to be
in conscious union with Jesus and in the peace and joy of
His Presence, I have had a spiritual thermometer, as it
were, that has enabled me to know how every thought, feeling, word, and act related itself to the increase or the
decrease of His conscious Presence and joy. So we are
taught by all experience, and everything works together
for our good. We not only have an external New Testament,
but an internal one. We know the things that make for
peace and can have all the peace of God that we are willing
to pass on to others.

CHAPTER V

THE WAY OF UTTER SINCERITY

‹‹‹‹‹‹‹‹‹‹‹‹‹‹‹‹‹‹‹‹‹‹‹‹‹‹‹›››››››››››››››››››››››

Truth in the high sense Jesus uses it is both the highest reality and the consciousness of this reality. It comes to us through the obedience of love. It sets us free from every form of bondage. The Spirit of truth is the Spirit of revelation guiding into all the truth. The Spirit of utter sincerity and truthfulness working by love opens our understanding and makes us good soil for the planting of the Heavenly seed and for bringing forth the Heavenly harvest.

As Maurice Maeterlinck puts it, "In owning our faults we disown them, and in confessing our sins they cease to be ours." The devil cannot stand for the full light of truth to be turned on in wisdom and love. He will go almost anywhere else with you, but not to full confession.

I have found in dealing with people, no matter what crimes they have committed, that whenever they have freely confessed them, they were set free from condemnation. When one tells freely on himself, not on others, he also calls forth sympathy and often secures forgiveness from others.

In the summer of 1905 or 1906 a young man came to see me whose face and bearing registered deep unhappiness. He told me that he had learned to steal in an orphanage where he had been sent after the death of his father and mother. When he was a student at Davidson College, North Carolina, he had stolen from everyone who had befriended him, including the president of the college.

When he came to Macon he asked money of Pastor

Rutherford Douglass of the First Presbyterian Church. Douglass, instead of giving him money, took him to his home. While in the home he stole some jewelry. After putting these facts before me he asked, "What would you advise me to do?" I told him that the highest for him to do was to write to all the parties that he could not see personally, telling each of them the truth and asking for the opportunity to make restitution as soon as he could get a position that would enable him to do so. He replied, "I am going to do it." I furnished him the paper and envelopes. As I remember, he brought me fourteen letters to post. Everyone he had stolen from forgave him and forgave the debt, and wished him well. Mr. Oscar Crockett, when he heard what the young man had done, offered to give him a position. The boy made good and told me years afterward that the full confession and the offer to make restitution cured him from even the desire to steal.

During the time I was dealing with this young man, another young man had been coming to see me rather frequently who said that he was seeking to regain his health. Providentially I told him about the other young man and how the telling of the truth had brought forgiveness and a position. He replied, "Dishonesty is my trouble." He explained that he had been appropriating for personal use some of the money due his employer. He added, "I am so miserable over the matter that it has made me sick." He left me saying that he was going to his former employer whom he had been defrauding and tell him the truth. In a few days he came back and reported that the good man, when he told him the truth, looked at him and said, "Do you want your old job back as collector?" The young man replied, "You couldn't trust me, could you?" He answered, "I had rather have a young man who has come clean as you have done, than to take chances with a new one." He was given such release and joy that his sickness disappeared.

Near that time, as my memory serves me, by seeking to use the technique of love and wisdom, the technique of

Jesus, I had the joy of seeing what might have developed into bad scandal nipped in the bud and bringing a blessing to all concerned.

In a certain city a young lady informed me that a young married man had said something to her that was not just the proper thing. I sent for the young man. He denied it. I next asked for the young man and his wife and the young lady and her sister to meet me at a certain place where our meeting would not attract attention or suspicion.

When we met I read from the Sermon on the Mount and we all knelt in silent prayer. Then the young man arose and said, "I did not tell you the truth this morning. The young lady did." He expressed deep regret for the thing he had said to the young lady and for not having told me the truth. That ended the whole matter. Nobody outside of the five ever had any hint of it. The way it was handled and the fine reaction on the part of all concerned worked much good to all.

In June, 1930, Willie Green was electrocuted at the State Farm. He was quoted in the papers as having said when he was brought to the State Farm about three days before he was to be electrocuted that he was not expecting any help except from God. This made a deep appeal to me.

I reached the State Farm early on the day set for his electrocution. He had confessed to the killing of not only the person he was sentenced for, but also of another person. God put him in such a spirit of release and good will that he was much concerned that no one else should suffer for any of the crimes that he had committed, so he was very careful to confess them all.

A few hours before he was to be electrocuted, when the colored men came in the death cell and commenced singing, he fell on his face and gave thanks that God had brought him to the place where he could face the death chair "unafraid." As he marched into the death chamber toward the death chair, he was singing "Amazing Grace." When he was strapped in the chair and soon before the death lever was pulled he said, "I see the angels coming for me." The truth that works by love had freed him from fear, even the fear of death, and seemingly had brought him to that place in God where he passed out of his natural body into his spiritual body without having any sense of dying.

Early in November, 1932, a father and son of a prominent North Georgia family were at the Georgia State Farm to be electrocuted. I was asked by relatives to be present with them on the day set for their electrocution. I went very early and was told upon arriving that the young man had made an effort to cut his throat with a safety razor blade a very sort time before I arrived. He almost succeeded. I had not been with him long before he told me the story of his crime in ghastly detail. It was not premeditated, but resulted from a quarrel and a fight growing out of a card game. His father, he said, had nothing to do with the killing and only helped in the effort to hide the bodies. If they had told the truth from the beginning, the son would most likely have received not more than a life sentence and the father only a few years' imprisonment. By denying any connection with the killings and by seeking to fasten them upon an innocent party, they both received the death sentence. The jury suspected the worst and gave them the worst.

After the young man confessed completely and asked the Lord for forgiveness, he entered into joy and release. The Governor of Georgia was making political speeches in North Carolina on the day of the execution. The authorities at the State Farm put off the electrocution until near the last minute in order to put the matter before the Governor. As I could not get to the Governor myself, I pled with the doctor to advise him to put off the electrocution, which he could have done until time for the young man's confession to produce its right reaction. But the word came from the Governor to proceed with the electrocution if the young man's physical condition made his electrocution possible.

I talked to the father, who was nearest to the death chamber, while his son was carried in the arms of one of the prisoners and put in the death chair. The father was about the saddest looking man into whose face I have ever looked. He said to me, "Surely I cannot be condemned for having tried to help my boy." After the son was put in the death chair he sent a message to his father telling him "good-bye" and that he was "ready to go," and that he hoped that his father was also ready.

The truth told even at that late hour brought to the young man release, joy, the witness of forgiveness, and the assurance of eternal life.

It has been my good fortune to see many forgiven by society after they had told the truth, and gave promise of giving themselves to the Good Life. This usually occurs when the offenses are not extreme and almost always occurs when the person has the grace and wisdom to confess and ask forgiveness in advance of having been accused. It is glorious to tell on yourself and the quicker you tell the better. When society refuses to forgive and show mercy, God shows all the more mercy and gives all the greater victories. All who tell all and forgive all, are forgiven all. The truth told in love never fails to bring release, freedom, joy, and often bliss, ecstasy, and glory.

Utter sincerity in dealing with ourselves makes us merciful in dealing with others; after we dare to see the worst in ourselves and to share it with others, we are set free from the temptation to be hard on others. The people who are hard on others have been too light on themselves. It is nearly impossible for them to keep from suspecting in others the bad they know about themselves.

The people who have power have come to sincerity. After you have brought yourself to the light and the whole of your life into the fresh air of confession and have gone to walking in the light, you will also enter into marvelous fellowship with Jesus Christ. The Spirit of Jesus Christ and the love of Jesus Christ cleanses you from your sins. There is no cleansing for those who live in the dark. If it were possible to cleanse them by their continuing in darkness, they would soon be dirty again. In the light there is only love and forgiveness and cleansing. The light has no condemnation even for the darkness; but as long as one remains in the dark, he is condemned by the darkness. The life of the Spirit in Jesus entirely frees from the law of sin, condemnation, deadness, dryness, and death.

Moreover, those who attain to sincerity are invariably alive and interesting, those who are insincere are dull and uninteresting. The truth makes you alive, makes you interesting and makes you free. It gives a mastery and charm all its own. It also gives a delightful sense of humor. I believe it was Mark Twain who said that he did not mean to be humorous, he just told the truth and for such a rarity people went to laughing. The truth told in good spirit causes the mind to laugh and the spirit to rejoice.

Sometime in 1931, as I remember, this interesting and humorous thing occurred at the Georgia State Farm. The sheriff of one of our Georgia counties brought to the State Farm for electrocution a man by the name of Gay. The sheriff had such faith in Gay that instead of delivering him to the officials, he bade him good-bye outside of the prison gates and without saying a word to anybody, drove off toward home.

Gay finally managed to get by the gate-keeper and enter the prison. After he had warmed himself by the stove of the officials, one of them asked him, "Is there anything that we can do for you?" Gay replied, "Well, I am up here to be electrocuted."

The officials not only had a good laugh about it, but thought it too good to keep among themselves and shared it with the *Macon Telegraph*. The *Telegraph* played it up as first page news. I sent the story to the Governor and said in my letter to him "that a man of such daring honesty as Gay's does not belong in the electric chair." He and the Prison Commission and the public generally must have felt the same way. Gay was not electrocuted. The last time I saw him, he was a trusty and one of the gate-keepers at the old State Farm.

As E. Stanley Jones has said, there are three grades of laughter, the first being the laughing at one's own jokes, the second being the laughing at other people's jokes, and the third laughing at one's own self. A still higher type of laughter is the laughter of joy, the laughter of victory, the kind of laughter that filled the mouth of the Children of Israel when they returned from captivity to Zion. There is, too, a high laughter at the stupidity of the devil. And there is a laughter in the Spirit when God admits the spirit into seeing the happy things of Heaven that might give offense to the mind. There are things so good that our intellect might be afraid of them. With me both my spirit and my mind are permitted to enjoy already some of the high humor and laughter of Heaven and of Jesus' way of turning the laughter of wisdom, love, and victory upon all enemies for the purpose of doing them all possible good. You can't laugh the laugh of Heaven until you enter into the boundless good will of Heaven.

The wisdom and divine humor of God is seen in how He has outdone everything, in the interest of everything, in its effort to escape His loving purpose. To achieve what he imagines to be his own interests man will resort to complicated schemes which in the end only increase his troubles, whereas the essentially simple scheme of God lies right before us as large as life and just as visible if we will only look with the eyes of little children and not insist, in adult pride, that everything be as complicated as possible. After all, the universe is fool proof, but the joke is that only the fool does not see it. Happily, when he comes to himself, even the fool will laugh at himself for his tremendous and futile effort to outwit God and his own good. Then he can share with the laughter of the love of God, which brings man to wisdom even through his own folly.

Once when I was in Evansville, Indiana, ministering in much joyous laughter, a teacher of a Bible school stood up saying, "Mr. Moseley, I want to ask your forgiveness. The first time I heard you I was offended at your laughter and did not come back. My wife kept on coming and has been much blessed. I had had the feeling that true religion could not be so joyous and have so much laughter in it." I replied in effect that I had wondered about all this laughter myself, but if we wanted to continue to laugh we knew where not to go, the way that leads to weeping and bitter tears, and we knew the way to go, the way of love and good will to each and to all. Then Frank Buglo read these verses from Psalm 126:

"When the Eternal brought the exiles back to Zion,
We were like men who dreamed:
Laughter filled our lips,
Shouts of joy were on our tongues;
The very heathen said,
'The Eternal has done great things for them.'
Yes, he had done great things for us,
And we rejoiced at it."

(Moffatt's translation)

In this instance as well as in many others, the Lord first gave me the experience of the thing that is biblically orthodox and later made known that it was biblical. All who go His way of love and of immediate discipleship, know each other and greet each other across the centuries. You must be led by the Spirit and have the experiences of the Bible to understand them. Study without practice does not get anyone anywhere except into the dryness, deadness, and hardness of the letter.

The Spirit gives life and only those led by the Spirit come up into divine sonship.

CHAPTER VI

THE WAY OF JOY, BLISS, AND GLORY

‹‹‹‹‹‹‹‹‹‹‹‹‹‹‹‹‹‹‹‹‹‹‹‹‹‹‹‹‹››››››››››››››››››››››››››

Joy, bliss, and glory are the blessedness of being in union with Jesus, living with Him in the Spirit and the in-flow and out-flow of His love. Jesus, while taking upon Himself our sorrows and burdens and sins and diseases and mortality in order to give us His holiness, health, and immortality, had even unto the shadow of the cross so much peace and joy that He gave both as possessions to His disciples. After explaining to His friends that they must be in the same close union with Him that He was with the Father and as the fruitful branches are with the vine, in order to bring forth the fruit of Heaven, and that they must love each other as He loves them, He tells them, "I've told you this that my joy may be within you and that your joy may be complete."

After Jesus conquered death and all that causes and goes with death and ascended into the fourth realm, union with Him has meant all the joy and bliss and glory anyone has been capable of receiving and manifesting. Luke tells us, "The disciples were filled with joy and with the Holy Ghost." As W. E. Moody says, "They were filled with joy because filled with the Holy Ghost. Where one is the other is also." Joy is not excitement or mere emotion. "It is calm delight." As Moody puts it, "To be joyful is to be calmly happy."

It is even better to be in union with Jesus today than it was yesterday and it will be still better tomorrow. We are enriched by the every experience of Jesus and will be increasingly so forever. We will also be enriched by every enrichment of everyone in union with Him. New qualities of joy will be continuously ours who are in fellowship with Jesus and with each other.

I realize that by His grace and by my late coming I have a quality of joy and bliss that far better friends of Jesus who came earlier did not have. Everyone entering in these late hours of God's great harvest-day receives something new which he contributes to all the rest. In this perfect way of Jesus, the last and the least become the first and the greatest in their contribution to all the rest.

Jesus gives the joyous way of seeing and reacting. Even those who came before Him in time but walked in His light, the "light that lighteth every man coming into the world," had a measure of His wise, kind way of meeting the disagreeable with the desirable. Socrates had so much of His spirit and enlightenment that some of the earlier Christians referred to him as "a Christian born out of due time." Socrates knew that no evil could befall a good man anywhere, so he was not disturbed by anything that his age did to him. One could even detect a note of thanksgiving in Socrates that it was he, and not some other man, who married the quarrelsome Xantippe. He was aware that he knew much better how to deal with her and get good out of being her husband than would any other man of his time. Socrates never complained of anything, not even that his fellow citizens voted his death because he was such a spiritual gadfly that he made them uncomfortable in their way of life. Plato, his greatest pupil, seeing how Athens dealt with her best citizen and the best man he ever knew, prophesied with great accuracy that when the perfectly just man appeared he would be sent to the cross.

In our own days, Emerson, a rare union of the wise humanist and of the Christian spirit, delights us and causes our minds to be perpetually smiling, often laughing, at the way he saw and reacted towards the whole drama of life. This wise and kindly way of seeing and reacting produces the highest kind of humor. In this sense, Emerson is our greatest humorist. More recently the finest qualities of insight that have come to us through men like Mark Twain and George Bernard Shaw have been due to the leavening of the mind and Spirit of Jesus.

The finest insights and attitudes everywhere are essentially Christian. Many of the plays of Shaw you would not care to read at all, were it not for the flashes of wisdom that are profoundly and brilliantly Christian. Shaw has said substantially, "Men who did not understand Jesus nailed Him to a stick of wood, but somehow he got hold of the right end of the stick and if we are ever going to have a decent world, it will have to be in terms of what Jesus sought to make it"; and is forever seeking to make it, we should add.

In whatever befalls us, the way we react and act toward it is all-important. It is not what we have done or been, but the way we feel about it and what we would do now, that counts. Even in the physical realm it is the use that we make of things that determines our place in the natural kingdom as well as in the spiritual. People may even sink and drown in a thing so excellent as water. But this is not the normal use of water. In the realm where Jesus lived and is leading us as we follow on, water is just as good to walk upon as the solid earth. In like manner, people will sink in despair in a situation that is just opportunity for another. We are here to be educated to meet everything in the right spirit and turn it to our good and to the good of all the rest. As we do this, our joy is beyond bounds. To the overcomer, everything is opportunity.

On the way to perfect everything which is our high call and predestination, we may have the joyous assurance that everything is working together for our good and that even when we fail to choose His best there is always provided the necessary whale to preserve us from drowning until we repent, rededicate ourselves, and call on our God. Then we are spewed out on dry ground and given the new chance.

Even what we call the present is not determined by the past nearly so much as what we call the past is determined by the present. As we become new, the present, past, and future become new with us. Since what we call the past and the future are part of the present, all redemption must be in the present. That the present not only gives interpretation and meaning to the past, but actually determines it, would have to be true for the Kingdom of Heaven to be at hand as a present possibility for everyone desiring to enter and willing to repent of and leave on the outside everything that has kept him on the outside.

If the past determined the present, only those who had in the past conformed to the laws of the Kingdom could enter; but if the present determines the past, it is what we desire, will, think, and do at this moment that determines the effect of our past upon others as well as upon ourselves. The Kingdom is open always to all ready to yield and respond to Jesus and to His good Spirit and to His way of life as love.

Those early Christians were so much in the Spirit that sees and reacts wisely and joyfully that if they lost their money or had their goods despoiled they would shout about it, so rich were they with imperishable riches. You could do the worst to them, and they would give thanks for the privilege of suffering with Christ. They realized that the needs of their persecutors were so especially great that they sought to manifest to them an unusual measure of the love of Christ that they too might be brought to Him and to His salvation. This kept the early Christians hidden away in Christ and made them lights to those in darkness.

There was nothing you could do to those early Christians who were in the Spirit of Jesus and in His victory without adding to their joy. Consider, for example, Saint Paul. It did not matter how much suffering was put upon him, you would hear him singing out, that afflictions which are light and but for a moment are working all the greater glory, while we look to the perfect unseen which is eternal and which changes the things that are seen more and more into its own likeness. If it looked as if he would lose his body he rejoiced at the thought of entering his spiritual body. Still he recognized that it was preferable for his imperfect house or body to be "clothed upon" rather than unclothed, so that all that was mortal might be swallowed up by life.

God is to be tremendously glorified and the Kingdom of Heaven immeasurably enriched by the Lord's redemption extending to the visible body and the visible universe. But happy is one in union with Jesus, for if he leaves his body here, he will come back for it later. His resurrected and immortal body will give concrete expression to his Spirit and spiritual body.

When the early Christians were martyred they had a way of facing martyrdom in such admirable spirit that they were not only kept in heavenly places in Jesus, but often won to the faith and love of Jesus the very ones who put them to death.

In the Spirit of Jesus and in fellowship with Him there is a joy and a bliss that nothing can take away. The martyrs who met their martyrdom in the Spirit of Jesus, even while in the lions' mouths or while being stoned, were in much of the joy and bliss and glory that Jesus entered into after His resurrection, ascension, and glorification.

Stephen, the first martyr and possibly the first disciple ready to meet martyrdom in the love of Jesus, was permitted to see Jesus while being stoned. No wonder that Stephen's face shone like an angel's.

Christianity spread because these early disciples were so in the Spirit of Jesus that they converted their persecutors. The early Christians knew that whether they lived or died, they were the Lord's, and were assured that even if they did not come to the bodily likeness of Jesus through ascension they would through resurrection.

The tragedy of most present-day persecution arises from the fact that the persecuted do not have enough of the love and the Presence of Jesus to convert their persecutors.

Suffering has to be done in love to have vicarious virtue. Suffering without love is tragedy. Suffering with love is salvation, not only for those who suffer, but also for those who cause the suffering.

We are not ready for manifest victory until we have the Spirit of victory in seeming defeat, we are not ready for Heaven at hand until we are so disciplined and yielded to Jesus that we manifest Him in His love under sorest trials and temptations. As Campbell Morgan once suggested in a sermon on "Our God is a Consuming Fire," the same fire that is bliss and Heaven for the saint, might be hell fire to the unpurified, until purified.

Those who are poor in spirit, those who feel their utter dependence upon Jesus, those who look to Him and yield to Him, realizing they are nothing apart from Him, but everything in union with Him, are already in the Kingdom of Heaven. Those who are persecuted for righteousness' sake because of their likeness and not because of their unlikeness to Jesus, those who love back and bless back, and meet all evil with good are already in the Kingdom of Heaven. The Kingdom of Heaven as a present experience is righteousness and love and peace and joy and bliss and glory right in the midst of the Kingdoms of this world.

Tolstoi, who failed to find Jesus in the popular churches and in the conventional life of his aristocratic associates, found Him in the lives of the humble and in the New Testament. Before he found Him he said he desired to die, and was sorely tempted to make the effort to get out of life. His son told me some years ago that at that period of his father's life, his father and the family sought to have all weapons of destruction kept out of reach.

But the elder Tolstoi found every time he was tempted to commit suicide that before he made the attempt the thought of God would come to his mind and with the thought of God would come the desire to live. Finally the revelation came to him that since the thought of God gives the desire to live and takes away the desire to die, GOD

IS LIFE, and with this revelation the desire to die was taken away never to return.

I have found the Lord everywhere I have looked for Him, and especially in sick rooms, in prisons, in death cells, and in every meeting of evil with good.

I have seen the Spirit of Jesus enable ignorant colored boys who had committed murder and were under sentence of death to make their execution day fearless, joyous, and victorious.

Lucius Jolley, a young colored man with very little education and a low order of mentality, and who at times suffered fits resembling epileptic seizures, received the death sentence for killing his wife. All the experts who examined him were of the opinion that he knew the difference between right and wrong, and was therefore legally sane, and a proper subject for the electric chair.

I was with him for hours on the Sunday afternoon before the Thursday or Friday set for his electrocution. This, as I remember, was in May, 1931. Up to that time he had been resistant to the Spirit and was in much fear. But he told me the next morning that during the night he heard a voice saying unto him, "Don't let the devil get you." This caused him to turn whole-heartedly to Jesus and brought to him His great salvation.

When I went to the jail the next morning I was told that Lucius had asked the authorities to telephone me and get me there as quickly as they could. He told me how the Lord had saved him and taken away the fear of the electric chair and added, "It would be all right for them to come and get me now and bury me alive if they want to." He was happy almost beyond belief.

Later in the day, or on the following day, I took a specialist in mental and nervous disorders to examine him. The doctor sought to comfort him and said to him, "Lucius you have had a good time in life haven't you?" Lucius replied, "I ain't had no good time until the Lord saved me. I am having a good time now." This joy of the Lord continued until the end. He chatted happily with me and others on the morning of his electrocution and made requests to us about his funeral. He seemed to be utterly fearless in the face of death.

James Barker, a colored boy about nineteen or twenty years old, received the death sentence and was executed in 1930. He was very humble and transparently sincere. The crime was not nearly so bad as it was made out by the state. James entered into a precious sense of forgiveness and into an unusual love for everybody. Later he received the baptism with the Holy Spirit. After that he lived much in the Spirit and was used to help his fellow prisoners.

The morning that he was electrocuted, I asked him if there was anything he would like to read. When he said there was, I handed him my Bible. He turned to Romans 8:35 and read these magnificent words: "Who shall separate us from the love of Christ? Shall tribulation or distress, or persecution or famine, or nakedness or peril or the sword, and it is written, for thy sake we are killed all the day long, we are counted as sheep for the slaughter, nay we are in all these things more than conquerors through Him who loved us. For I am persuaded that neither death or life, nor angels nor principalities, nor powers, nor things present, nor things to come, nor height nor depth, nor any other creature shall be able to separate us from the love of God which is in Jesus Christ." This was a reality to him. He faced the death chair in the witness of the Spirit that he had already passed from death to life, that he had nothing to fear and everything to look forward to with hope and joy.

The greatest manifestation of God's love and light that I have ever witnessed in jail, in death cell, or in death chair, or anywhere else was that of Robert Jones, previously referred to as the colored boy who told the truth to the bottom and who never asked for any help except to get forgiveness and more of Christ. When he entered jail in September, or October, 1927, he could scarcely read. He told me that he knew a few letters and words and by starting with these and with God's help, he learned to read unusually well and pored over the New Testament.

He had a marvelous experience of conversion and later received the baptism with the Holy Spirit, and became the most effective witness and preacher to prisoners that I have known. When they took him to the State Farm for execution late in June, 1928, I wrote to the kind and cultured chaplain, E. C. Atkins, of this unusual boy. I suggested that he make good use of him to minister to the prisoners.

Robert was furnished money so that he could get anything to eat that he might desire. When I reached the State Farm the morning of his electrocution, June 30 (I had been before the Governor making the hardest fight that I had ever made for anyone to get Robert's sentence commuted), the chaplain told me that Robert was the most extraordinary person who had ever been sent there for electrocution. He informed me that the first night he was there one of their hardened criminals brought to Robert's death cell was converted. The next night three were converted and the last night everyone that the chaplain could get in the presence of Robert was converted. The chaplain expressed the conviction that if the state would permit Robert to live he would become the greatest colored man of his time, even greater than was Booker T. Washington.

During his days at the State Farm Robert prayed and fasted. He was so in the Spirit and in the joy of the Lord that he did not even ask me if there was any hope of his sentence being commuted. A short time before the officials were due to take him to the death chamber, I handed him my Bible and asked if there was anything that he wished to read. He turned to the intercessory prayer of Jesus and read it better than anyone I had ever heard read it before. In his elevation and wisdom he had something of that which made Socrates so interesting, and also a larger measure of the Spirit of Jesus than anyone else I have ever seen facing death.

After he took his seat in the electric chair and was asked

if there was anything he would like to say, he started off by saying, that he hoped that all of those present would repent and go where he was going. Looking around and seeing the sons of the man he had killed, he told them that he did not mean to kill their father, but was sorry that he struck him, and that he wanted them to forgive him. He went on to say that he was not the same person who struck the blow that resulted in the old man's death, but if they wanted to kill him for what the former man or the old nature did, it was all right. He assured them that they were only killing his body and not killing him. Robert was way ahead of me that morning, and way ahead of the rest. The chaplain said he had never seen anything like it; neither had any of the rest of us.

I explained to those who were to pull the death levers, as I had also to the Governor, that Robert had entered into such union with Jesus that whatever they did to him ranked with Jesus the same as if they had been present in the days of Jesus and did it unto Him. So far as I was concerned I could no more pull the death lever than I could have driven a nail in the hands of Jesus. Seemingly with the approval of the Spirit I referred to the death chair as being "a hellish thing." For a time it seemed that the authorities could scarcely proceed with their horrible business of putting to death this remarkable boy. After the cap was put over his head and just before the death lever was pulled, we heard Robert saying, "I'M IN HIM AND HE'S IN ME."

Through union with Jesus and in the out-flow of His love and in the meeting of all evil with good, there is great joy, bliss, and glory even in seeming defeat, shame, and crucifixion. By entering into and manifesting a spirit of victory in the presence of seeming defeat, we are made ready for manifest victory.

CHAPTER VII

MANIFEST VICTORY

◄◄◄◄◄◄◄◄◄◄◄◄◄◄◄◄◄◄◄◄◄◄◄◄◄►►►►►►►►►►►►►►►►►►►►►►►►

Jesus was so sure of perfect manifest victory for Himself, for us and for all, that He would not make the least compromise with evil and imperfection to make the victory apparently easier, quicker, and less costly to Himself. While as yet He is the Only One Who has attained this victory, which is His predestination for each of us who goes His way, every advance and attainment made by Him and by everyone is made for all.

Through fruit-bearing union with Him we are already participating in His achieved perfect everything and are on the way to manifest victory.

Every miracle of His Spirit, of His love, and of His power is beating back and conquering the kingdom of satan and bringing into manifestation the Kingdom of God, of perfect everything, for each and all. The perfect everything that is to be in manifestation has not only been achieved by Jesus, but is being achieved continuously by every victory of good over evil, of light over darkness, of love over hate, of life over death, and of the Spirit of Christ over the spirit of the anti-Christ.

The Kingdom at first must of perfect necessity be more in the unseen than in the seen; otherwise we would miss the Jesus way of attainment and become victims of the anti-Christ way of putting appearances above reality. Yet the victory is not complete until it becomes manifest in the realm of the seen and the self-evident. The realm of manifest victory is what we have designated as the fourth realm or the empire of the human-divine, the empire of the Son of Man in His glory.

As sublime as was Jesus on the plane of His incarnation as the divine-human, or as the Son of God in humiliation, the new creation of manifest victory does not begin to emerge until His resurrection, ascension, and glorification as the Son of Man. To use a rare interpretation of Saint Paul by Albert Schweitzer, Jesus' coming up from among the dead is the first mountain peak of the new creation to arise from the old. The resurrection of the righteous dead and the rapture of the prepared living will be the next peaks to emerge in the great progression toward a whole creation from the old, a new creation bringing with it the old purified, redeemed, transformed, and enthroned as the human, visible, tangible, perfect everything.

As my friend, Dean E. M. Highsmith, of Mercer University, expressed it recently when I was talking over these things with him, "God Himself seems to have chosen self-objectification as the basic technique of creation." From the highest free necessity of His own perfect nature, He chose self-objectification in creation, in redemption, and in the attainment of His divine completeness in us. Nothing but manifest victory on the plane of the human-divine, the plane where Jesus is, could fully please God and please us.

> Death, be not proud, though some have called thee
> Mighty and dreadful, for thou art not so;
> For those whom thou think'st thou dost overthrow
> Die not, poor Death; nor yet canst thou kill me.
> From rest and sleep, which but thy picture be,
> Much pleasure; then from thee much more must flow;
> And soonest our best men with thee do go—
> Rest of their bones and souls' delivery.
> Thou'rt slave to fate, chance, kings, and desperate men,
> And dost with poison, war, and sickness dwell;
> And poppy or charms can make us sleep as well
> And better than thy stroke. Why swell'st thou then?
> One short sleep past, we wake eternally,
> And Death shall be no more: Death, thou shalt die!
>
> (John Donne)

Here it is seen that nothing has really died but death, that nothing is defeated but defeat, that nothing is destroyed but destruction. Everything that is perfectable, everything that desires, aspires after, feels out for and responds to the perfect is to be brought to visible, concrete, manifest perfection.

This final victory may come with great joy and rejoicing as well as through suffering, travail, and tribulation.

"The first come through love; the next come through supplication and intercession; the next come through suffering; and the last come through tribulation; but all come."

The easy, happy way is to come through love. There is no definite amount of suffering required, only enough to teach us the wisdom of yielding and responding happily to the will, wisdom, and perfect everything of God.

It has always been true that when the desire has been intense and persistent for Jesus and His salvation, there has been the reward of manifest victory. From now on if we are sufficiently wise, receptive, and responsive to God, there will be more and more victory without the necessity for travail and tribulation. Even persecution is to be overcome increasingly through the grace and wisdom of love, and to be overcome for the perfecting of the persecutors as well as for the persecuted.

All of the acts and accents of the Holy Spirit, and all of the responses to the Spirit previously reported, really belong in this chapter, and the following achievements of the Spirit have in them special hope and prophetic significance as to the way all relationships of men and of life may be brought to harmonious fulfillment.

In the spring of 1905, an unusual business man at the head of one of the largest business firms of Montgomery, Alabama, asked me to give him the best help I could to meet a personal temptation and if possible to save his business from being thrown into a receivership which was threatened because of the ill-will of a business partner who had a small financial interest in the business, but nevertheless had it within his power to put the business in the hands of a receiver. This rare man had formerly befriended this young man who had turned against him, seemingly without cause.

I told the distressed man to pray for the highest good of the young man and his family, as well as for himself and his family. The wife thought this was an unreasonable prayer, but I believe she joined us in praying it. I asked the man with the fine spirit to say to him, whenever the young man said anything that he could not answer in the good spirit and in wisdom, that after he prayed he hoped to be able to give him the right answer.

Sometime later I received a telephone message telling me that a crisis had been reached and asking me to come to Montgomery the next day. When I reached the station the next evening about seven o'clock, the friends met me at the station in manifest joy. The wife said, "The highest thing you said to pray for has come to pass. Today the young man came to my husband and said, 'Since you want me to get out of your business, I am going to get out in the right way.' My husband melted down in gratitude and tenderness and said, 'If you feel this way about it, I don't want you to get out.'" The two men had a happy reconciliation. They then telephoned to their families and the whole threatened personal tragedy and harm to the business had been turned to the good of all concerned, as well as to the good of the business. Months afterward, Mr. ——— told me that there had never been anything after the peace making but a pull together.

The following achievement of Jesus' way of love is yet another instance of its power to bring understanding out of strife.

A man who was blessed when yielded to the good Spirit, and a roaring lion when yielded to the other Spirit, came to a meeting in Philadelphia where I was ministering, apparently determined to voice in the open every grievance, real and imaginary, that he had against another member of the group.

For a time he remained in a back room where the member whom he was accusing came to him seeking peace and his accuser's deliverance. I also left the meeting for a time to see if I could achieve anything with him. I apparently failed. A little later the enraged man came into the meeting determined to make his accusation public. I told him that as soon as he yielded to the good Spirit, he could have all the time he desired and freedom to say everything he cared to say, but that I loved him too well to let him talk until he was delivered by surrender to the good Spirit. He was a very large man and determined to take charge of the meeting. He must have weighed about two hundred and twenty-five pounds, while I weighed only about one hundred and twenty-five. But the Lord gave me not only grace and boldness, but seemingly more power than the large brother.

He said to me, "Why don't you call a policeman?" I replied, "I appeal to God, not to Caesar." A little later a very Christian woman joined me in the effort to get him to repent of the wrong spirit and to yield to the Spirit of Jesus.

He said to us, "I know you two love me." All the rest loved him, too, and instead of condemning him, they were praying for him. A little later the Spirit began to work upon him. He said, "I guess I'm the worst one of all." That was great progress. He then went to the member whom he had been accusing and asked his forgiveness and told him and the congregation what good points he had. He next went to his saintly wife, knelt before her and told her how wonderful she had been through everything, and asked her forgiveness.

His whole spirit changed. Later he went from person to person, kneeling before each of them and asking forgiveness. The devil had left him for a season and angels were ministering unto him. He became the mouthpiece for some of the best preaching I have ever heard. I was made aware that the man could never be the same again and that the group of blessed friends had been given the secret of how to turn threatening situations to manifest victories. We have not found God's will in any situation until we find the highest possibility of good for everyone concerned.

I have a very interesting, vital friend, Andrew D. Urshan, whose Apostolic Christian Church is at 296 West 92nd Street, New York City. Soon after he received the Holy Spirit in Chicago, miracle after miracle attended his ministry. Later, he and others associated with him in the Chicago work, came to Macon to hold a meeting. In high conscientiousness he felt that I should denounce, as coming from beneath, a religious philosophy and way of life that seemed to me to have much good in it. I refused, and for a time he separated himself and his group from me, until the good Spirit that I sought to manifest took effect. A while later he wrote me, fearing he had sinned against the Holy Spirit. I replied that he was much too conscientious. Thus the Lord handled the situation in a way that I feel led to the grace and heroism in which Friend Urshan was used to overcome persecution and to deliver a blessed company of Christians out of what seemed a situation that must lead to death, during a bloody persecution where the Mohammedan Turks were slaughtering Christians without mercy.

Immediately prior to the First World War, Urshan received a definite call through the spirit to go to his native land, Persia, as a missionary. It was made known to him in what desperately dangerous straits he would be. Before they were told of his intentions, his friends began to have visions of the dangers and persecutions that were ahead for him. He felt such need of supernatural help for his difficult task that he studied the list of the gifts of the Spirit as given through Saint Paul and, feeling that he could ask for only one of these gifts, was uncertain which to ask for, as he would seemingly need them all. Then the Spirit within made known to him the more excellent way, the way of perfect love, or charity. He prayed for this and in answer he was filled with the love that was melting and transforming, and that brought with it miraculous grace and wisdom.

When he returned to Persia, he began his work. All kinds of false reports had gone ahead of him. The Lord was so much with him that the worst was stirred up in those yielding to the wrong spirit. Those yielding to this spirit wanted to kill him, but could not.

Later, when the Russian army withdrew and the Turks swept into the part of Persia where he was ministering, these same people who had been persecuting him and trying to kill him, confessed that they knew he was right and they were wrong, and they sought his help in the face of the bloody persecution facing them. Many Christians were slaughtered. Urshan and the company with him, awaiting death for Christ's sake, pledged themselves to God and each other to bear faithful testimony even to death. Urshan felt it was the leading of the Spirit to make an effort to escape to a place of safety. He did not know then that there was such a place near them.

Their deliverance was so miraculous that I went to New York recently to obtain an exact statement of the details. Urshan not only told me the story, but gave me his *The Story of My Life*, from which I shall quote.

When he and his company of some seventy-five Christians came out in the open:

"Men came on horseback with their guns and spears ready to kill. We prayed and the Lord told us to run in front of the people who were with us and to fall on our knees in front of the horses with our hands uplifted to Heaven and to say repeatedly, "Jesus, Jesus, Jesus." This I and the brethren did and when the horses were close up to us, the men told us to get up. They asked for my overcoat and my brother Timothy's watch, which we gave them. They didn't do us any harm and seemed so friendly to us that they even told us if we would go in another direction we would be safe. . . .

"As we went on a little further we saw the Mohammedans

destroying the people. Suddenly a man came before us, one
of the religious men, his eyes red as blood. He looked as
though he would drink the blood of the Christians. As I
looked at him I saluted him in the Turkish language and
said, 'God's mercy be with you.' Then the Spirit led me to
confess the sins of our nation. I told him we were real Christian people. His heart was touched. He stood and looked
at me and almost wept. He said, 'Young man, I'm going to
deliver you. I will give my life to take you safely to the
American quarters. . . . I cannot take you safely by the
regular road, it is filled with thieves but you must follow
me.' The woman with us said, 'Oh, brother Andrew, he is
deceiving us. He will take us off into some lonely place and
kill us.' I said to him, 'They say you will take us into some
secret place and behead us.' He swore by Mohammed that
his life should be written in his blood if he let anybody
touch them. I said to the people, 'Let us trust God. He will
make them take us to the place of safety.' The man took
everyone of us safely to the city, not one of us was touched,
bullets flew around us, but none were hurt, not a single girl
harmed. Around us people were being killed, stripped
naked, we saw terrible sights, dead bodies lying around,
dogs eating their faces, girls taken from their fathers and
mothers, wives from their husbands, but we, about seventy-
five souls, were unharmed."

"Love never faileth."

Everything else fails and the failure of everything unloving prepares for the love of Jesus to be tried that it
may win.

From the very nature of God and the things of God and
from the very nature of evil and the things of evil, God and
the things of God must win. Manifest victory has not only
been achieved in the experience of Jesus but is being
achieved in the experience of every one in union with Him.
Ultimate manifest victory is predestined; God is working
everything together for its achievement in us and in the
creation. We are spoiled for everything else. Try everything

else, enter all other doors and nothing but the perfect everything of God for us can satisfy us. All experiences teach us that life only *works* in one way—the way of God.

Evil and imperfection have no power to hold us and have to let go when we choose Jesus and His perfect everything for ourselves and for all. I had a verification of this years ago in dealing with a very strong character who was both kind and domineering.

Both the kindness and the domination continued for years and there seemed no escape. But the very hour that I dedicated myself to be led by the Spirit and to turn away from all particularism of religion, this kind and domineering friend increased in kindness and ceased to be domineering.

This dedication to be led by the Spirit not only set me free from the sense and fear of being dominated by this particular friend or by anyone else, but also was the last blow to the friend's own dominating spirit. Until we give ourselves to be led by the Highest, it seems well that we are subject to all the things that contribute to make us happily willing to be led by Him.

The things of God, like God, are omnipotent as well as omnipresent. Take, for example, a mathematical truth or fact, like two plus two make four. This truth has all power to destroy every guess and answer to the contrary, while every false guess about this fact has no power to destroy the fact. Light has power against darkness, but darkness has no power against the light. All that is needed is more light and enough light in order to get the lights shining everywhere. Love has all power over hate and hate has no power over love. Heaven has all power to conquer hell and hell has no power against Heaven. Christ is omnipotent against anti-Christ, while anti-Christ is impotent against Christ.

The victory is so glorious that all of the education and overcoming required to bring it are as nothing. While God has the power of special intervention and miracle to hasten it, He seems to desire for the most part to achieve it by the way of the cross and by all of the steps necessary for its attainment by our own free and happy choosing. It may not be so long as it appears that it might be, for things that require much time for preparation have a way of bursting forth suddenly, like the blooming of flowers, and the rising of the sun. God works suddenly in achievement and gradually in preparation.

Everywhere the forces of imperfection and destruction move rapidly; God takes all the time necessary for growing and perfecting the things that are His, particularly the saints. Man can kill a tree and build a cabin quickly; God chooses to take plenty of time to grow His trees and to build His temples. He could grow and build by miracle, but He chooses upon the whole to grow and build by our joyous free will.

The victory is not something that can be forced as dictators force their wills upon their subjects. It is something we choose happily and give ourselves in joyous partnership to attain. God makes us free and all of his achievements are in terms of bringing us to the same kind of freedom that He has for Himself. His perfect everything is an attainment as well as a gift. The bride makes herself ready. We are given power to overcome, but we, through union and coöperation with Him, do the overcoming.

The way of attainment, being for the most part by the way of the Cross, rather than by miraculous intervention, requires repentance, even death, and the leaving on the outside of everything that has prevented entrance to the Kingdom and ineffable fruit-bearing union with Jesus. Everything that is evil and selfish hates and fights the Cross, hates and fights against its own death which is inescapable.

Moreover, manifest victory as well as every unseen victory in spirit, has to be attained by perfect means. Since the means appear in the end, the Kingdom of love cannot be attained except in the Spirit and technique of perfect love. Humans are slow to see this and slower to put it into practice. You cannot end war with war. You cannot end hell with more hell. If you could, the hell remaining would be worse than the one you first had. If you could destroy Satan by the spirit and weapons of Satan, we would have a new and worse Satan in you than the one you had destroyed.

Jesus and his perfect everything can only be manifested as we make ourselves like Him in Spirit, motive, purpose, and way of life. There is no advantage in gazing up into the heavens, there is great advantage in making yourself heavenly. Those who really look for Jesus in manifest victory and desire to be manifested with Him are making themselves and seeking to make everything, ready for this manifestation.

We have to desire, hunger, and give ourselves to all that is implied in the coming of the Kingdom of God, the manifestations of Jesus and our manifestation with Him on the plane of the human-divine. All this has to be by our happy choosing. The father of the prodigal son was too wise to try to hold his son by anything but love. He even furnished him the substance, the health and everything else to squander on harlots and for the whole of his experience away from home. He had to do this to be good enough to assure the son's return and to keep him after he returned. The Father not only provides for the feast and the everything when we return, but has also provided everything for the journey away from home. Evil, having no capital of its own, has to do business on the capital of God. Anti-Christ having no appeal in himself, has to imitate and create the illusion that he is the Christ in order to do business even for a season.

The friends listening in are laughing. Happily from now on the laugh will be heard and turned more and more on the one who has in the past laughed so much at us. As Emerson put it, in essence, since everyone reaps according to his sowing, the devil instead of being really wise is, after all, an ass, the superlative ass.

Evil holds on, not through any power of its own, but by imitating and utilizing the good. As Plato saw, if a band of robbers was wholly bad, the robbers would destroy each other before robbing any of us, but by utilizing the coöperative spirit and technique which they draw from the good, they continue their business for a time and only for a time, and only a very short time, in comparison with the eternity of the good.

The thing that delays manifest victory most of all is that those who claim to love Jesus and His way of love supremely, hold on so long and so tightly to self and to the love of honor, power, money, and are so slow in making their profession a reality.

It is the so-called best citizens who love self and their vested interests more than they love God and the best things for them and for all who put up the most stubborn resistance to God and His perfect everything. It was the so-called best citizens who put the cup of poison to the lips of Socrates, who persecuted the prophets, who crucified Jesus, and who opposed just reforms and advances of His Spirit of love and way of life. These so-called best citizens are the strongest set of all against God's very best for them and for the whole of life. But they, too, must be won. It will cost much and will require time, but it will be worth infinitely more than it costs.

As we have seen, in previous chapters, the victory is to be visible, tangible, and concrete. It is to be the fulfillment, the harmonization, the perfection, the perfect use, the utter satisfaction, and the glorification of every contributing factor and realm. The natural, the spiritual, and the divine-human are to be absolutely fulfilled, harmonized, and glorified together in the human-divine, in the glorified Jesus.

I have entered into new enrichments and happier realms by the dictation and writing of this report of my Quest. The best and most vital parts of it have been dictated spontaneously. Time and time again I have been balked until I would take time for sleep, and for the refreshing and the renewing of the body, which the Lord seems to be far more concerned with than we are ourselves. Then I have invariably received the insights and clarifications I was feeling for.

As James Russell Lowell found that he always made his best speeches on his way home after he had spoken to audiences, so I shall in the days to come be rehearsing in my mind far better books than this one, but the things in it given by the Spirit, the things that succeeded in getting themselves reported without too much human coloring are flashlights from the light that lights every life coming into the world and that focuses the truth of eternity in time and in terms of the needs of our time. Some of these truths are without apparent human coloring.

Be led by the Spirit. Center yourself on Jesus and His way of life in love. Overcome all evil with good. Intercede for and dedicate yourself to bring pure good alone to everybody and everything. Welcome the whole of Jesus into the whole of your being and life activities. Receive the full, free, and freeing control and baptism of the Spirit. Gladly repent of and die to all that has kept you from entering and abiding in perfection, ineffable, fruit-bearing, and transforming union with Jesus, who is God's perfect everything on the plane of our needs and comprehension. Be always manifesting Him and overflowing with His perfect love to each and all. You will abide in Him perpetually and increasingly as you choose to manifest Him and His perfect love perpetually and increasingly.

To me the future is bright with promise. The darkness of the night through which so much of the human race is passing is bringing out the stars. The devil hath great wrath, precisely because he knows his days are short. With confidence I expect soon to see the dictators of anti-Christian views and systems, now waging the most hellish war of all history, no longer objects of terror and hatred, but of pity and compassion. War is on its last as well as its worst legs. Our selfish, stupid, competitive ways of life, responsible for unemployment, war, and all the man-made hells on earth, must and will be supplanted by what W. H. Kilpatrick calls "some common-good system." We face a new era; "life," says Kilpatrick, "beckons us as never before."

Life, like water, is wonderful to drink, wonderful to swim in, wonderful to be cleansed by, but dangerous to sink in. It would be tragic if it were not for the loving provision of rescue, even if it requires the help of Jonah's whale. Life calls for overcoming or being overcome. The overcomer is like the artesian well and like a river flowing from the very holy temple of life itself. He throws off and knocks back every would-be adversary. Those who, by meeting evil with evil, fail to overcome are like suck-holes that draw in all the evils about them. If we could overcome the bloody dictators by out-doing them with their spirit and weapon, which is the spirit of anti-Christ and the weapon of hell, we would thus in overcoming them be overcome ourselves and would be worse than they are. Thus life contrary to the good will and sense of Jesus of right necessity becomes worse; but life in Him and in His immeasurable love and wisdom ever becomes better.

Better still, Jesus, as glorified man, from the realm and throne of achieved, manifest, perfect everything for the everything of everybody and everything, is to be fully revealed and manifested, and we and the creation are to be manifested with Him in the likeness of His perfect nature, Spirit, body, and dominion.

So the quest for God's best clarifies itself and becomes His quest and ours for Manifest Victory.

"The best is yet to be."